WRIGHT BROTHERS, WRONG STORY

ALSO BY WILLIAM HAZELGROVE

Shots Fired in Terminal 2:
A Witness to the Fort Lauderdale Airport Shooting
Reflects on America's Mass Shooting Epidemic

Al Capone and the 1933 World's Fair

Forging a President: How the Wild West Created Teddy Roosevelt

Madam President: The Secret Presidency of Edith Wilson

WRIGHT BROTHERS, WRONG STORY

HOW WILBUR WRIGHT SOLVED THE PROBLEM OF MANNED FLIGHT

WILLIAM HAZELGROVE

 Prometheus Books

59 John Glenn Drive
Amherst, New York 14228

Published 2018 by Prometheus Books

Cover design by Nicole Sommer-Lecht
Cover image of glider © Science History Images / Alamy Stock Photo
Cover image of Orville *(left)* and Wilbur *(right)* © Bettmann / Getty Images
Cover design © Prometheus Books

Inquiries should be addressed to
Prometheus Books
59 John Glenn Drive
Amherst, New York 14228
VOICE: 716–691–0133 • FAX: 716–691–0137
WWW.PROMETHEUSBOOKS.COM

22 21 20 19 18   5 4 3 2 1

Library of Congress Cataloging-in-Publication Data

Names: Hazelgrove, William Elliott, 1959- author.
Title: Wright brothers, wrong story : how Wilbur Wright solved the problem of manned
    flight / by William Hazelgrove.
Description: Amherst, New York : Prometheus Books, 2018. | Includes bibliographical
    references and index.
Identifiers: LCCN 2018031181 (print) | LCCN 2018033863 (ebook) |
    ISBN 9781633884595 (ebook) | ISBN 9781633884588 (hardcover)
Subjects: LCSH: Wright, Orville, 1871-1948. | Wright, Wilbur, 1867-1912. | Haskell,
    Katharine Wright, 1874-1929. | Aeronautics—United States—History—20th century.
    | Inventors—United States—History—20th century. | Aeronautics—United States—
    Biography. | LCGFT: Biographies.
Classification: LCC TL540.W7 (ebook) | LCC TL540.W7 H392 2018 (print) |
    DDC 629.130092/273 [B] —dc23
LC record available at https://lccn.loc.gov/2018031181

Printed in the United States of America

Once again for Kitty, Clay, Callie, and Careen

"For some years I have been afflicted with the belief that flight is possible to man. My disease has increased in severity and I feel that it will cost me an increased amount of money if not my life."

—Wilbur Wright to Octave Chanute, 1900

CONTENTS

PREFACE: THE WRIGHT MYTH

I t is hard to get flesh and bones on these two men. They come to us as stick figures in vests and white shirts, with their hard shoes hanging off the back of their flyers. They seem to not be of the earth and have few worldly desires after the desire to fly. Historians tramp from the Outer Banks to Dayton, Ohio, then to the Smithsonian in Washington or to the Ford Museum in Dearborn, Michigan, to see the Wrights' bicycle shop. And after seeing the *Wright Flyer* in Washington or the markers in Kitty Hawk, they sit down to write the "Wright story."

It is a fact that the two men in the derbies have eluded historians and the rest of us for a long time. They were elusive men, after all, and so the questions linger behind the legend and the façade of the two Arrow collar young men who dazzled the world in 1903. History would have us believe that the Wright brothers were one in the same: Somehow, *they both* invented manned flight. They both had the same epiphanic moments while working on their gliders in Kitty Hawk. They both studied birds and deduced that wing warping was the key to controlled flight. They both worked out the complex aeronautical data that went into determining the amount of lift, the shape, the very design of a wing that would enable them to ascend to the heavens.

Their father, Milton Wright, set the bar early on by declaring to a reporter they were as "inseparable as twins."[1] Wilbur and Orville have been treated as two sides of the same card, and that card solved all the problems men had been wrestling with for at least the last century in their effort to leave the surly bonds of Earth. The mantra of shared responsibility, shared credit, shared genius, shared effort, and shared eureka moments begins with their father. After clashing with his own church and losing a pivotal legal battle, the bishop saw the world as evil and the family as good, and he believed that the family must be united. As Lawrence Goldstone, author of *Birdmen: The Wright Brothers, Glenn Curtiss, and the Battle to Control the Skies*, described,

"They [Wilbur, Orville, Katherine] came to believe in the essential depravity of mankind. The world beyond the front of their home was filled with men and women who were not to be trusted."[2]

In the eyes of their father, there must be no fissures between the siblings, especially the boys; the brothers, Wilbur and Orville, were to be equal. Period. But the old, crafty man of God let it slip toward the end that Wilbur was the man who was the real force behind the evolving science and art of flying. In a letter to Wilbur, he wrote, "Outside of your contacts and your aviations, you have much that no one else can do so well. And alone. Orville would be crippled and burdened."[3]

Milton knew who the real intellectual force was, the silent genius who solved the head-scratching physics of riding invisible air currents into the sky. It was Wilbur. But this was lost quickly under the bishop's philosophy, which colored his sons' view of the world. His beliefs that the world was inherently evil and untrustworthy, and that all must be unified against it, meant no one would be singled out. There could be no division apparent to the outside world.

This philosophy was the guiding light of the Wright brothers as they lived, and death would cement the Wright myth. Wilbur's early death from typhoid fever in 1912 ensured an obfuscation of the truth by leaving behind Orville to scatter the breadcrumbs for others to follow. These breadcrumbs begin with Fred C. Kelly in 1943. A journalist who had written many articles on the Wright brothers, he had become a close friend of Orville. He was the one man who would explain to the world how the Wright brothers flew.

The very title of Kelly's biography of the Wright brothers throws up a red flag: *The Wright Brothers: A Biography Authorized by Orville Wright.* This lets us know right away that this is Orville's version of events and not Wilbur's. The biography is a picture of perfect 50 percent partners. Orville would approve every word of the Kelly biography, ensuring the mantra that they equally broke the code of flight. They were to be the two men in derbies walking side by side with their brains adjoined. No man was smarter than the other. No man solved what the other could not. Kelly set the bar for all historians to follow—from every children's book to David McCullough's latest effort aptly titled *The Wright Brothers.*

But it gets worse. When reading the Fred Kelly biography, one quickly realizes it is not a biography of the Wright brothers but of Orville Wright.

Orville is on every page in spirit, and many times he is literally dictating large swaths of prose in first-person narration. Orville's name appears 337 times in Kelly's biography while Wilbur's name appears 269 times.[4] Almost a quarter less than his brother. Biographical information is given as if there is one Wright brother: "At the age of twelve, while living in Richmond, Indiana, Orville Wright became interested in wood engravings."[5] So begins chapter 3, in which we are given the biography of Orville, with Wilbur often referred to only within the plural *Wright brothers*. The entire tone of the Kelly biography is one that pays tribute to Orville with fuzzy references to Wilbur.

Orville is painted throughout as the nascent genius inventor, with Wilbur in the background: "Orville even found time during this period for experiments having nothing to do with bicycles. . . . He made a new kind of calculating machine for multiplying as well as adding . . ."[6] Kelly then throws Wilbur a bone with the line, "What will those Wright boys be doing next?"[7] This is Kelly pleasing Orville in the worst way, with a bit of Capraesque Americana.

The Kelly story goes like this. The brothers' interest in flight begins with a toy helicopter Milton brought home. Orville would cement this fact in a deposition six years after his brother died: "Our first interest began when we were children. Father brought home to us a small toy activated by a rubber spring which would lift itself into the air. We built several copies of this toy, which flew successfully. By 'we' I refer to my brother Wilbur and myself."[8] The "we" became gospel with Orville Wright—*Thou shall not use the singular when the plural will do*. Kelly took it to high art by submerging Wilbur into "the Wright brothers" or referring to him as "they." Great pains were made to obliterate Wilbur's use of the singular "I" for the plural "we" in his early letters. *We* invented the airplane. *We* called the Smithsonian for information. *We* cracked the code of aeronautics. *We* wrote Octave Chanute. *We* are equal in the eyes of the world. This is the beginning and the core of the Wright myth.

So, as children, they became fascinated with the toy helicopter and the way it would fly to the ceiling. Orville would say he had equal interest in the toy and wondered how man might fly one day. They both lost their mother. They both had a father, Bishop Milton Wright, who was rarely home. They both had a sister, Katherine, who had strong relationships with other women and looked after the brothers *their entire adult lives*. No one ever moved out of the original family house. Neither brother had a sexual relationship the world knew of. This would be explained by Wilbur, who said, "I don't have time for both a wife and an airplane."⁹ Kelly laid cover for both by saying neither brother had time for marriage. Neither did their sister have time for a husband; and when she did care about sex and finally married in her midfifties, Orville would punish her for marrying by refusing to see his sister until she was on her deathbed.

They both dropped out of high school. They both became interested in printing and started a newspaper. Then they both got into the business of making and fixing bicycles. They both became interested in flying and requested information from the Smithsonian. You can feel Orville looking over Kelly's shoulder as he writes, "Knowing that the Smithsonian Institution, at Washington, was interested in the subject of human flight, they decided to send a letter to the Smithsonian, asking for suggestions of reading material."¹⁰

The most egregious example of Orville's heavy editorial hand is evident in the invention of wing warping by Wilbur. In Kelly's biography, this breakthrough is given a fifty-fifty status, with Orville having an equally inventive moment: "Why, he [Orville] asked himself, wouldn't it be possible for the operator to vary the inclination of sections of wings at the tips and thus obtain force for restoring balance from the difference in the lifts of the two opposite wing tips?"¹¹

They both then built a glider. They both went to Kitty Hawk four times and built a wind tunnel. In the Kelly biography, Orville is purported to have built an early wind tunnel to check facts given by Wilbur at the Society of Engineers in Chicago. Then, in 1901, Kelly has Orville encouraging Wilbur to continue with his experiments when he declares, "Not within a thousand years will man ever fly!"¹² Then, on December 17, 1903, in Kitty Hawk, North Carolina, Orville flew a plane under its own power for twelve seconds. Done.

The Orville Wright version of how powered flight was invented is there for all time, with all its strictures, obfuscations, and creations. Our main ruler for comparison to the Kelly biography are *The Papers of Wilbur and Orville Wright, Including the Chanute-Wright Papers, 1899–1948*. In their own words lies the truth of what really happened at Kitty Hawk and afterward. It is not really Kelly's fault. Wilbur had been dead for thirty years, and Kelly was working with essentially one source, one voice: Orville Wright. And Orville had the power to censor anything or cancel the whole project. Kelly had no access to the letters of the brothers or the correspondence between the engineer, Octave Chanute, and Wilbur Wright that lies at the very heart of the invention of the airplane.

Historians generally lead with the Kelly thesis, and the Wright brothers are left alone to leak sawdust like the mannequins in the museum in Kitty Hawk. The latest and most popular biography is David McCullough's, and he sets up the relationship right in the beginning: "As others in Dayton knew, the two were remarkably self-contained, ever industrious, and virtually inseparable. . . . They lived in the same house, worked together, kept their money in a joint bank account, even thought together."[13]

So, the die is cast and the Wright story is told of two cardboard men who had no foibles, no strange passions—two men who lived with their father and sister their whole lives until Wilber passed and Orville bought a mansion for the three of them to live in. The brothers were not gay, or at least we have no evidence that they were, yet they eschewed all women because of shyness, supposedly, or because it would interfere with solving the problem of manned flight. This is taken as part of the Wright mythology. "In one significant respect, the three youngest Wright children set themselves apart from their contemporaries. Wilbur was twenty-nine in 1896, Orville twenty-five, and Katherine twenty-two. They were ripe for marriage yet none of them showed any interest in the opposite sex. They seemed bound by an unspoken agreement to remain together and to let no one come between them."[14]

This mythology protects the brothers from being gay, the sister from being a lesbian, and the father from being an overbearing ogre who only wanted his children home and who turned his daughter into his dead wife and foisted upon her the role of servant in waiting while admonishing his three children that the world was evil and only the family could be trusted. As Tom Crouch wrote in *The Bishop's Boys*, "Sex was a subject on which the entire family maintained silence. This was expected in any late Victorian American household."[15]

Still, one must wonder why three healthy adults would eschew any sexual relations or any known relationship outside the family. Charlie Taylor, the mechanic who would build the engine for the *Wright Flyer* in 1903, would later say that Wilbur "would get awfully nervous when young women were around . . . if an older woman sat down beside him before you know it he would be talking . . . but if a younger woman sat next to him he would get fidgety and pretty soon would get up."[16]

Charlie Taylor would finally surmise that Wilbur was "woman shy."[17] Katherine would get engaged at college and keep it from her father until she broke it off, and even then she would not tell him. When she did marry, finally, in her fifties, Milton was gone and Orville would never forgive her.[18] Orville's only known courtship was with a friend of his sister's, Agnes Osborn. "There were evenings of chess and romantic boat rides on the old canal. Agnes's younger brother, Glenn, the proud owner of a Wright bicycle, remembered that Orville came calling dressed in his best suit, and loved to play practical jokes on his sister."[19] It would come to nothing, but this at least gives us a glimmer of a man with desires like anyone else. Orville even went to a party that a high school friend later described: "Orville sat in a straight-backed chair just inside the parlor door all evening, genially aloof from our games of Kiss the Pillow, Post Office, Forfeits and other stimulating enterprises."[20]

You can imagine everyone having fun while the bishop's son sits. His strongest known relationship will be with his brother and his sister, until she marries. Freud would have a field day. This information at least pumps some blood into these historical characters who have not changed in history since Kelly's biography in 1943. If we were to keep score, Wilbur came the closest to living up to his father's implied wish of asexual children, with Orville a close second and then Katherine. Bishop Wright held up the two older sons in the family as evidence of what happened to those who ventured out into the world and married. Reuchlin and Lorin, the older Wright brothers, had married and had children and entered into a depressed economy. In *The Bishop's Boys*, Crouch points out that "Wilbur watched his two older brothers with interest and a great deal of sympathy. Reuchlin and Lorin were talented men with more formal education than most of their contemporaries, yet both gave the impression of being constantly overwhelmed by responsibility and circumstance. They suffered from chronic poor health and seemed to be perpetually on the brink of failure."[21]

The world was not to be trusted. No wonder Orville and Wilbur would spend most of their life after their historic flight in litigation, proving to the world they had flown first and they should be rewarded handsomely. Bishop Wright's grown children were there to serve him when he returned from his travels, which consumed him to the point that he would not alter his schedule even for his dying wife. It was especially unfair to Katherine: "The dutiful daughter who devoted her life to caring for the widowed father was the epitome of female virtue in the life and literature of the period. Yet it is safe to assume that few widowed fathers were as demanding as Milton Wright."[22]

It is as if a child's book is the bible of the Wright brothers' story and all characters must remain one-dimensional, misanthropic, and stunted, if not emotionally incestuous. But this is all brushed under the Wright rug and has remained the inconvenient dust under the clean tabula rasa of the Wrights' story; it is to be retold and accepted with the same blind faith that George Washington did cut down a cherry tree and that Ben Franklin flew a kite with a key and discovered electricity.

Wilbur and Orville Wright are portrayed as perfect men, and, in that perfection, we are given characters who think and act as one. They are given to us as men who have little flesh and blood. "Like their father, they were always perfect gentlemen, naturally courteous to all. They neither drank hard liquor nor smoked nor gambled and both remained, as their father liked to say, 'independently republican.' They were both bachelors and by all signs intended to remain so."[23] They seem to be men devoid of bodily functions. No one uses a bathroom. No one secretes anything. Sister Katherine is treated the same way: "Younger than Orville by three years, she was bright, personable, highly opinionated, the only college graduate in the family and of the three still at home, much the most sociable."[24]

In short, she was the perfect post-Victorian spinster. The famous picture in Kitty Hawk on December 17, 1903, only complicates matters. In this photo we see the *Wright Flyer* leave Earth for twelve seconds, with Orville Wright at the controls and Wilbur looking on. It was a coin toss and a bad maneuver that handed this historic moment to Orville. This is what history has delivered to us.

It goes against the gospel of Wright to say that Wilbur Wright invented the mechanical system of control for manned flight and rewrote the science of aeronautics that was required to produce a wing capable of enough lift and an airplane with enough control to carry a human being into the air; in short, Wilbur Wright *invented* the plane that would carry his brother for the first twelve seconds of human-powered flight on December 17, 1903. And yet Orville was his partner. He did join Wilbur in this great adventure and did help him physically build the airplane. He helped him build the wind tunnel that reset the basic data of manned flight. He did fly the plane for twelve seconds on December 17, 1903. In a way, that was fitting. Wilbur could observe his plane leaving Earth under its own power; and, in that moment, he has the satisfaction that his vision, his theories, his calculations, his years of work produced a machine that could lift a man and fly like the birds he studied so intensely.

Now if we go with that supposition, then we must turn the Wright myth on its head and shake out the falsehoods. The first one is that these two men, separated by five years at birth, were the same. As Lawrence Goldstone wrote in *Birdmen*, "They may have been alike, but they were not the same. Wilbur is one of the greatest intuitive scientists this nation has ever produced. Completely self-taught, he made spectacular intellectual leaps to solve a series of intractable problems that had eluded some of history's most brilliant minds. . . . Many subsequent accounts have treated the brothers as indistinguishable equals, but Orville viscerally as well as chronologically never ceased being the little brother."[25] Author James Tobin takes it one step further: "It is impossible to imagine Orville, bright as he was, supplying the driving force that started their work and kept it going from the back room of their store in Ohio to conferences with capitalists, presidents, and kings. Will did that. He was the leader, from beginning to end."[26]

Then there are the personal differences. In *Birdmen*, Lawrence Goldstone points out that "as family correspondence makes clear, Orville's relationship with Wilbur was a good deal more complex than is generally assumed and after his brother's death, Orville was never able to muster the will to pursue their mutual obsessions with the necessary zeal."[27] The strange, insular relationship of the three children, and Katherine's strong relationships with other women her whole life, screams out some sort of androgyny that historians have chosen to ignore. Orville was fastidious, if not obsessive, about his appearance. A niece, Ivonette, recalled that he always knew what clothes to wear. "I don't believe there was ever a man who could do the work he did in all sorts of dirt, oil, and grime and come out it looking immaculate."[28] Argyle socks and low-topped shoes were a favorite among the brother who always wore a dapper suit, with his shoes shined to a high gloss.

As Tom Crouch wrote in *The Bishop's Boys*, "His pale complexion was a matter of choice—and some pride. During the three years when they returned from Kitty Hawk each fall tanned by the wind and sun of the Outer Banks, Orville would immediately go to work bleaching his face with lemon juice. Carrie Kaylor Grumbach, the housekeeper, remembered that Orville would have gone pale again weeks before his brother."[29] Further suggesting that Orville was effeminate, George Burba, a Dayton reporter, described Orville's hands as "small and uncallused."[30]

The impression of Wilbur is very different, he seemingly had little regard for his appearance besides the basic uniform of high collar, tie, and coat. Katharine spoke of having to watch him to make sure his clothes were clean. Wilbur had a darker complexion with a strong jaw. A French journalist wrote of Wilbur, "The face is smooth shaven and tanned by the wind and country sun. The eye is a superb blue-grey with tints of gold that bespeak an ardent flame."[31] An English reporter would observe his "fine drawn weather-beaten face, strongly marked features, and keen observant hawk like eyes."[32] So it would seem that Orville resembled an early century metrosexual; Wilbur was the silent, masculine type; and Katherine was androgynous, if not a lesbian. One thing is clear: they were not asexual.

If there is a smoking gun in the Wright myth, it is Wilbur's voluminous correspondence with the aeronautical scientist Octave Chanute that is so technical it gives the lay person a headache. Chanute was Wilbur Wright's mentor, though Wilbur would fight against that impression all his life. But it was Wilbur who went to the symposiums of the day in Chicago and related theory and the progress in Kitty Hawk with a lantern-light slide presentation at Chanute's invitation. It was Wilbur who wrote the first articles for aeronautical journals of his experiments at Kitty Hawk. Wilbur was viewed early on as the pioneer breaking the boundaries of known aeronautical science. Wilbur and Orville both participated in the *building* of the *Wright Flyer*, but Orville was the mechanic while Wilbur was the designer. It is telling that three years after Wilbur's death in 1912, Orville sold his interest in the company they had formed.[33] Without Wilbur the Wright brothers ceased as an entity driving the science of powered flight forward.

This is not the story we want to hear. Pluralism bespeaks of combined effort. We like to believe that two brothers were behind our ascent to the sky. The artist is a quirk of nature. The genius, an aberration. Most live in the terrestrial world where people work together to solve problems. Wilbur Wright as the lone inventor of flight has little appeal versus the mechanical mannequins side by side in the sheds at the Wright Memorial. This appeals to our national team approach. America is a team. We will solve our problems together. But there is always the visionary: from Jefferson to Edison to Bell to Oppenheim. There is a force behind that moves like a savant in a dark room. Every great movement or advancement in human history has the force of one man or woman behind it. Others may help; they may codify; they may construct; but it is the magician who creates something out of nothing. Destiny is but a singular tap on the shoulder.

This great work was Wilbur's invention of *controlled flight*. "The first U.S. patent, 821,393, did not claim invention of a flying machine, but rather the invention of a system of aerodynamic control that manipulated a flying machine's surfaces."[34] The visionary of this control system was Wilbur Wright. The story of flight in Kitty Hawk is the final arbiter.

But it gets worse for the historian trying to decipher fact from fiction. In 1912, Wilbur Wright died of typhoid fever and Orville did not die until 1948, which gave him a very long time to shape history. The younger brother is torn by conflicting interests. He wants to protect the legacy of Wilbur and himself as the inventors of powered flight, but he also wants history to know that *he was an equal partner*. He gets into a fight with the Smithsonian Institution, and this leads to the strangest unknown episode of the Wright story: the holding for ransom of the 1903 *Wright Flyer* by the British for twenty years. The epic fight of Glenn Curtiss and the Smithsonian Institute versus the Wright brothers is part of the drama and subterfuge that is the *real* history of the Wright brothers.

Here are the facts we know.

The United States in 1900 was on the edge of greatness when Wilbur went searching for the perfect place with the perfect wind flow to begin experiments toward a final goal of manned flight. The Gilded Age had ended but left a nation crisscrossed by railroads, with a national market in place and an industrial economy just warming up. People were leaving the family farms and heading for the cities to make their fortunes. Men like Andrew Carnegie and J. P. Morgan made enormous untaxed fortunes and proclaimed what was good for business was good for America. William Jennings Bryan had lost the presidential election to William McKinley but had shown that populism was a force to be reckoned with. Theodore (Teddy) Roosevelt had returned from the Wild West twenty years before and became president in 1901 after President McKinley was assassinated by an anarchist.

Henry Ford was getting ready to churn out cars like boxes of cereal.

Inventions on every front were the news of the day, with wireless telegraph connecting remote ships to the shore. America was in an amazing spot. The West had been declared closed in 1890. The US Industrial Revolution was producing goods on a scale that was unthinkable. Everyone all over the world wanted to go to America, and in New York Ellis Island had become the revolving door to new opportunities in the new land.

Against this heady backdrop, a moody and depressed young man named Wilbur Wright had grown bored with making bicycles and started to read about attempts to fly. He had gone so far as to write to the Smithsonian for all information regarding flight and then asked the National Weather Service where he might find the most suitable winds for testing airplanes. The reply came at once, a remote fishing village that wasn't even a village, on the outer banks of North Carolina, called Kitty Hawk. Wilbur had never heard of this strange place seven hundred miles due east of Ohio. But he decided then and there that he must go to Kitty Hawk and immediately begin testing a kite glider he had been working on above the bicycle shop.

Kitty Hawk was the wilderness in 1900. Wilbur Wright would go to this remote fishing village once in 1901, twice in 1902, and once in 1903. A final return to Kitty Hawk for testing in 1908 was more of a victory lap to get ready for a flight test for the United States Army. But it was those first four visits, with the resulting laboratory for testing the planes that were built and the answers found there, that hold the secret to why a man in a high collar was able to do what up until then only the winged creatures of the earth could accomplish.

The Outer Banks and Kitty Hawk in particular were inaccessible except by boat. There were seasons to deal with, and Wilbur had no patience for such things, so he set out at once to go *by himself* to inspect this strange, windswept land of sand dunes and the few fishermen eking out a living. Isolation is what most men who had been to Kitty Hawk talked about. This didn't matter. Wilbur would crate up the glider he had been building and ship it to this remote fishing village. Then he would go to Kitty Hawk to check out this strange enclave on the eastern seaboard. Wilbur Wright was thirty-three, and his pursuit of flight would be the ultimate young man's adventure.

This is what we know. Now let's turn the Wright story upside down, crack the myth open, and see what falls out. We should start with author John C. Kelly, the man who is the architect of all that follows. The real story is more fascinating than the myth, but, after all, truth is often stranger than fiction.

PREFLIGHT

"No bird soars in a calm."

—Wilbur Wright, 1901

1914

The Great Flood

The 1903 flyer had been dismantled and packed away. The wooden crates stored in Dayton, Ohio, behind the bike shop in the shed looked like nothing. The crates were not marked and had been there for eleven years. The shed held bicycle parts, bicycles, wheels, tires, tools. The large wooden crates were an imposition, really. They were bulky and took up a lot of the space. The floor of the shed offered no real protection against the elements. Rain leaked down onto the crates occasionally from the roof. The men who had put the crates in the shed had long since forgotten them. Wilbur had died in 1912, and Orville was busy and traveling. So the crates with sand in the bottom from 1903 in Kitty Hawk, North Carolina, remained silently moldering.

The rain began on Easter Sunday, March 23, 1914. Dayton, Ohio, was a sitting duck positioned between the intersection of the Miami, Stillwater, and Mad Rivers, along with Wolf Creek, which was always flooding. Already six times before, waters had rampaged through the streets of Dayton. This would be the worst, with torrential rains blanketing the area, swelling the rivers and creeks, and meeting in downtown Dayton. Then the earthen dam of the Laramie Reservoir in Shelby County collapsed, sending a wall of water surging toward Dayton. A levee along Stratford Avenue breached at four o'clock on Monday, with more breaks along East Second and Fifth Avenues.[1]

The Wright home and bike shop were in the crosshairs, and so was the shed. So was the flyer.

1

THE BIOGRAPHER — 1942

Fred C. Kelly smoked and drank his cold coffee. Awful. Cigarettes and coffee kept him going usually, but he felt a fatigue that even nicotine and caffeine couldn't mitigate. He lit another cigarette and blew the smoke out, tiredly watching the blue undulations float over his typewriter. He parked the cigarette and bent over his typewriter, his notes surrounding him. Man had flown thirty-nine years ago, and there was not one diary, not one book written by anyone to explain how it had happened. No one had written a biography of the Wright brothers.

Kelly picked up his cigarette and read over what he had written that day. He had known the man a long time. He had published his first interview with Orville, "Flying Machines and the War,"[1] in an issue of *Collier's* in 1915. His sense of humor had won over the inventor of the airplane, and he had published many interviews and articles on Orville Wright, as long as they didn't dig too deep. He had been thinking of a biography for a long time, and the 1939 article for *Harper's*, "How the Wright Brothers Began,"[2] gave him an opening.

Kelly used that as a basis and got Orville to sign on with one stipulation: he would approve every single word. Kelly began sending pages to Orville and getting back crossed-out sections. It was going to be a long process. As one family member said, "writing a book with Orville Wright looking over your shoulder would not be an easy task."[3] It wasn't. He had to nudge Orville every step of the way just to respond to the pages. But it was all worth it. It would put Kelly's name on the map and maybe make him a rich man, or at least able to pay the mortgage.

Kelly leaned back in his chair. He had written a humor column for the Cleveland *Plain Dealer* for five years and then a column for the *Statesman* in Washington, DC, for eight years. That's when his career took off with his "Real and Near" column that ran for eight years and was the first column ever to be syndicated. He had done a little bit of everything and even served as a special agent for the FBI in World War I. Then he bought a farm in Peninsula, Ohio, and took whatever came his way.[4] Kelly saw himself as a journalist first, but he was open to other things, one of those other things was to write the only account of how the Wright brothers flew at Kitty Hawk.

Kelly wasn't a historian, and writing anyone's history was tricky, but writing someone's history who insisted on reviewing every page was almost a sleight of hand. He had to be very careful. Anything personal was out. Orville Wright wanted it to be technical, but Kelly was a writer, and he knew nothing about aeronautical science. So, it was touch-and-go. Orville was moody, and Kelly was walking a tightrope every day. Still, he couldn't believe his luck. He alone was writing the definitive biography of the two men who had cracked the Rubik's Cube of flight thirty-nine years before.

It was hard to deal with Orville, but even harder to deal with his secretary, Mabel Beck. She was "fiercely devoted to him ... acting as a buffer between Orville and the rest of the world. Anybody—whether business associates or family members—who wished to speak with Orville at his office had to go through Mabel first, and her attitude made it difficult, particularly for many of his business associates."[5]

She had given the journalist Earl Findley the kiss of death years before and fired him when he really needed the money and had put in a lot of work. He had been a good friend of both Wilbur and Orville, and Katherine Wright, the sister, had been on Finley's side initially: "I've been talking to Orville about it and he says that he would only be interested in a carefully written, accurate account of their work. . . . We are now of the opinion that you could write such a book, if you had time enough to devote to the work."[6] Findley and another reporter had worked for six months on the first draft of the book and sent it to Orville for his approval. At the time Orville read the manuscript, he was in bed with severe back pains. "This manuscript is too personal and chatty," he told Mabel. "Send it back. I would rather have the sciatica."[7] Mabel told Findley exactly that.

But if you wanted to get to Orville or you wanted information, then Mabel Beck was the conduit. Kelly had made a point of being nice to her at every opportunity, and that wasn't easy. The truth was, "Mabel had complete charge of the papers, and she let him see only what she chose to and often hindered his work."[8] Kelly had known Orville for over twenty years, but that didn't matter. Orville had known Findley for a long time when he gave him his walking papers. Even Charles Lindbergh couldn't get Orville to commit to a biography. He had visited Orville a month after his flight and then tried to straighten out the whole Smithsonian thing, and, when that didn't work, he tried to get him to agree to a biography.

Lindbergh gave up and wrote in his diary:

> It is a tragedy, for Wright is getting on in years, and no one else is able to tell the story as he can. It seems that Wright does not trust anyone to tell it properly. The words and phrases people use in telling the achievements of Orville Wright and his brother are never quite satisfactory and never of sufficiently comprehensive accuracy. . . . There are many writers who would be glad to do a book in cooperation with him but the writers do not understand aviation enough to suit him. He prefers a technical person. . . . I am afraid the book will never be written.[9]

So Lindbergh had bombed out along with Earl Findley.

The phone rang. Kelly swore and stubbed his cigarette. He walked across the room and picked up the phone.

"Fred . . . it's Orville."

Kelly had a bad feeling. Usually it was Mabel who called him. Orville told him he wanted to stop and would pay him for what he had done so far. Kelly stared at his typewriter and jammed his hand down into his robe pocket. He should have kept writing for the papers. His payday was going right out the window. He rubbed his forehead, staring at the bare trees outside his office.

"Let me ask you a question, Orville. . . . Would you have given up on the morning of December 17, 1903?"

Orville was silent then chuckled.

"No. I guess not. Okay. Let's continue."[10]

Fred hung up and breathed deeply. He went back to his typewriter. He was halfway done. He had almost suffered the same fate as Findley. He had passed every page to Orville and accepted all his edits, censoring, and strange suggestions. He wasn't going to write anything that Orville didn't want him to write—but there were questions, there were the secrets under the black ice that threatened the Wright legacy. There was the fight with the Smithsonian that had been going on for twenty years and was a symptom of Orville Wright's obsession with making sure that history treated him fairly.

Kelly didn't really write what he began to suspect. It was like a creeping virus, but he knew if he breathed a word of it, there would be no publication. Orville would see to that. The way Kelly saw it, Orville had thrown snake eyes more than once. He had been the one who flew the airplane in the photo in 1903 because Wilbur had been unsuccessful the day before and they had to make some adjustments. The world would see Orville lying down in a twenty-five-mile-an-hour wind, fighting to keep the plane aloft, while John T. Daniels snapped a picture that showed Wilbur running alongside. And then Orville drew the ultimate card when he survived typhoid fever and Wilbur didn't. Neither brother had ever put pen to paper. Neither brother had said this is the way it happened, so there was a vacuum. Orville could say this is how it happened, and no one could question him. The dead asked no questions.

Kelly stared at his typewriter, feeling the fatigue again of the past year—too little money, too many cigarettes, too much coffee. The writer's life was killing him. He was exhausted, and now all his work could be for nothing. Orville Wright had gone off on one of his spells, the same spell that put him in a knockdown fight with the Smithsonian Institute and a refusal to give them the 1903 *Wright Flyer*. Kelly slumped down in his chair. There was a war, and he should have been covering that, but he had thrown his career aside for this once-in-a-lifetime opportunity. He was going to set the bar for historians to follow one hundred years down the line. He was no historian, that was for sure, but he could tell a story.

He looked over his notes. Orville had shipped the 1903 *Wright Flyer* to London fourteen years before, and now it was deep below ground while the bombs from the *Luftwaffe* pounded London into dust. The very technology that allowed the Germans to rain hell from the skies was being bombed by them. The Smithsonian desperately wanted the *Flyer* back. America wanted the *Flyer* back. President Roosevelt wanted the *Flyer* back. Lindbergh wanted the *Flyer* back. The country needed it to come home. And Orville Wright was the man with his finger on the button. Even if he gave in, it couldn't come across the ocean until the war ended, lest a German U-boat send it to the bottom of the Atlantic.

The truth was Orville had crossed his arms like a petulant child. It all came down to what really happened in 1903. Sometimes Kelly thought Orville saw his own personal legacy in danger of blowing away like the shifting sands he and his brother had walked almost forty years before. Kelly lit another cigarette and stared at his manuscript. He was willing to play ball, but if Orville was going to pull the rug out from under him, maybe he should just tell the real story. He really doubted he could ever finish with Orville flip-flopping back and forth. That's the thing with history: it really belongs to who tells the story first. Everything else that follows is held up against that first story. But the real story, that was something else.

The only thing that mattered to Orville Wright was to get the Smithsonian to say that he and his brother had built the only plane that could fly in 1903. If someone could solve that for him, then Orville would be forever in his or her debt. Secretary Charles Doolittle Walcott of the Smithsonian had his back against the wall. He needed to bring back the plane. He needed to get the *Flyer* back from London. Kelly rubbed his chin. It would look really bad if he published the book and everyone read about how the Smithsonian had lied and forced Orville to send the *Flyer* to London.

Maybe he should let Secretary Abbott over at the Smithsonian know what was coming. There was the real story, but Abbott would want this thing put to bed before publication. Kelly shook his head. It was a pity. The real story would be a hell of a lot more interesting. Mabel Beck knew the real story, but she would never talk. She knew where all the bodies were buried. He would finish this chapter and write Abbott a letter. Who knows, he, Fred Kelly, might just be the man to bring back the plane that had flown at Kitty Hawk, North Carolina, in December 1903.

2

THE LETTER—1948

He was a boy whose father sold whiskey from a baby carriage that he made in his home. His father would wheel the buggy around with the baby and reach underneath the wool blanket for his customers, making one delivery after another. It was the Depression then, 1935, and everyone made any money they could. John Wohlganger was thirteen now; he shined shoes and made deliveries for a dry goods store. One of his customers was Orville Wright, who always demanded his shoes be spit shined, and then inspected the shoes very carefully before tipping.

His laboratory and office at 15 Broadway in Dayton was famous. The local boys liked to hang around and get glimpses of the man who had invented the airplane. "Orville Wright's office was not on street level. The front entrance was recessed, and there were stairs to the front door. The office part of the building was made with red wire-cut bricks with deep-set mortar joints. The shop part of the building was of cement blocks on street level," John recalled years later.[1]

John had to pull himself up on a ledge in the alley just to get a glimpse of Orville Wright in his white smock, and he didn't want Ms. Beck to catch him. Her face was winter. The commandant of Orville Wright. Nobody got to Orville Wright without going through Ms. Beck. She was the gatekeeper, secretary, assistant, centurion, guard, troll, and protector of the surviving inventor. Even the family had to go through Ms. Beck, and they hated and feared her but appreciated what she did for Orville. In her memoir, Ivonette Wright Miller, niece of the brothers, wrote, "She felt the power of her position and seemed to want to alienate everyone from Orville in order to have his full attention to herself."[2] Niece Sue Wright once had her car serviced at a garage near the laboratory. Since she had a long wait, she decided to wait in a comfortable place. She rang the bell at the laboratory. Mabel opened the door.

"Is Uncle Orv here?" Sue asked.

Mabel frowned. "You mean Mr. Wright?" she asked coldly.[3] "Wait here. I will see if he is in."

She disappeared into Orville's office. Sue said she heard her say to him, "It's Sue."

"She never would speak to any of us if we met on the street," Sue recalled. Orville's brother Lorin's daughter later wrote, "she became more and more possessive. She knew that with her knowledge of the Wright story she had a job for life. Knowing Orville, she was sure he'd never make a change."[4] Even so, John Wohlganger liked to watch the inventor: "During the three years I shined Orville Wright's shoes, I got to know him rather well. He was always dressed to perfection; he usually wore a black suit and black shoes; his shirt was white with a stiff collar."[5] "Shoe shines at that time were five cents, and Mr. Wright usually tipped a nickel. He was most particular about the shine and inspected his shoes all around the soles and heels before he paid me."[6]

One day, John was making his way down the alley when he decided to peek in the window. To get to Orville's office, he had to jump up and grab onto the brick ledge with his fingers and hoist himself up. John grabbed onto the cold bricks. It was January and just a few flakes were wisping down. Mabel Beck was sure to be around, so he would just raise his eyes over the ledge and get a quick peek.

The boy pulled himself up ever so slowly. It was 1935, and his meal of beans and cheese and prunes wasn't sitting well. Bricks, bricks, then the glass. He raised himself up until his eyes crested the sill and his head appeared in the window. There was Orville Wright in his smock. He had on his shined shoes that John had just worked over the day before. The boy stared, his eyes growing, because sitting on Mr. Wright's lap was Mabel Beck. "Here is what I saw. . . . Mr. Wright was sitting in his office chair facing North Broadway. He had his white smock on. There was Mabel Beck, sitting across Orville's lap, [her body] facing me. She had on a long-sleeved, light-colored blouse and a dark skirt. The reason she couldn't see me was because her eyes were closed. She and Orville were kissing."[7]

The unmarried woman with the close brown hair and the air of a school marm was now *kissing Mr. Wright.* John felt his face burn. The two adults couldn't see him, because their eyes were closed. The inventor was leaning back in his chair, and Ms. Beck had her legs crossed like a young girl. The boy felt his breath leave, and then he dropped to the ground and ran as fast as he could down the alley. John Wohlganger would not speak of what he saw for sixty years.

The woman the boy had seen was Mabel Beck, the daughter of Charles Beck, who was a machinist, and his wife, Lena, who lived in McPherson Town and then moved to Dayton in 1897. Mabel graduated from Steele High School in 1907 and then worked for three years at Moses Cohen's Furnishings and Hats. Mabel at eighteen was pretty, with dark hair and a plump figure. Moses occupied the ground floor of the United Brethren Building. On the thirteenth floor was the Wright Aeronautical Company. Roy Knabenshue had been hired to head up an aerial team of fliers for exhibitions. He stopped into the store, and Mabel Beck waited on him.

"I need to hire a secretary," he told the young woman. "I like your looks and the way you do your work, but you would have to type and write shorthand."[8]

Mabel jumped at the chance, took a course in typing and shorthand, and then went to work for the Wright brothers. She was Wilbur's secretary until he died in 1912 from typhoid fever, then she became Orville's secretary.[9] The world would never see Orville again unless it saw Ms. Beck first. Orville soon gave her a picture of himself that Mabel had framed and kept on a bedside table. She was there when Charles Lindbergh came to visit. She was there when the great flood of 1914 buried the *Wright Flyer* and she and Orville dried out the muslin canvas and recovered the wings.[10] One did not speak of Orville without Mabel.

They were always together, right up to the day on January 27, 1948. Orville was working in the laboratory with Mabel when he suddenly stopped talking and slumped in his desk chair. With pinched mouth and pale skin it looked like another heart attack. Orville had suffered a mild heart attack back in October 1947 while running up the steps of a building. He had been careful, ever since, not to push himself. Mabel frantically called Dr. Allen Horwitz across the street, who rushed over and examined Orville. It was a stroke that left Orville unconscious for the entire ride in an ambulance to Miami Valley Hospital.[11] Mabel would never see him again. Orville died three days later. He was seventy-seven.

Now he was dead. They were all dead—Wilbur, Katherine, Milton, and now Orville. The Wright brothers, the Wright clan, were gone. Poof. Dust. History. All that was left were their planes, and one in particular held the world in thrall. Death had brought the question to bear about the destiny of the 1903 *Flyer*. Everyone assumed Mabel Beck would be the executor and possessor of the will:

> Family and friends assumed that Orville had named Mabel Beck as the executor of his estate and waited patiently for the secretary to produce a will. When nothing happened, Harold Miller proceeded to Orville's bank to check on the will's whereabouts. Bank officials then contacted Orville's lawyer, Charles Funkhouser, who produced the will. To everyone's surprise Orville had named Miller and Howard Steeper, both nephews by marriage, as his executors.[12]

The two nephews studied the 1937 will "and discovered the passage deeding the machine to the Science Museum [in London] unless Orville had revoked the clause with a letter indicating his new disposition."[13] Orville had said there was a letter. The 1903 *Flyer* had gone to England, but there was no letter saying what to do with it. Probate Court Judge Love ordered Harold Miller to look for the letter, and he began with the most obvious person. It was as if that grim, tight-lipped Mabel Beck had just walked into the room and once again blocked access to Orville Wright. The woman who had given one biographer his walking papers and kept close rein on the second was back. The centurion at the gate was there again.

There had been whispers of something more between the inventor and his secretary for years. That would explain a lot. She was the only person Orville would trust to be the keeper of a letter that would change the course of history. But she had disappeared after Orville Wright's death, and no one could get hold of her. Miller finally tracked her down at the home she shared with her sister. Mabel acknowledged that there was a letter "but refused to produce it."[14] The keeper of all knowledge, the woman who held the answers, was not going to give up Orville's final wish concerning the most important plane in the world.

Mabel Beck had the letter and was keeping it. She had become the final footnote to the story of the invention of the airplane. A story that began back in 1884.

3

THE MURDERER—1884

I t was cold. The boys puffed breath and scraped the ice with their steel skates. The pond in Dayton, Ohio, was frozen down several feet. Boys with hockey sticks had discovered it long ago, and the shaved ice that now sprayed up had been accumulating for weeks. The games were rough, but there were rules. Oliver Crook Haugh knew no rules. He was older and the bully of the block, if not the town. His teeth constantly ached. Later, historians would say that cocaine tooth drops might have precipitated the invention of flight.

Or maybe Oliver Crook Haugh was insane. Before he was electrocuted in 1906, he claimed to have proven that two personalities can exist in one person: "All that I do know is, that if I die for these crimes, I shall have at least established the proof of the theory on which I have always insisted—that two beings, one of good, the other of evil, may exist in the same man, and in that respect at least I shall have rendered a distinct service to posterity."[1]

More likely Oliver Haugh was a full-blown psychopath, but the cocaine tooth drops certainly didn't help. There was no regulation for drugs then. Old ladies mixed cocaine with water and became horribly addicted. Opium was in abundance. Coca-Cola would make its mark by giving everyone a boost of cocaine that was still found in the coca leaves used in its recipe up until 1929 and corner the market on soda.[2] An apothecary was there to give opioids to whoever had a nickel to buy them, and doctors need not get in the way.

Oliver was fifteen when Wilbur met the boy who lived down the street in Dayton. They had skated before together. The Wright brothers were known as well-dressed, quiet young men who were the younger two sons of Bishop Wright, a well-respected man of the town. So, the three young men were on the frozen pond again playing hockey with the sticks flying. Haugh didn't dress like the Wrights. He wore no tie. He dressed like a laborer and was already known as the neighborhood bully, and he had the build of a man, if not a football player. Wilbur was eighteen. He had excelled in his classes, and there was talk of him heading off to Yale. "His schedule of classes would daunt a modern honors student: Greek, Latin, geometry, natural philosophy, geology and composition with general scholastic averages of 94, 96, and 95 for the first three terms."[3]

Wilbur enjoyed riding the high-wheel bicycle, excelled at gymnastics, and even sang with an informal social club known as the Ten Dayton Boys as their youngest member. He was said to have a fine bass voice. A childhood friend, John Feight, recalled that "he played on the Central High football team and was one of the swiftest runners in the school."[4] Wilbur was tall, slight, and fresh-faced; his grey eyes betrayed a luminous intelligence. His father was a successful bishop in the church and while not wealthy, the Wrights occupied the top rung of the middle class. This trip to the pond was a childhood skate before stepping into the adult world of the East. But here was Haugh skating toward Wilbur like a comet of doom.

Wilbur skated away from the boy-man zeroing in on him like a later fighter pilot. Maybe Haugh had it in for Wilbur. The preacher's kid. Smart. Well-dressed. Well-spoken. Everything Haugh was not. The weather was getting colder, the breath from the boys steamed into the clear December evening. The skates cut the ice with the steel blades grooving what would be iced over again when the next thaw came. Haugh was physically stronger than boys his age and bigger than Wilbur, who was facing off in front of him. Maybe he had the puck and maybe he didn't, but Haugh lifted his wooden hockey stick straight into Wilbur Wright's face and shattered his upper teeth and broke his jaw. History was altered with the teeth and the blood on the ice. Wilbur went down to his knees while Haugh skated off. It would later come out that not only did Haugh enjoy the cocaine drops, but he drank and used other drugs that landed him briefly in the Dayton Asylum for the Insane.

Oliver Haugh would go on to become a doctor and along the way was accused of several murders. He was probably a serial murderer, but there were no forensics to link him to his victims.[5] When he was finally electrocuted in 1906 for killing members of his family and then setting their home on fire, it was estimated that he had dispatched at least sixteen people. Wilbur returned home to be fitted for false teeth and have his jaw set.

But the damage went far beyond the physical. Something that Wilbur had not seen before—evil—had entered his world. His father, Bishop Wright, wrote in his diary, "A few weeks later he began to be affected with nervous palpitations of the heart which precluded the realization of the former idea of his parents, of giving him a course in Yale College."[6] The pain in his teeth and his jaw was unending. There was no Novocain, and Wilbur would not take the opioids that others so willing did for anything from a headache to a hangnail. Yes, there had been a physical blow with real damage, but the psychological blow was life-changing. Stomach issues began to haunt the young man as he convalesced in the Wright house with his mother, Susan, who was dying of tuberculosis. The dying light of winter was all around him now. The evil in the darkness. The pain. Then depression. Wilbur Wright began a spiraling descent into a physical and psychological breakdown that would last for three years.

Many late-nineteenth-century families succumbed to a singular event that left lasting consequences. Medical science did not understand the connection between the psychological impact of many diseases and injuries. Bishop Wright's brother had suffered an attack of dyspepsia that left him without his "wit in conversation and public speaking."[7] The family prescribed immediate prolonged rest for Wilbur, known as "the rest cure," which was medical science's answer to all problems for which there was no easy answer. Wilbur became a semi-invalid recluse; he did not leave his home. His view of the world had been shattered along with his jaw and teeth. The evil that was Haugh had touched Wilbur, and he recoiled with heart palpitations, chronic indigestion, and a full-blown depression that made him a loner who became obsessed with caring for his mother. He became the caretaker of the hospice. Was it the confluence of two horrible moments of his life that destroyed all dreams of college, of Yale, of going into the bigger world of the East? Was it the sudden realization that his mother was dying and that he, too, could die? Whatever it was, the journey into the dark night of the soul had begun for Wilbur Wright.

Milton Wright would sum up the incident in 1913 with a cryptic entry in his diary: "The man who threw the bat that struck Wilbur became one of the most notorious murderers in the history of Ohio."[8] The hockey stick was a bat, but this could become semantics. Whatever the weapon, it altered Wilbur Wright's life right there. No longer was he the bright, energetic eighteen-year-old headed out for college. He became a moody, reclusive, sickly young man.

The world had proved that his father was right about everything. There was evil out in the world, and only the family was a refuge. Retreat. Retreat. Leave the evil world as the good bishop admonished. Milton Wright would be described as "isolated and combative . . . not adept at the skills required to make friends and influence people . . . reconciliation, negotiation and compromise . . . were foreign to him."[9] In time, the same would be said of Wilbur.

Born in 1828 in a log cabin in Indiana, Bishop Wright was the son of Dan Wright, a farmer who had fought in the Revolution. Dan married Catherine Reeder on February 12, 1818. As Tom Crouch cited in *The Bishop's Boys*, "Milton Wright took great pride in the fact that his mother was the product of two first-generation Ohio families."[10] Of Milton's father it would be said, "he was grave in countenance, collected in his manners, hesitating in his speech, but very accurate."[11] He didn't drink or smoke. The apple did not fall far from the tree. Milton joined the United Brethren Church and preached his first sermon at age twenty-two. The Protestant Brethren church believed in "the abolition of slavery, women's rights, and the opposition to Freemasonry and its secretive ways."[12] The church and Milton were one, and he hit the road and never looked back while spreading the good word. After he became a bishop, he was mostly gone from the family and instructed them from afar in long epistles: "Make business first, pleasure afterward, and that guarded. All the money anyone needs is just enough to prevent one from being a burden to others."[13]

All that Bishop Wright required was that a hot meal, a warm bed, and a loving family await him after his long journeys. He would insist on this even when his two sons became world-famous and his daughter had passed into middle age. The trick was to keep everyone at home, and it was a godsend that Wilbur had become his wife's caretaker. That rendered Milton free to continue traveling and have the hearth fires burning when he returned.

Milton was crafty that way. His older sons had not done well. Reuchlin and Lorin had married and had families, but neither man prospered and both were in chronic distress over money and health. They had children, wives, and homes, but they were on the brink of disaster. In 1889, Reuchlin headed West to Cincinnati, then took a job with a lumber company in Kansas, and then a job with the Kansas City, Memphis, and Birmingham Railroad. His baby died and after thirteen years he returned to Dayton still unable to provide for his family.

Lorin headed West as well and ended up in Coldwater, Kansas, forty miles southeast of Dodge City. He took on the Western life with a hat and a gun but found the brooding isolation heavy. Looking out of a window in town, he saw a wolf loping down the street through the snow. He would head back to Dayton and for the rest of his life tell stories about the Wild West, a failure in all but fables. The bishop could now point and crow, *You see! This is what comes of going into the world!* Wilbur would slink in the background of his father's edict. Evil follows man in the world. Milton Wright could point to the two older brothers and say to his daughter, Katherine, and his younger sons, Orville and Wilbur, *You see what happens when you venture into the world? It is not to be trusted. Better you stay under the family roof, where all is safe and secure.* Wilbur—who was still in pain and still suffering from the assault, the psychic pain of his mother's demise, and his own personal hell—could offer no rejoinder. Risk was to be avoided at all costs.

The economy was not strong in the 1890s. "All across America young people were finding it much more difficult to strike out on their own than their parents and grandparents had. Times were hard."[14] This might have contributed to the Wright brothers abstaining from an interest in women and family life in general. Orville eventually wanted to establish himself as a printer, and the only way to do that was to remain at home. Wilbur had entered a dark land and taken up the role his father left vacant with his incessant traveling for the church. He was the young man adrift now with no direction, no compass to govern his life, just the caring for his mother and his own wounded soul.

Could there be any more desire to escape from the harsh realities of life than this three-year journey into the heart of darkness? This was at a time when there were no psychoactive medications. There was no therapist standing by to administer the answers to the basic questions a young man might have as to why he was brutally assaulted. This all went toward crafting Milton Wright's view of the world. Milton could go out in the world and do God's work, but his daughter and her two brothers should keep him company when he returned. This would be even more true when Susan Wright died. The bishop saw his life as a potentially lonely road, and he would cultivate his daughter to stand in for his wife, and his sons to never marry, to never leave. Even when Wilbur was at the zenith of his fame as the inventor of powered flight, Milton sent him letters, reminding him, "the ties of blood relationship are more enduring and more real."[15]

More real than what? Than becoming world-famous and eventually wealthy. Milton was a covetous old sinner in that he was psychologically castrating his children. He would record in his diary, "there is much in the papers about the Wright brothers. They have fame but not wealth yet. Both these things, aspired after by so many, are vain."[16] Neither Orville, Wilbur, nor Katherine would have a family life outside of Milton's orbit. When Katherine did attempt to do so later in life, she was cast out by Orville in the vein of the father. Bishop Wright was the star of the household, and even the invention of manned flight could be seen as frippery. He was a one-man wrecking ball against perceived depravity and would even split with his own church and throw in with the old conservative faction against the more progressive elements.

In his pictures he is a man with a bad comb-over and an Amish beard; he seems pious, self-absorbed, and judgmental. Even the death of his own wife would not slow his travels, though she was the angel in his life. The bishop would later acknowledge that Wilbur's care for Susan allowed him to continue his traveling. This was far greater than the invention of the airplane, and the bishop framed it all in the glory of God and himself: "His mother being a declining, rather than suffering invalid, he devoted himself to taking all care of her, and watching and serving her with a faithfulness and tenderness that cannot but shed happiness on him in life and comfort him in his last moments."[17]

Susan Koerner, born in Virginia, was brought West by her father, who was a German wagon maker. If her sons were mechanical, then it was because of Susan Wright. She was mechanically inclined and could create toys out of things around the house and treasured anything her boys made. When she met Milton Wright, she required him to wait three years before accepting his proposal of marriage. She was a woman who wanted to be sure. Her pictures are dour. She is the bishop's wife, the woman who must endure. Smart and painfully shy, she would give these traits to her son. The Wrights moved around as Milton's career required and as he spent six of every twelve months on the road. His wife quietly packed up the family as they moved from Fairmont, Indiana, to Millville, Indiana, where Wilbur was born in 1867, and then to Hartsville, and, finally, in 1869, to Hawthorne Street in Dayton Ohio, where Orville came into the world in 1871.

In every picture she is plainer, more tired, and more the enduring woman of the late nineteenth century. Then, in 1877, they moved yet again to Cedar Rapids, Iowa, and finally back to Dayton in 1884. Dayton was then becoming the modern city of the Midwest, with electric streetlights and a growing population of 40,000. Abraham Lincoln had spoken there in 1859 in front of the courthouse, and now a brand-new library was being constructed. Industrious and growing, the populace needed a new railroad station. The bishop would continue to travel six months out of the year, but this was home. There was no running water, and baths were taken in a tub on the floor of the kitchen. The boys grew up with Abe Lincoln austerity, though they were better off than the log cabins of the plains. Gas fireplaces provided heat for the entire house, and everyone had to keep their doors open at night to stay warm. Out back was an outhouse and a well and a shed for the horses. Their father had been born in a log cabin, and the Wright brothers were not that far removed—at least in sprit.

But this was where Wilbur Wright's three years of isolation provided a very different education. Slowly, surely, he began to emerge. He became the ghost prowling the upper floor of the Wright home, carrying his mother down the stairs. The stoic who would never say much began to awake. His intelligent mind would not be snuffed even by a crazed, cocaine-jazzed psychopath. Evil altered his life but didn't destroy it. The eighteen-year-old young man began to read his father's books between bouts of caring for his mother: "There could be found the works of Dickens, Washington Irving, Hawthorne, Mark Twain, a complete set of the works of Sir Walter Scott, the poems of Virgil, *Plutarch's Lives*, Milton's *Paradise Lost*, Boswell's *Life of [Samuel] Johnson*, Gibbon's *Decline and Fall of the Roman Empire*, and Thucydides. There were books on natural history, American history, a six-volume history of France, travel, *The Instructive Speller*, Darwin's *Origin of Species*, plus two full sets of encyclopedias."[18]

It was a house of readers, with Milton setting the tone. Wilbur began to systematically read and educate himself in the great quiet of the empty house during the day. He was no longer attending high school. Officially, he was a dropout, as was his brother later. His life had been turned upside down, and for the next three years the life of the mind would take precedence over the physical life. The man who would emerge from these three years would cement his distrust of the world outside. His interior life became preeminent, and maybe it was here the great escape of Wilbur Wright began to take hold.

A schoolmate would later say, "the strongest impression one gets of

Wilbur Wright is of a man who lives largely in his own world, not because of any feeling of self-sufficiency or superiority but as a man who naturally lives far above the ordinary plane."[19] One must live in one's own world to do what others cannot. Wilbur Wright began to fly alone at a very early age. Between 1886 and 1889, the bishop's library became his escape, and his father later noted the homeschooling he approved of: "He ... used his spare time to read and study, and his knowledge of ancient and modern history, of current events, and literature, of ethics and science was only limited by the capacity of his mind and extraordinary memory."[20]

Milton had already violated his tenet he would adopt after the first successful flight—that of his two sons being equal in mind and spirit. Oliver Haugh had murdered Wilbur's sense of purpose and left him adrift, but he had also provided space for a greater life purpose. Wilbur did not know it, but he was an artist. Haugh had made him become the artist without a calling, not confident in mind or body. His rehabilitation over three years in his father's house would produce a very different person who would escape ultimately by leaving the earth.

Wilbur had at one time considered teaching and had written his father, "I have always thought that I would be a teacher. Although there is no hope of attaining financial success as might be obtained in some of the other professions or in commercial pursuits, yet it an honorable pursuit, the pay is sufficient to allow me to live comfortably and happily and is less subject to uncertainties than almost any other occupation. It would be congenial to my tastes and I think with proper training I could be reasonably successful."[21]

But that went out the window with the decision not to go to college. Years later, before taking up flight, Wilbur would write, "I do not think I am specially fitted for success in any commercial pursuit even if I had proper personal and business influences to assist me. I might make a living, but I doubt whether I would ever do much more than this [run a bicycle shop]. Intellectual effort is a pleasure to me and I think I would be better fitted for reasonable success in some of the professions than in business."[22]

In 1889, Susan Koerner Wright died. Wilbur's self-imposed three-year isolation ended, and Orville, now eighteen, decided to build a printing press in the back shed with some spare parts. He had dropped out of his last years of high school and enlisted his brother Wilbur in his venture, and they began to publish the *West Side News*.

Orville had a checkered past in school. In eighth grade he had been sat up front so his teacher could keep an eye on him. "Orville was not an outstanding student, but he got by. His ninth-grade marks included a 79 in Latin, an 86 in Algebra, and a 92 in botany."[23] Instructor William Werthner didn't see anything remarkable in Orville Wright, who was "a quiet, reserved boy, faithful in his work, but not strikingly different from the rest." The year of his mother's death, Orville decided he would not return to high school for his senior year. The bishop, curiously, said nothing, probably seeing the public school as an institution that pulled his children away.

Orville didn't care about school anyway. He saw a publishing empire where his older brother saw drudgery. Still, he was his younger brother, and Wilbur was always mindful of his role to take care and look out for him. "My father and brother, seeing my determination to become a printer, managed after a while to get a small printing press for me,"[24] Orville would later write. The bishop noted that, "Before long the printing operation had taken over the summer kitchen at the rear of the Wright house, and the boys were accepting commissions for the job printing of handbills and advertising circulars, as well as letterhead, business cards, envelopes and tickets."[25]

Orville shows a prowess early on in construction of all things mechanical. He built his first press out of "a damaged tombstone, buggy parts, scrap metal, and odd items scrounged from local junkyards."[26] His second, larger press consisted of "four-foot lengths of firewood, while the framework of a folding buggy top was used to ensure a uniform pressure of the type on each sheet."[27] An office at 1210 West Third Street was secured, and the firm of Wright and Wright was in business. Classmate Paul Laurence Dunbar, who later rose to international fame as an American writer, briefly edited the *Dayton Tattler*, a weekly newspaper printed by the Wrights.

A Chicago pressman stopped by and examined the homemade press. Ed Sines, an employee of the new company, recalled that the pressman "went back into the press room, stood by the machine, looked at it, then sat down beside it and finally crawled underneath it. . . . He got up and said, 'Well it works, but I certainly don't see how it does work.'"[28]

Even though they together formed the firm of Wright and Wright, it was Orville's baby. The paper had changed its name to the *Evening Item*, and Orville felt they were doing well, but he picked up on his brother's indifference: "I've been making [$]2.00 to [$]3.25 a day in the office but I have to divide it with Will so that when the week is over I don't have much left. Will's working on the press, at least he says he is, but I can see little signs of it from the appearance of things."[29] Little brother was questioning big brother's commitment. The truth is business bored Wilbur, while Orville found business and mechanical challenges absorbing.

Wilbur would later write to his father that he was thinking again of going to college: "I have thought about it more or less for a number of years but my health has been such that I was afraid that it might be time and money wasted to do so, but I have felt so much better for a year or so that I have thought more seriously of it and have decided to see what you think of it and advise."[30]

The printing business ran its course about the time a national craze took over America that, at least for Wilbur Wright, would eventually lead to the building of the first airplane, namely, interest in the bicycle. The advent of the safety bicycle, an improvement over the high wheelers, lead to the opening of the Wright Cycle Exchange and then the Wright Cycle Company, where they would manufacture their own brand. Wilbur would be the reluctant partner until another catastrophic event involving his brother would alter his life again.

Wilbur Wright had been cast adrift by a madman and then fell under the tutelage of a father who, with the certitude of John Brown, believed that outside the family evil lurked. Business would be another prison for the man without direction. Escape had to be a terrestrial concern, if not an existential mission. In the gloom of his father's parlor in those years of physical and mental anguish, Wilbur must have looked out the window and seen the birds soaring on the wind and thought to himself . . . if only he could fly away.

STEAM BUGS—1896

Newspapers changed everything in 1896. "The linotype machine, curved stereotype plate, and high-speed rotary press"[1] allowed a publisher to set an enormous amount of type in a short time. Mass-produced newspapers demanded news that excited and titillated. The sports section was born and became the dominant section of a paper. William McKinley was running for president against William Jennings Bryan. Bryan traveled the country and gave six hundred speeches while McKinley stayed home and gave speeches from his front porch.

America was taking a breath before the Great American Century just around the corner. In Detroit, a mechanic built a car in the shed behind his house. He worked for Thomas Edison's new company that was busy electrifying cities and suburbs. The young man was a little odd and kept to himself, spending all his free time in the shed. When he was finished, he couldn't get his machine out the door. Henry Ford had to take apart his shed to free his new car.

The hard news was one thing, but Americans also wanted to be entertained. Funny news was born with the first comic strip, *The Yellow Kid*.[2] But there was nothing funnier than those crazy men who build machines and then tried to fly them. People all over the country read their papers and drank their coffee and followed the antics of men who ran off cliffs or hillsides, were pulled behind horses, or jumped off fences or roofs, or into the sea. Nobody could fly, but then Alexander Graham Bell said that powered flight was just around the corner. People listened to him as they listened to his phone, Edison's phonograph, and eventually large wax discs that recorded voices. Maybe man could fly, but nobody seemed to be able to do it.

Then Alexander Graham Bell and Secretary of the Smithsonian Samuel Pierpont Langley took a train to Quantico, Virginia, and then they took a boat to an island in the middle of the Potomac. Langley was a self-taught engineer who had switched to astronomy, built a telescope, toured Europe, then returned as an assistant at the Howard Observatory, followed by the United States Naval Academy and then Pittsburgh, where he became a professor of physics and director of the Allegheny Observatory. Over the next two decades, he would perform experiments, build a whirling arm device, disprove Newton's hypothesis that flight was impossible, and assert that motorized flight *was possible*. He landed an assistant secretary position at the Smithsonian, and when the secretary died, following the normal method for career advancement, he became the secretary of the Smithsonian Institute.

Bell and Langley stepped ashore and headed for the Mount Vernon Ducking Club, a very exclusive hunting club for Washington elite who worked just forty-one miles away by train. The two men passed the club and traveled down to a marsh, where a flat-bottomed boat was anchored. "Dubbed the *Ark* by the press, the strange craft featured a wooden structure almost as wide and long as the boat itself built on the deck. Four large windows on either side of the deckhouse were sealed with heavy wooden shutters. A spidery wooden superstructure on the roof supported a single twenty-foot rail extending over the rear of the boat."[3] It looked like a launching platform for a large bug.

Secretary Langley was thick-bodied, imperious, and known to be bluff, and he had younger assistants perform the experiments he supervised. Imperious is the right word for this man, who insisted that the nuts and bolts on his airplane models be polished, and who gave detailed instructions that were then followed by contradictory instructions. He was the secretary of the Smithsonian, an august, even somewhat-glamorous position in Washington. Alexander Graham Bell had sought him out to discuss science, and the science he wanted to discuss most was that of flying. Langley was way ahead of him, having published *Experiments in Flying* in 1891. It was a sensation even if the basic data of powered flight would prove to be disastrously flawed. No matter, Bell was an articulate and brilliant man. If he wanted to talk with Langley, then he must be brilliant too.

Langley was all about the experiment. Aeronautical data simply was not that important. It took power to fly; of this he was certain. No need to build gliders when one could build a fully powered, steam-driven model that, if it flew, would simply be a matter of size. One just built a bigger model to carry a man. None of the rubber models his assistants built took to the air, but Secretary Langley was confident that *power* was the key. Build a powered model and it will fly. The aerodromes were constructed out of spruce and pine, with a silk covering for wings. A small steam engine brought the aerodromes in at around thirty pounds. A launching system was devised and put on top of the houseboat, the *Ark*, and the Potomac was selected as the site.

Three initial aerodromes were just too heavy, and the steam engine too small. Langley didn't bother with those. Instead, he had his assistants, of which there were many, build two more aerodromes. "Tandem sets of wings fore and aft of the motor set in a dihedral—in an upward slant from the body forming a V—did well in simulations and, with a cruciform tail, provided the proper stability."[4] All that was left to do was fly the models, which some said looked like steam bugs.

Some workmen took the two visitors inside the boat, and on a table in the deckhouse were two silver models numbered 5 and 6. This was the cutting-edge technology of the moment. Ten years in the making, these two models were designed to fly. They might have been viewed as art, "glistening with copper pipes, brass fittings, and thin walled steel fuselages."[5] Fourteen-foot tandem wings with a steam engine at the center powered twin propellers. A delicate insect, these two models had yet to fly at all. The secretary of the Smithsonian asked the workmen several questions. He was now sixty-two, bearded, august, and the foremost authority on the new science of aeronautics.

Experiments in Aerodynamics was published by the Smithsonian in 1891, and Langley set the bar by stating boldly, "The most important general inference from these experiments . . . is that . . . mechanical flight is possible with engines we now possess."[6] Langley's critics laughed behind his back. For the last five years he had been building models that shot off the catapult on his boat and went right into the water. Too heavy, too weak, and underpowered, the first rubber-band-powered models nosed into the deep green of the Potomac. Then the steam-powered models followed: when hurled off the catapult launching system, the gleaming man-made insects whined, smoked, and puffed steam like crazed locomotives, and then splashed into the mighty river and sunk. Langley went back to the drawing board and made adjustments. Now Aerodrome 6 was ready to launch, and no less than Alexander Graham Bell was there to observe.

Langley had taken on two new assistants to help build the machine that would fly. Edward Charles Huffaker, "a Tennessean who went by E. C. was a forty-year-old slovenly, tobacco-chewing engineer who had submitted a paper in 1893, 'The Value of Curved Surfaces in Flight,' to the Congress on Ariel Navigation."[7] Octave Chanute, another self-taught engineer who was making headway on his plans to fly, recommended him to Langley. Huffaker drove Langley crazy with his habit of spitting tobacco juice by his desk, but put him to work on devising the airfoil configuration on the model.

Augustus Moore Herring, born in Georgia, was a trained engineer who had worked for Octave Chanute as well and built two gliders before being hired by Langley to work on the aerodrome. Herring only lasted eight months, complaining that Langley took all the credit for his accomplishments, but he had made "invaluable contributions to the design of Aerodrome 6, particularly in the wing configuration and tail assembly. Without his participation, Langley would have no chance."[8] Both men would appear again down in the sands of Kitty Hawk, North Carolina.

The catapult was ready. A powerful streetcar spring would shoot No. 6 down the rails and hopefully into the sky. It was 1:10 in the afternoon of May 6, 1896. A gentle breeze stirred the Potomac. A superintendent of the Smithsonian carpentry shop was behind the machine. He pulled the lever and "one of the guide wires holding the frail wings in place snapped now on launch, allowing the left forward wing to bend sharply up."[9] The aerodrome shot down the rails, puffing and whining, with the propeller spinning madly, then arced to the left and sank with a sad plop beneath the tranquil waters. Secretary Langley puffed on his pipe. He was the secretary of the Smithsonian, and he was embarrassed, but he had been here before. They fished out the model from the water. The propellers were smashed and the engine damaged. Number 6 would not see the air again. Bell waited patiently while model No. 5 was put on the catapult. A Smithsonian photographer stood by. He had missed a shot of model No. 6. It had gone down into the water too fast. Secretary Langley, whose face was red and brow furrowed, let the photographer know he better not miss the shot with No. 5.

Alexander Graham Bell knew that experiments often failed initially and stood silent while the workmen fired up the boiler on the model to develop 150 pounds of steam. The propellers began to spin and quickly reached their top speed. The Smithsonian photographer readied himself. This time he would get a shot before No. 5 disappeared beneath the sparkling green water.

An assistant pulled the release again, and No. 5 shot down the rails and disappeared over the side.

Langley and Bell stared anxiously, expecting to hear the telltale gulp of failure, when they heard a whine, and a gleaming silver insect rose up above the deck not unlike some alien creature. Langley and Bell watched, open-mouthed, as the model did something none other had ever done before: it caught the wind and began to climb in a slow-building arc. The unmanned steam-engine plane began a slow, circling glide and went around the houseboat twice. The whine was that of an automated insect, and to the men on board it sounded like the new century just around the corner. They were speechless as No. 5 ran out of steam and then settled back into the water and landed on the Potomac. The steam-powered model floated, turning ever so slightly in the current. The plane—they could call it that now—had flown 3,000 feet at a speed of 25 miles an hour.[10] The men on the boat cheered, and Langley shook hands with Bell. By God! By God! The plane had flown!

Alexander Graham Bell would later give an account to the newspapers: "The aerodrome or flying machine resembled an enormous bird soaring in the air with extreme regularity in large curves, sweeping steadily upward in the spiral path, the spirals with a diameter of perhaps 100 yards, until it reached a height of 100 feet in the air at the end of a course about a half of mile." The great inventor then added, "to my further surprise, the whole, instead of tumbling down, settled as slowly and gracefully as is possible for a bird to do, touched the water without any damage, and was picked out immediately and ready to be tried again."[11] Bell was telling the world that a model plane had been built and had flown. They flew the model again in the afternoon, and it did the same thing. The laughter behind Langley's back ceased. The black spot on his reputation that had threatened to fester into being just another crank had blossomed into the vindication that heavier-than-air flight was possible.

There were pictures and articles in the newspaper, and it is hard to say whether the great gliding man of his time, Otto Lilienthal, over in Germany, knew about Langley's success, but he probably did. He was about to jump off another cliff and was ready in his "flannel work shirt, twill knickerbocker trousers with padded knees, heavy brogans, and a close-fitting skull cap."[12] He looked like an early-century football player with his stocky build, red hair, and full beard. He would basically wear his twenty-foot bi-plane, with his legs hanging down for takeoff and navigation. He had flown two thousand times in his hang gliders, and now he was going to fly for Robert Wood, a correspondent for the *Boston Transcript*. His son and a mechanic helped him on with his wings while the correspondent took notes:

> So perfectly was the machine fitted together that it was impossible to find a single loose cord or brace, and the cloth everywhere was under such tension that the whole machine rang like a drum when rapped with the knuckles. . . . Here was a flying machine, not constructed by a crank, to be seen at a county fair at ten cents a head, or to furnish material for encyclopedia articles on aerial navigation, but by an engineer of ability . . . a machine not made to look at, but to fly with.[13]

The reporter Wood readied his camera. Lilienthal was already world-famous for his glides, and the pictures that he shot around the world. He was ready-made for the new age of mass communication, and the newspapers ate up the photos and descriptions of the "Flying Man," as he had come to be known. Unlike Langley, Lilienthal did not believe man would fly from building steam-powered models. Man would only fly by ascending into the sky himself and learning how to fly or at least how to glide. The air must be tamed, and control must be wrestled from the chaos of the invisible air currents he rode with regularity. The American papers loved the strange, bearded German acrobat in the padded knickers. The papers published the photos and reports on front pages. It was the perfect blend of daredevil, science, and oddity, with a tinge of humor.

Lilienthal crawled under his wings and wiggled his way into a set of "cuffs that would give him leverage on the machine,"[14] grasped a bar near the forward edge of the wings, and stood "like an athlete waiting for the starting pistol."[15] The stocky German ran forward off the edge of the hill and was immediately lifted off into the sky. He passed over the reporter's head fifty feet below and then went into a wide left turn, kicking his feet to right the wings. The wind was strong, and the German's beard was smoothed back. He had tamed the air and enjoyed the ride. Lilienthal passed over some haystacks and in a bit of drama kicked the hay with his feet and then kicked his feet straight up, putting the nascent airplane into a mild stall, he then floated down to Earth.

The reporter was over the moon: "I have seen high dives and parachute jumps from balloons . . . but I have never witnessed anything that stung the nerves to such a pitch of excitement or awakened such a feeling of enthusiasm and admiration as the wild and fearless rush of Otto Lilienthal through the air."[16]

Then Wood tried the glider. Lilienthal positioned him on the hill, and then he began to run with the heavy wings. The wings caught the wind, and Wood was lifted: "The feeling is most delightful and wholly indescribable. The body being supported from above, with no weight or strain on the legs, the feeling as if gravitation had been annihilated"[17] The reporter left Lilienthal to write his article and sing the German aviator's praises.

The following Sunday, Lilienthal went gliding on August 9, 1896. He again took off from the edge of a mountain. The wind was stronger than before, and he shifted his weight forward to keep the plane level. Still, the lift was too much and the wings turned up. Lilienthal kicked violently forward to head off the stall, but the glider lost all life and turned down. The German was too far forward and became a missile headed for the ground. The glider then turned on its back and plowed Lilienthal head-first into the ground, snapping his neck. He had fallen fifty feet when his glider stalled. He died the next day in a Berlin hospital. The news made headlines all over the world. The Flying Man had died. It was the summer of the flying men, and there was one more man who was about to tempt fate—Octave Chanute.

Two months before, on June 22, 1896, Chanute took a train from Chicago to Miller, Indiana. He had just read of Langley's success and was anxious to get his own glider unloaded. Octave Chanute looked like a trimmer Burl Ives. With a white Van Dyke goatee, a cherubic face, and piercing blue eyes, the French-born Chanute moved his family to Kansas City after working in New York for very little pay on the Hudson River Railroad. He contracted out to design the bridge crossing the Missouri River and established his reputation as an engineer with national prominence. In 1873, he became chief engineer for the Erie Railroad. On a family trip to Europe in 1875, he began to read about aeronautics. He was always puzzled with the way wind affected a roof or the bridges he built over rivers.

After 1884, he retired and began to scour libraries and institutions for any information on anything to do with aeronautics or flying. He sponsored aeronautical sessions at meetings of the American Association for the Advancement of Science. These meetings at Buffalo and Toronto were responsible for getting Samuel Langley interested in solving the problem of heavier-than- air flight. In 1893, Chanute organized the International Conference on Aerial Navigation, to be held at the Columbian Exposition World's Fair in Chicago that year. [18]

Wilbur and Orville Wright would go to the fair in the spring of 1893, but they said nothing about Chanute's conference. Still, we have men who would solve the problem of flight in close proximity to each other ten years before manned flight would be solved. Like moths drawn to a light, Wilbur and Chanute were both extremely intellectually curious, and the World's Fair of 1893 brought culture and science together. Chanute's conference on flying caught the attention of the newspapers, and he found himself at the center of many stories.

The Pittsburgh *Dispatch* summed it up this way: "The Chicago Conference undoubtedly marks the new era in aeronautics. It brought together many scientists and engineers who have been seriously working on the problem of flight. . . . It is no longer considered to be the hobby of cranks."[19] Chanute then published *Progress in Flying Machines* in 1894, and it quickly became the most up-to-date text to consult for any would-be aviators. Chanute then had several gliders built according to his design and hired Edward Huffaker to build and fly his glider. Having previously worked for Langley, Chanute enlisted another Langley refugee, Augustus Moore Herring. He used a multi-wing design that brought workers to refer to his plane as the Katydid.

Chanute was sixty-four years old and was not looking to kill himself in a glider. Herring made the flights at the Indiana Dunes. The dunes had been born over thousands of years and were gigantic, soaring hills that rose up from Lake Michigan like two sand-colored mountains. Wind was erratic, though, and in the heat of summer there was often no wind at all. The sulfurous smell of the steel mills of Gary, Indiana, wafted over with the whistles of passing freight trains headed for Chicago. Chanute waited patiently in the stifling heat while his two identical gliders, the Lilienthal and the Katydid, were launched. Neither plane responded to the controls and flew only one hundred feet. Herring then came up with a small, monoplane kite that flew very well. Chanute wanted a glider built on the same principles, and Herring suggested a cruciform tail that would move for stability. This would predate a major Wright brothers' improvement by seven years in terms of using a rudder on the tail of a plane.

Flight testing back at the dunes began again after Lilienthal's death. They began with a triplane glider but quickly removed one wing. Their glides now grew to 359 feet. They continued flying into September, with newsmen from Chicago recording every flight and making Chanute a public celebrity. Now that the Flying Man was dead, someone had to fill the news cycle, and why not another flying man of a more refined ilk? A sort of flying professor. Octave Chanute, with his small, white beard, was just such a man, and the space reserved for the German pioneer now was given to the men flying gliders in the Indiana Dunes. Chanute became sunburnt, and his joints ached, but he appreciated this new drug, fame. Still, he wouldn't fly himself. He would leave that to younger men.

As a younger man, Wilbur Wright read every word about Langley, Lilienthal, and—more important—Octave Chanute, while quietly nursing his brother Orville back to health from typhoid fever in 1896. He would write a letter to the flying professor, Chanute. Meanwhile, the War Department, with President McKinley's backing, gave the secretary of the Smithsonian, Samuel Langley, fifty thousand dollars to build a large-scale version of his aerodrome that had circled over the Potomac. Never had public funds been spent on trying to solve the problem of manned flight. It was an amazing endorsement of Secretary Langley and the Smithsonian. It was incredible. People had just gotten used to that invention that had overtaken America, the bicycle, and now there was going to be a machine that flies with a man on board. Good God!

TYPHOID—1896

I t may have been the well at the back of the bike shop. That well was quickly sealed, but it was too late. Orville went down in August 1896 with typhoid fever. The dreaded disease of the nineteenth century would kill Wilbur in sixteen years. In Chicago in the late nineteenth century, a typhoid epidemic broke out just before the 1892 Columbian Exposition. Human feces was the problem. Food or water tainted with feces became a potential carrier of the disease.

> Indeed how could there not be typhoid in a city with 40,000 privies and people who wouldn't connect to the sewer even when threatened with legal action.... The four-mile tunnel came on line in December, 1892. Typhoid deaths had begun to fall in 1893, partly due to the cleaner water from the tunnel but probably also due to the new public awareness about boiling or filtering the water. Work on the huge Ship and Sanitary canal project, which was to famously turn the Chicago River around and send its waters and Chicago's sewage down to St. Louis instead of into Lake Michigan, had begun in September 1892.[1]

Chicago would reverse its main river to combat the disease and keep people from drinking contaminated water. When this didn't work, city engineers built water cribs, which were giant intakes situated a mile out in Lake Michigan, for drinking water to get clear of the sewage along the lakefront. The extremely high fever from typhoid produced delirium and, many times, organ failure. During the Spanish-American War, more men would die from typhoid than were killed in combat. Training camps with poor sanitation were often the culprit.[2] New York and other cities had typhoid outbreaks when drinking water was contaminated with raw sewage. It was the disease of terror in the late nineteenth century, with no antibiotics to stop the ravaging disease marked by death in many cases.

In the late summer of 1896, Orville was confined to bed, with his temperature spiking to 105.5°F. Dr. Spitler was called to the house but could do little beyond confirming that it was typhoid fever. Medical science had no weapons at all for any sort of infection, and the best anyone could do was try to keep the patient hydrated and strong while the fever raged and delirium set in. Typically, in the first week, the fever rises dramatically with a cough, maybe a bloody nose, while the white-blood-cell count plunges. In the second week, the fever hovers around 104, and rose-colored spots break out all over the torso. Delirium is now a constant, earning typhoid the nickname "nervous fever." In the third week, diarrhea takes hold, the appetite vanishes, and the spleen and liver are enlarged. Patients often succumb when organ failure sets in.[3]

The bishop was nowhere to be found. He was traveling for church business and instructed Katherine and Wilbur from afar. They were to put Orville in the best room and sponge him "gently and quickly with least exposure, followed by rapid friction . . . boil the water you all drink, and set in ice water to cool. Use the best economy about rest. Be temperate in articles eaten. Be regular."[4]

For the month of September, Wilbur stayed by Orville's bed, along with his sister. This allowed him to once again sink into books. During the last few years, Wilbur and Orville had been consumed with their bike business, with no time to read anything. The bicycle in 1892 was the link between the horse and the automobile. As Tom Crouch explained in *First Flight*, "It marked the first convergence of technologies crucial to automobile production, ranging from electrical welding and work on ball bearings to experience with chain and shaft transmission systems, metal stamping technology and the manufacture of rubber tires."[5]

The first bicycle business in America sold "high-wheel ordinaries," which were the large-wheel bikes that only the brave could sample. The "safety bicycle" had two wheels of the same size and allowed everyone to now ride the contraption that was better, in many ways, than riding a horse. Orville quickly purchased a bicycle and determined their next course: fixing and manufacturing bicycles.

Millions of bikes began pouring out of American factories in 1895.

People could now pedal to work or go out for long rides in the country. The technology that was used for bikes would later be used in cars and then planes. It was a craze, with the church and moralists warning against the degradation that would follow bicycles. Strangely, the biggest moralist of them all—Bishop Wright—would have no objection to his sons' new business. Now children could leave their neighborhood out of the view of their parents. Children were going for a bike ride when they should be reading their books. In fifteen minutes, children could be over a mile away from their parents. Later, cars would be attacked for the very same reason. Mobility was equated to moral decay, and at the very least it meant sex. Nobody cared about the outrage, though, and bicycles swept the country and swept up the Wright brothers.

In a prescient article published by the editor of the Binghamton, New York, *Republican* on June 4, 1896, he predicted that the flying machine would probably be invented by bicycle manufacturers: "The flying machine will not be in the same shape or at all in the style of the numerous kinds of cycles, but the study to produce a light, swift machine is likely to lead to an evolution in which wings will play a conspicuous part."[6] That summer, bicycling and flying were dominating the news. Swift, balanced, rolling on air-inflated tires, people did feel like they were flying. Others saw a more direct relation.

James Howard Means wrote in the *Aeronautical Annual*, "it is not uncommon for the cyclist, in the first flash of enthusiasm which quickly follows the unpleasantness of taming the steel steed to remark: 'Wheeling is just like flying!'"[7] Wilbur and Orville purchased bikes and went for long rides on the roads outside of Dayton. One can see Wilbur taking Means's next words to heart when he would later write, "to learn to wheel one must learn to balance . . . to learn to fly one must learn to balance."[8] He would equate the control of the bicycle with the control of an airplane.

In 1893, their company, the Wright Cycle Exchange, started doing business by offering to sell and repair bikes. The Wright brothers opened at one location and then moved to a bigger one as business improved. But Wilbur and Orville diverged again: "Bring up the subject of the shapes of handlebars or types of pedals on early safety bicycles and his whole face lights up," a contemporary would later recall.[9] He was talking about Orville. Wilbur, we can be sure, was bored to distraction. In a letter to his brother Lorin, he spelled out his problem, though he speaks in the plural sense.

In business it is the aggressive man who succeeds who continually has his eye on his own interest. . . . Business is merely a form of warfare in which each combatant strives to get the business away from his competitors. . . . There is nothing reprehensible in an aggressive disposition. . . . I entirely agree that the boys of the Wright family are all lacking in determination and push. That is the very reason that none of us have been or will be more than ordinary businessmen. . . . There is always a danger that a person in this disposition will, if left to depend upon himself, retire into the first corner he falls into and remain there all his life struggling for bare existence. . . .[10]

In other words, Wilbur did not want to fall into "the first corner" or any corner. This he knew after crawling out of his three-year journey into the dark night of the soul. At this point, he is the artist without calling. He knows what he doesn't want to do, and that is any type of business. This is a split in the Wright-brother motif of combined aspirations. Orville would have been quite satisfied to be a printer or the owner of a prosperous bicycle company. The intellectual boredom was not there for the younger brother, but it was there for Wilbur. So, like every man who has not found his calling, his destiny, Wilbur was looking for the path, the challenge that would satisfy the intellect that could have taken on Yale and that had burned through Milton's library for three years.

Then fate took a hand again with Orville becoming ill. It would be a month before he could sit up, but it was during Orville's illness that Wilbur began to read about the death of the German glider, Otto Lilienthal. It is here he would pin his interest in flight: "My own active interest in aeronautical problems dates back to the death of Lilienthal in 1896 . . . and led me to take down from the shelves of our home library a book on Animal Mechanism by Prof. Marey, which I had already read several times."[11]

Common lore has it that Wilbur began to read to Orville about the glider's demise, and this seeped into the deliriums of Orville, and he emerged as his brother, intent on solving the problem of manned flight. The truth is that caring for his brother gave Wilbur time again to think and wonder and to contemplate something commensurate with his own intellectual, spiritual, and existential needs. Besides the fabled helicopter toy that caught the two brothers' imagination, this is the first time Wilbur Wright considered the problem of human flight.

So, while Orville slept or tossed and turned in delirium, Wilbur read about the German pioneer. Lilienthal, like many early pioneers, had a day job manufacturing steam engines and was a mining engineer by trade. He had some money, and this helped put flying squarely in the realm of an expensive hobby. Men trying to fly had to be careful; history was littered with cranks and nuts who had jumped off castles, cliffs, boats, and hills, all to either perish or suffer severe injury. Even Wilbur, years later, would remark that flying was his hobby and the bicycle shop was most important. This was just cover—it is much easier to tell people that flying is just something on the side, when most people saw flying as crazy. In the late nineteenth century, anyone attempting to ascend to the heavens was clearly insane, in the view of most middle-class Americans. The analogy today would be someone dedicating his or her life to time travel; the technology did not support the ambition in either case.

But Lilienthal was deadly serious and had built up to a dozen gliders. He was the perfect late-nineteenth-century flying enthusiast joining athleticism with a quest to fly like the birds. His wings were shaped like a bird and made of white muslin, with a large rudder protruding off the back of the glider. Wilbur read about Lilienthal taking a running start off the side of Rhinower Mountains, a range about two hours by train from Berlin. Running off the side of the mountain, he would be lifted from the earth. Hanging down like a praying mantis, he kicked his legs one way or the other to go left or right. It was crude and very dangerous, but Wilbur recognized immediately that this red-haired maniac was *flying*. The only things he lacked were an engine and, more important, *control*.

Lilienthal was savvy enough to have pictures taken of himself while in flight, setting the bar for all would-be aviators to follow. If you do fly in the air, make sure you record it so the world can know what you are up to. This was not lost on Wilbur Wright. Lilienthal's glides had made him world-famous, and when he crashed on August 9 in one of his favorite gliders, it was national news. He broke his neck and died the next day, at the age of forty-eight, but he left behind an admonition for the young man looking for a path in life: "It must not remain our desire to acquire the art of the bird. It is our duty not to rest until we have obtained a perfect conception of the problem of flight."[12]

Wilbur had his charge. While his brother lay writhing in the damp sheets on Hawthorne Street in the hell of typhoid, the man who had found nothing in this life to engage him since before the assault by the murderous Haugh now had something as big as his mind's capacity to wonder and scientifically attack a problem. Like the writer who finally finds the theme, the subject that will become the book of his life, Wilbur now had the ultimate engineering problem that had to be solved. Man must fly, *man could fly*, and it was up to him to crack the code of powered flight.

This was not a bicycle that had to be fixed or a business that had to be managed. This was something so complex, so varied, so *unknown*, that Wilbur would have to find out every known fact and start from there and then, like Lilienthal, jump off the side of the mountain to see where he would land. Once he had the bug, there was no turning back. Man should fly. It was in his grasp, but no one had put the pieces together. He knew this intuitively. Was it destiny? Maybe. Teddy Roosevelt had survived three years in the Bad-lands of the Dakotas, and there were cowpunchers who told him one day he would be president. Wilbur Wright knew this was his destiny, yet there were no markers of aeronautical greatness for others to recognize. It was simply a complex mechanical, spiritual, life goal. It was big. Bigger than anything anyone could imagine at the time. It was perfect for the man who had gone inward for three years and emerged with a tabula rasa, a blank slate of ambi-tion and intellect. Here is where he would engage the world. This would be his San Juan Hill to climb. It would be his point of contact before he would take to the air and leave Earth forever. To fly would be the ultimate escape from the terrestrial hell of humans, pettiness, evil, concerns, and responsibili-ties. The world had seemed strange and demonic during his journey into the dark night of the soul, and yet he had to enter back into it. There would be no family for him. No partner. No woman. He would commit himself to the holy grail of manned flight and improve the world.

Wilbur looked up from the paper and looked at his brother Orville, now sleeping. It was October, and he had survived the worst of it, but it would be weeks before Orville could leave his bed. Wilbur would need assistance. He had built a printing press with his brother and then bicycles, but they were both Orville's projects. Now Orville could come along with him. He would take his younger brother along for the ride. If they were on a ship, he would be the navigator and Orville would man the tiller. But he would set the course for both.

Wilbur immediately dove into his father's book *Animal Mechanism*. He would base all of his initial science on the winged creatures who had already solved flight: birds. Étienne-Jules Marey, a French physician, had become fascinated with birds thirty years before and had drawn a line between winged flight by birds and man: "How frequently has the question been raised, whether man must always continue to envy the bird and the insect their wings; whether he too may not one day travel through the air as he now sails across the ocean."[13]

From the beginning, Wilbur saw flight as a problem of control. The science was there. Air could lift a creature and could lift a man, but the bird could control the air currents and ride them at will; man had a bad habit of getting killed when he went aloft. Wilbur then discovered J. Bell Pettigrew's treatise, *Animal Locomotion or Walking, Swimming, and Flying with a Dissertation on Aeronautics*. These writings centered on birds and more specifically the birds' *wings* as the key to solving the problem of flight. This makes perfect sense to us now, but would-be aviators had been busy for fifty years strapping on rockets and feathers, and creating bouncing, flapping machines that went nowhere. Time would prove that Wilbur differed from men who believed flight was a matter of power. Strangely, no one had taken on the simple concept of a wing. How does it provide lift, and how does one control that lift?

Wilbur fell back into his old mode of reading while the invalid Orville slept. Wilbur had done so with his mother for three years, and now he used the hiatus to uncover the thoughts of other men who had contemplated taking to the air. He continued, and, as Orville recovered, he gave the books to his brother. Did Orville take to these dense studies of birds and theories on flying? Maybe. But it's telling that Orville left no paper trail of any interest in flight at this point. The bicycle shop was booming, and one cannot imagine Orville taking too big a detour from being the enterprising Yankee to go solve the problem of flight. He probably thought Wilbur's interest in flight would pass; besides, they had a new line of Wright brothers bikes to get out the next year. But Wilbur took the next step.

It is one of those moments when a path is chosen. Reading books on birds and ruminations on winged flight is one thing, but to pass from the amateur to the professional systematically approaching a problem to be solved speaks of secret intent. A cool day found Wilbur alone in the house. The clock on the mantle ticked, the locomotives were whistling and clacking as they hauled freight into the interior of the country. It was the last year of the nineteenth century, 1899, and the last day of May. His father, Milton, and his sister, Katherine, had left to put flowers on Susan Wright's grave in Woodland Cemetery. Orville was at the bike shop, of course.

Wilbur slid down into a chair and faced his sister's slant-top desk in the parlor. He picked up the fountain pen and positioned the stationery emblazoned with *Wright Cycle Company*. The sun slanted in the West and drummed across the wide-plank floor. He was in his high collar and tie and a plain gray vest. He had exhausted the books he could get his hands on, and he needed more. Research cries out for volumes, the thirst for knowledge where there was none before. By trade he was a bicycle manufacturer and mechanic. A high-school dropout. A man who had veered from life for three years with no plans and then followed the whims of his brother half-heartedly. That was it. He only possessed the keen intellectual curiosity that is the hallmark of any man or woman who pursues the life of the mind. He began to write, his fountain pen scratching the rude paper.

> I have been interested in the problem of mechanical and human flight ever since as a boy I constructed a number of bats of various sizes after the style of Caley's and Penaud's machines. My observations since have only convinced me more firmly that human flight is possible and practical. It is only a question of knowledge and skill just as in all acrobatic feats. . . . I am about to begin a systematic study of the subject in preparation for practical work to which I expect to devote what time I can spare from my regular business. I wish to obtain such papers as the Smithsonian Institution has published on this subject and if possible a list of other works in print in the English language . . . I am an enthusiast, but not a crank in the sense that I have some pet theories as to the proper construction of a flying machine.[14]

Wilbur then asserted his belief "that simple flight is possible at least to man and that the experiments and investigations of a large number of independent workers will result in the accumulation of information and knowledge and skill which will finally lead to accomplished flight."

The letter went off to the Smithsonian and ended up on Richard Rathbun's desk. He was an assistant to Secretary Samuel Langley, and since the flight of the aerodrome, the Smithsonian had been besieged with letters from would-be aviators. Wilbur was requesting anything on aeronautics, "such papers as the Smithsonian Institution has published on this subject, and if possible a list of other works in print in the English language."[15] It is amazing Rathbun replied to the letter that had been drafted on Wright Cycle Company stationery. A bike mechanic who wants to fly. Sure.

A reply came back from Rathbun, who had passed the letter on to a clerk who supplied a list of books and pamphlets on aviation:

> They were reprints of articles originally published in the *Smithsonian Annual Report*: Louis-Pierre Mouillard's *Empire of the Air*; Otto Lilienthal's "The Problem of Flying and Practical Experiments in Soaring"; Samuel P. Langley's "Experiments in Aerodynamics"; and E. C. Huffaker's on "Soaring Flight." Rathbun also suggested James Howard Means's the *Aeronautical Annual*." The Langley could be purchased for one-dollar postage included.[16]

Wilbur placed the order for Langley's *Experiments in Aerodynamics*. These writings were those of Octave Chanute and Samuel Pierpont Langley. Both men would be the twin pistons of Wilbur's future. One man would open the world for him while the other would be the lynchpin to a descent into darkness. Langley had funding and had managed to launch his model-sized steam-powered insect with wings from a catapult atop a houseboat, and the invention flew amazingly for a half a mile. Langley was convinced he was close to solving manned flight. All he had to do was build a bigger aerodrome and put a man aboard.

Wilbur learned that the great minds of the country were working on the problem of flight. Many were eminent scientists, with Alexander Graham Bell and Thomas Edison heading the list. They all had money and resources that Wilbur Wright could not possibly hope to possess. Another possible inventor, Hiram Maxim, had sunk a cool $100,000 into developing a flying machine that crashed on takeoff. It is worth noting here that the lack of money will be Wilbur's greatest advantage. It brought caution, methodology, and the slow cracking of the nascent science of aeronautics. There could be no frippery, because Wilbur couldn't afford any. Efficiency was uppermost. He had to isolate the central problem of flight before attacking the whole. This was the machine age, and men believed that a powerful engine could solve all problems. They went right past the central problem of lift. After all, since birds flew from rapidly flapping wings, it would follow that if a machine flapped just as rapidly, it should fly. Some pursued this idea and were immortalized a hundred and ten years later in YouTube videos of jumping cars.

Also, people tended to die while trying to fly; and this, along with the contraptions that kept crashing, going into the sea, or falling apart on takeoff, kept the art of flying squarely in the lunatic fringe category. Death ended most of the nascent aviators' short careers. The science of aeronautics was not advanced, because there was no methodology. Like the trapeze artist in the circus, the man attacking flight in the late nineteenth century took the flying leap first and worried about the science of flying not at all. It was a mechanical problem that would be solved by trial and error. The error was costly and usually deadly. It was as if manifest destiny of the skies had been declared. If the birds could fly, so should the white man. All he had to do was leave the ground and figure it out as he flew through the air. Such hubris would sink the *Titanic* a dozen years later. But who would risk life and limb on something so foolish and dangerous? Technology was crude, and this led to machines shaped like ducks and one that had nitroglycerin pellets being ignited for thrust. Nothing worked, and—after the notices of another aviator's death—the newspapers of the time declared: "It is a fact, that man can't fly."[17]

But this was also the age of invention, and with the new century came innovations that would change everyday life. A man named George Eastman had perfected an everyday camera called the Kodak, and Isaac Merrit Singer came up with the first electric sewing machine. People could now go high up in buildings in New York because the Otis Elevator Company had produced something called an elevator that hoisted people up to the heavens. Motorcars were being built all over America, and manufacturing in general was taking off with mass production and a populace ready to buy on easy credit. Change was in the air, and exploration was still the passion of the time.

In the letter sent to the Smithsonian there is no mention of Orville Wright. There is no use of the plural "we" that would later be applied to all correspondence. As the historian Tom Crouch would write in *The Bishop's Boys,* "In later years the brothers would claim that Wilbur had simply written 'I' when he meant 'we' but Wilbur was aware of Orville's touchiness about an equal division of labor, profits and credit. Had aeronautics been a joint interest in 1899, Wilbur would have spoken in the plural."[18]

The truth is that the letter was from Wilbur because it was *his desire* to fly. His brother had no interest in flying. Even in letters to his father announcing his intention to go to Kitty Hawk, there is no mention of Orville. Why should there be—it was not Orville's idea or his quest. He wrote to the Smithsonian, "*I have been interested in.* . . . *I am about to begin.* . . . *I wish to obtain*"[19] His father would maintain that Wilbur had "drawn" his brother into the "flying problem." Wilbur was thirty-two years old in 1899. He poured over the known data of flight from the Smithsonian, reading Chanute's, Huffaker's, and Langley's findings. He obtained a copy of Chanute's *Progress in Flying Machines*; located copies of the *Aeronautical Annual* for 1895, 1896, 1897; and read through the back issues of popular magazines in search of articles on flying machines.

Wilbur Wright was a man on a mission. He would jump off where others had left off. The problem was that a lot of the information contradicted data gathered by one aviator to the next. He would later write, "Thousands of pages had been written on the so-called science of flying, but for the most part the ideas set forth, like the designs for the machines, were mere speculations and probably ninety percent was false. Consequently, those who tried to study the science of aerodynamics knew not what to believe and what not to believe."[20]

The school of one was in session. Langley and Chanute had some success with planes that had flown in brief spurts, but they did not really know how they did it. The man reading in Dayton, Ohio, the bicycle mechanic, wanted to know how a wing provided lift. What was the math behind it, the equation that would tell him how a wing lifted itself into the air? How did it work? Wilbur wanted to know how a plane could then be controlled. Secretary Langley just assumed stability was a given, and other "aeronautical investigators regarded flight as if it were not so different from surface locomotion except the surface would be elevated . . . the flying machine remained essentially level in the air . . . leaning or rolling to one side seemed either undesirable or did not enter into their thinking."[21] Octave Chanute was not sure anything would fly and believed in slow, methodical planning. Wilbur read on, looking for answers.

For now, his letters led with the singular "I." The plural "we" that would punctuate later Wright correspondence is conspicuously absent. It is a slipup that Orville would correct forty-five years later.

INVENTORS—1900

The century had turned, and Glenn Curtiss finished the last adjustments to his motorized bike. Hammondsport, Steuben County, New York, was a small, tranquil town in the first year of the new century, with summer breezes flapping green awnings over the general store. Down on Main Street, everyone was waiting for the show. Glenn Curtiss ran the bicycle shop over on Pulteney Street. He had dropped out of school in the eighth grade and never looked back. He liked anything mechanical. He loved bicycles, and riding faster than the cars puttering down the street gave him a thrill. All bikes went faster than cars in 1900.

The awning flapped again in the summer wind, undulating G. H. CURTISS—BICYCLE SUPPLIES—SPORTING GOODS. Glenn leaned over the bike. He was a muscular, lanky, quiet young man of twenty-three with a bushy mustache, and he was perpetually reading about engines and electricity, anything that moved something along. People always thought he was chewing, ruminating, trying to figure out how something worked and how to improve on it. The early twentieth century offered up to young men a fountain of inventive spirit, with bold strides in mechanics, electricity, and that outlier—flight—being made every day. Glenn was a natural mechanic and perfectly suited in demeanor and intellect for his time.

Curtiss stood up and wiped his brow. He finished up with the bicycle that was now motorized with an engine he had built from some mail-order engine castings. People would stroll into the shop and watch him tinker with the engine, trying to improve and modify the power plant for the bicycle. "The thing did not even come equipped with a carburetor, and so he made one out of a tomato can and a gauze screen. More tin cans were soldered into service for other uses, attached, wherever there was a place for them to hang."[1]

Glenn pushed the motorcycle out the door. Proprietors and customers emptied out of the stores to watch. Dust blew up from the street. Glenn fitted his goggles, got on the bike, and began to pedal down the street; he intended "to pedal the transmogrified bicycle up to a speed where the motor could be started by engaging the transmission belt."[2] Glenn pedaled and pedaled around the park square, but the engine did not engage. People began to laugh at the long-legged man pedaling then stopping to adjust before pedaling again.

Glenn stopped by the post office and adjusted the spark. He was hot and sweating profusely. He saw some people returning to their stores. There were all sorts of cranks out there with automobiles that broke down all the time, or the hilarious accounts in the papers of men who tried to fly with jumping cars, chicken wings, or jet packs of rockets on their backs. Newfangled ideas were just that, and here was another one.

Glenn started to coast on a small downgrade and engaged the engine again. There was a backfire as the engine beneath his legs coughed to life and, like a demon, the engine shook the bicycle and then took off. Glenn felt the acceleration along with the wind as the engine with no throttle blasted along, just a wide-open, spitting hellcat screaming out a staccato of explosions, with the bike increasing in speed. The motorcycle was now tearing down the street for Lake Keuka. Glenn felt his hair blow back and the sweat cooling on his brow; he was trying to keep the handlebars straight while the motor shook and gulped air through the tin can, leaving behind a thick stream of blue smoke roiling in the summer light. This was amazing. He was flying along and not using any of his own power. He simply wanted to go faster and faster, and the bike was obliging, but there was one slight problem: no brakes.

The lake was now directly in front of him and Glenn had no choice but to jump off his motorcycle or take a swim. He rolled in the dust and watched his creation crash in the street, with the motor shooting out a series of final blasts before silence. The people along the storefronts stood open-mouthed, and little boys came running down the street. Glenn was now picking up the motorcycle. He had already decided to wheel it back to the shop and put on brakes—and then put on a bigger engine. He couldn't get over the feeling of whipping through the air on the bike.

Glenn Curtiss began to build more motorcycles with better engines. That was really his thing. He loved to make engines go faster by increasing the horsepower. People still laughed at him, until he began to win the motorcycle races. He went 64 miles per hour—at a time when an average speed of 30 miles per hour was considered fast. Glenn loved speed. The faster, the better. He won the endurance ride from New York to Cambridge, Maryland. His motorcycle motors became better and better. When he was thirty-one, he started his own company. He saw all technology as there for the taking. If he read or heard about someone's idea and it sounded good to him, then he used it. He was in the vein of inventors like Henry Ford, who used a basic mechanics approach to all problems and never thought about any idea or any innovation belonging to any one person. Innovation was in the air, the ether of the young century blowing down the hot summer streets of his hometown. That was how ideas were improved upon. One man took another's and made it just a little better. You couldn't trademark an idea or a technology. It was there for the taking. If a man wanted to use a soup can for a carburetor, then no one could tell him he couldn't do so just because someone else had done it before. That would be ridiculous. Nobody owned an idea. That would be like someone saying, "You owe me money for using my idea." To Glenn Curtiss, that made no sense. Ideas came to him in the dusk when he was working on his motors in his shop. He sure didn't expect someone to pay him for an idea. They could pay him for the motor, maybe, but ideas, like the wind, were free. This is at a time when other men were being paid for their inventions, and being paid very well.

Secretary Langley was now the preeminent man of science and aeronautics. The steam bug had flown over the Potomac. It was now just a matter of time before the secretary of the Smithsonian proved to the world that man could fly. Propulsion was everything now. Power was everything. Aerodrome No. 5 had proven to Alexander Graham Bell and others that Langley was the man who would solve the puzzle of flight. It was just a matter of size. Langley was feted from one celebratory dinner to another. Bell extolled his virtues. The Smithsonian saw it as a great feather in their scientific cap that the very leader of the institution should solve the problem of flight. It was the motherlode of recognition that the Smithsonian was truly the repository of all known science.

All Secretary Langley had to do was find an engine big enough and powerful enough to carry a man over the sparkly, green Potomac. The $50,000 the government had given him had come at an opportune time. Aerodrome No. 5

had flown just after the battleship *Maine* had blown up in Havana Harbor. The army and the navy saw war on the horizon and wondered if Aerodrome No. 5 might lead to an airplane that could be useful in the coming war. The army and the navy departments both agreed to kick in $25,000 for future experiments, not realizing the war would end as quickly as it did. Nonetheless, President McKinley wanted the experiments to go forward and the US Army Ordnance Department put in the full $50,000.

So, with money to burn, Langley went in search of a lightweight gasoline engine. He found Stephen M. Balzer, a machinist "who had designed and built the first automobile to run in the streets of New York."[3] The vehicle was powered by a three-cylinder rotary engine (that is, the engine revolved around its shaft). Balzer had been looking for someone to finance and market his automobile, and he saw Langley as a source of income to that end. Secretary Langley believed in lots of assistants and engineers to fill out his plethora of men who would make him look great by their innovations, and he asked the dean of the Cornell College of Engineering to recommend "the best young engineer he knew to become his assistant."[4] Charles M. Manley appeared at the Smithsonian on the eve of his graduation, to assist Balzer in designing the new motor. He was a small, lithe man with a high forehead and a diminutive mustache. Langley respected his intelligence and suspected he was more talented than Balzer, who had just unveiled his motor.

"Balzer's pattern was a 5-cylindered rotary engine the cylinders arranged radially, like the points of a star. It was to be air-cooled. When it was finally up to testing, this motor could produce no more than 8 horsepower when the contract called for a minimum of 12 horsepower."[5] Langley and Manley quickly combed Europe looking for another engine and, not finding it, returned to deal with Blazer's underpowered combustion engine. Secretary Langley had lost all faith in his original hire and paid off Blazer, leaving Manley to alter the engine and increase the horsepower. The engine was shipped to the Smithsonian, where Manley could work in secrecy.

As Cecil Roseberry wrote in *Glenn Curtiss: Pioneer of Flight*, "The first thing Manley did was convert it from a rotary to a static radial engine. The power picked up instantly. He made it water-cooled and gave it lighter pistons, along with other refinements. Ultimately the engine Manley installed in Langley's 'aerodrome' produced 52.4 horsepower."[6] The secretary had found the perfect assistant in Charles Manley. He was a brilliant man who was able to work under pressure and wanted not fame, but only to please his boss. Secretary Langley immediately cut off all information about his project to the outside world: "It is the practice of all scientific men, indeed of all prudent men, not to make public the results of their work until they were certain."[7]

The secretary let the grass grow long outside the carpentry shop, to stave off any curiosity about the airplane being constructed inside. Secrecy would become a hallmark of aviators and put the secretary of the Smithsonian on a collision course with another man who valued secrecy, Wilbur Wright, who guarded the privacy of his remote location for experimentation. For there was no place more secret than the barren sands of Kitty Hawk. When Langley's plane was ready, it would fly off the *Arc* on the Potomac like a flapping white bird ushering in the brilliant new century. Secretary Langley, like a lot of men of his time, felt the twentieth century would belong to America, and it would be fitting that he should conquer the skies for the Smithsonian and make himself the most famous man in the world.

SCHOOL OF ONE—1900

Wilbur rode his Van Cleve bicycle outside of Dayton. He wanted to test a theory on balance. He rode very fast down the farm road and then slowly took his hands off the handlebars. If someone had seen him, they would have observed a man in a tie and a brimmed cap with his arms straight out like Christ on the cross. Wilbur felt the wind passing over his body and kept his eyes straight ahead. Balance. He was perfectly balanced, and this was keeping the bicycle straight up. As long as he kept pedaling, the momentum kept the bike in a state of suspended animation. Balance and movement were in tandem. If he leaned to one side or the other ever so slightly, then the bicycle turned to that side. A plane must fly on the same principal, one of perfect balance.

Wilbur would later write, "I had asked dozens of bicycle riders how they turn to the left. I have never found a single person who stated all the facts correctly when first asked. They almost invariably said that to turn to the left, they turned the handlebar to the left and as a result made a turn to the left. But on further questioning them, some would agree that they first turned the handlebar a little to the right, and then as the machine inclined to the left, they turned the handlebar to the left and as a result made the circle, inclining inwardly."[1]

Wilbur put his hands back on the handlebars and turned around. He had to get back to the bike shop, but first he wanted to write a letter. He returned and put his bike in the back room. Orville barely looked up from his work on putting together the latest Wright Van Cleve bicycle. They had become manufacturers of bicycles, and this was very exciting for a while. Even though the bicycle shop had expanded to two locations and business was still good, Wilbur never quite gave up the idea of becoming something else: "I have always thought I would like to be a teacher. Although there is no hope of obtaining such financial success as might be attained in some other professions or in commercial pursuits yet it is an honorable pursuit."[2]

The life of the mind. Even though he and his brother had come out with two different models for bikes and business was doing well, this wistful man did not feel engaged. In fact, the bicycle craze had started to wane in 1897, and by the time Wilbur took his bike ride it had slowed. This gave him pause, but the truth was "he felt trapped in a commercial pursuit for which he was ill suited and which had not enabled him to develop his latent talents and abilities."[3]

Then, of course, fate took a hand on a late summer day. Maybe it was in the waning days of the bicycle craze, but a man came in for an inner tube, and Wilbur brought out the tube in a long cardboard box. After the man had left, Wilbur held the box in his hand and flexed it. He noticed that one end of the box flexed down, but the other side flexed up. He ripped the ends off the box, and the flexing became more apparent. Was this the prelude to the groundbreaking idea of wing warping?[4] How could a bird turn? The creature flexed its wings ever so slightly and veered right or left. This was surely truer than the helicopter that many point to as the pivotal moment that brought the Wright brothers to study flight. Some would hail this cardboard-box moment as the beginning of modern flight. The lore is he went home and showed it to his brother Orville, and they both agreed that wing warping was the key to aeronautical control. If this was a great moment in the journey toward flight, then Orville would certainly add the "we," if not in fact then in thought.

The Kelly biography puts Orville as the man who had this idea first, but there is no support for this. As Fred Howard wrote in *Wilbur and Orville*, "It was Wilbur who stumbled on the solution. . . . He sold an inner tube for a bicycle tire. He removed the tube from the long narrow box in which it came and while talking to a customer, began absentmindedly to twist the ends of the box in opposite directions. . . . It suddenly occurred to him that if a frail pasteboard box could survive such strain, it might be possible to twist the cloth covered wooden frame of a flying machine in the same fashion."[5]

It was Wilbur, not Orville, who then began to build a kite to demonstrate this new principal. Orville was fighting for business and building bikes, but Wilbur was taking every spare moment and going above the bike shop on West Third Street and constructing a kite of split bamboo and paper. His first laboratory was cold and unheated and dimly lit. Perfect. It was the first kite he had ever built, and this would be Wilbur's first aircraft. He based the kite on Octave Chanute's design for his glider, and built a biplane with two wings on top of each other. The nascent engineer trussed it together like a bridge with cross wires and vertical pine struts. The innovation was the two cords that would allow the wings to warp and could be controlled by someone on the ground. This was an aviation first accomplished by a man with no experience or training—the first ailerons fitted to an experimental kite or aircraft of any kind. This would become a point of contention years later.

Decades later, Orville would admit that he was not there but would speak of it as "we" and describe the flying wing very technically: "I was not myself present when the kite was flown. Wilbur gave me an account of the tests upon his return, and a few days later I was told about it by a couple of boys who were present. . . ."[6] Here again is where history is fudged. Orville had little to do with Wilbur's new obsession. His brother was building a kite above the bike shop in his spare time. Everyone had hobbies. So what? Similarly, the printing press was more Orville's than it was his brother's.

Orville wasn't there when Wilbur took the kite in August 1899 to a field outside of Dayton on a late windy afternoon. The scent of hay and earth rose from the field. Maybe some manure. America was transitioning still from a nation of farms to a nation of cities. Wilbur and Orville had flown kites in the same field with Wilbur's friend Ed Sines when they were boys, but this time it was just Wilbur with a very different kind of kite.

Now it was Wilbur feeding out the line and holding firm to the two control sticks. Small boys stopped on the edge of the field and stared up at the giant kite blotting out the sun as it was being flown by a man in a tie and high collar. A carriage clopped by. A dog barked. Adults did not fly giant kites in fields, as far as they knew. Wilbur felt the tug on the line. The kite wanted to fly and went higher and higher. It was time to see if his idea, which had been born in a moment in the bike shop with an inner tube box, might turn the kite. Wilbur held one stick steady and then began to pull on the other one.

As Fred Howard explained in *Wilbur and Orville*, "The big kite responded promptly to the warping of the wings. The wing with the positive angle lifted; the wing with the negative angle dipped."[7] Wilbur pulled on the stick again, and the kite flew right and then left. He was aviating, though he didn't know it. The control exerted over a bicycle was now being applied to a machine in the air. Wilbur pulled back again, and suddenly the lines went slack and all control was lost. The kite dove for the ground, and the boys dove to the earth. The lines pulled tight again, and Wilbur was able to correct the dive as the kite swooped upward. The stall that had killed Lilienthal was there. You could dance with the wind and you could court her, but she was a dangerous and fickle bride. Already Wilbur knew more than anyone else investigating aeronautics. Wing warping worked, and yet there was a great black hole in the center of navigating the heavens that could kill a man in seconds. This knowledge of risk would keep Wilbur Wright alive.

Wilbur pulled and watched the kite glide across the late-summer sky. The taste of pollen, a hint of autumn, as the kite flew back and forth under the control of a man who had never flown anything in his life, not unlike the sailor who takes to the sea with the natural ability and the feel of controlling a boat. How long did he fly the kite? No one knows, because he was the only one there, save for the boys. His brother was not there, and we are led to believe he went home and told Orville about the success of his wing-warping system. "According to Wilbur's account to me," Orville would testify years later (and then he inserted the "we"), "we felt that the model had demonstrated the efficiency of our system of control. After a little time, we decided to experiment with a man-carrying machine. . . ."[8]

This is highly doubtful. Orville was not interested in flying yet. His brother was just flying a kite, after all, but for Wilbur it was enough. Wilbur then did two things: he determined that he would next build a man-carrying kite, and he sat down and began to write a letter to the French engineer Octave Chanute. It was a bolt of inspiration out of the blue to contact the grandfather of aeronautics, but he needed someone who was further along in this new science, and more than that he needed a kindred intellect. Here is the curve away from the Wright-brother myth that Orville was Wilbur's primary sounding board. He was not. Octave Chanute was the link to the rarefied world of aeronautical science that Wilbur desperately needed:

> For some years I have been afflicted with the belief that flight is possible to man. My disease has increased in severity and I feel that it will soon cost me an increased amount of money if not my life. I have been trying to arrange my affairs in such a way that I can devote my entire time for a few months to experiment in this field. My general ideas of the subject are similar to those held by most practical experimenters to wit: that what is chiefly needed is skill rather than machinery. . . .[9]

Wilbur then laid out his plan to construct a tower of one hundred and fifty feet and to fly a large glider from the tower to gather data. After summarizing what he had learned from Lilienthal, he wrote a line that would later haunt him: "I make no secret of my plans for the reason that I believe no financial profit will accrue to the inventor of the first flying machine, and that only those who are willing to give as well as receive suggestions can hope to link their names with the honor of its discovery. The problem is too great for one man alone and unaided to solve in secret."[10] In time, Wilbur would reverse himself on both assertions. He would pursue financial gain for his discovery and invention of the first powered airplane, and he would become secretive to the point of his own detriment and the wrath of the world.

But here he is the supplicant. He needed openness. The sixty-eight-year-old engineer opened the envelope of blue stationery and read the bicycle mechanic's dissertation on the progress and prospect of manned flight. These five pages were the beginning of an official record that would track the invention of flight. Wilbur starts out by naming the two flaws that ultimately killed Otto Lilienthal. One, he didn't fly enough; he didn't have enough experience. Two, his method of throwing his weight around to guide his glider was wrong. Wilbur pointed out that birds do this with their wings and not their bodies: "The fact that in five years' time he only spent about five hours altogether in actual flight is sufficient to show that his method was never adequate. . . . My observations of birds convince me that birds use more positive and energetic methods of regaining equilibrium than that of shifting the center of gravity."[11] Wilbur then explained to Chanute his concept and his discovery of wing warping: "My observation of the flight of buzzards leads me to believe that they regain their lateral balance, when partly overturned by a gust of wind, by a torsion of the tips of the wings. If the rear edge of the right wing is twisted upward and the left downward the bird becomes an animated windmill and instantly begins to turn."[12]

This is the first time Wilbur mentions his discovery of wing warping to Chanute, and it shows his willingness to divulge what would turn out to be the pivotal invention of his method of control. This too will come back to haunt Wilbur years down the road and will lead to a permanent break between the two men. Chanute does not point out in his reply that this wing warping was never used before, and he does not mention it at all in his reply. This would become a salient point for what transpired after the flight of 1903.

It is interesting that, for the next six months, Wilbur will never mention his brother in his correspondence. In fact, for a long time, Chanute would be unaware of Orville Wright's existence. There was not the usual, "my brother and I"[13] or "we," that would pop up later in correspondence with other people. Wilbur's first letter of 1900 is a declaration of his aspirations: "For some years *I have* been afflicted with the belief that flight is possible to man. *My* disease has increased in severity and *I feel* that it will soon cost me an increased amount of money if not my life. *I have been trying* to arrange my affairs in such a way that *I can* devote my entire time for a few months to experiment in this field."[14]

This is a mission statement of Wilbur Wright. "Chanute's only clue to the existence of another Wright brother would be Orville's name in small type under that of Wilbur in the upper left-hand corner of the Wright Cycle Stationery letterhead."[15] Clearly, Wilbur was on a one-man mission to solve the problem of manned flight, and he would keep Octave Chanute to himself. It is rare to find a letter that passed between Orville Wright and Wilbur's new mentor, even as they closed in on the date of the first powered flight at Kitty Hawk on December 17, 1903.

Even in this first letter, Wilbur asks for advice that he would take and that would change the course of events: "I would be particularly thankful for advice as to a suitable locality where I could depend on winds of about fifteen miles per hour without rain or too inclement weather."[16] Chanute lost no time in writing back to the nascent inventor and pushing him away from the tethered-tower idea and toward finding some place where the wind blew consistently. Chanute responded: "The two most suitable locations for winter experiments which I know of are near San Diego, California, and St. James City, Florida, on account of the steady sea breezes which I have found to blow there. These however are deficient in sand hills and perhaps even better locations can be found on the Atlantic coasts of South Carolina or Georgia."[17]

This would begin a lifelong correspondence between Wilbur Wright and Octave Chanute on the aspects of aeronautical science that would have to be solved before man could fly. Let me say this again, this is the science of aeronautics that has to be worked out to produce controlled flight and then powered flight. Literally no one understood the real or correct math of lift for a wing, and here is where Wilbur Wright will shine as a pioneer. There is no "we" in this endeavor for Wilbur. He needed Chanute to find the path, and then he would use him to cast off the final shackles of known science and go it alone.

Like the writer of the novel, only one person can solve the unsolvable. In the over four hundred letters between Octave Chanute and Wilbur Wright found in *The Papers of Wilbur and Orville Wright*, it is but a school of one. Not unlike a great chess player who takes a novice under his wing, Octave was the chess player whom Wilbur needed to face down. Historians have painted Orville as this counterweight to Wilbur's dominant intellect, and this may be true in the mechanics, but for the heavy lifting, the sheer intellectual leap that was required for a man contemplating the complexities of a world where no man had gone, Wilbur needed an equal.

Octave Chanute would be a mentor, and though the student would rebel against this assignation once manned flight had been achieved, the proof is in the voluminous correspondence where theories were tested, discounted, and reinforced, where new theories were proposed and old theories destroyed. This was the life of the mind, and Wilbur needed a sparring partner, if not a guide: "There was only one person in the United States who possessed that kind of knowledge [aeronautical] and experience; that French-born Chicagoan, that former bridge builder and civil engineer, that semi-retired manufacturer of railroad ties and consultant in wood-preserving, Octave Chanute."[18]

The next thing Wilbur needed was a better place to fly, with a constant wind. Ideally an environment where a soft landing might mitigate some of the dangers of experimenting with a glider that no one had ever flown before. He wrote to the United States Weather Service to see if they knew of such a place. He received the *Monthly Weather Reviews* sent from the Weather Bureau and saw the winds at Kitty Hawk, North Carolina, were of sufficient strength. He wrote to the Weather Bureau there and another letter came back from William Tate:

> Mr. J. J. Dosher of the Weather Bureau here has asked to me answer your letter to him, relative to the fitness of Kitty Hawk as a place to practice or experiment with a flying machine. In answering I would say that you could have nearly any type of ground you could wish, you could for instance, get a stretch of sandy land one mile by five with a bare hill in center 80 feet high, not a tree or bush to break the evenness of the wind current. . . . We have telegraph, communication, and daily mails. If you decide to try your

machine here and come, I will take pleasure in doing all I can for your convenience and success and pleasure.[19]

Wilbur decided on Kitty Hawk for his glider experiments. Chanute then invited the young bicycle mechanic to come visit him in Chicago: "If you have any occasion at any time to be in this city, I shall be glad to have you call on me and can perhaps better answer the questions that have occurred to you."[20]

Wilbur wrote back to Chanute: "When next I am in Chicago I shall without doubt accept your kind invitation to see you personally and till that time while I shall not inflict upon you a voluminous correspondence about mere theories and untried experiments, I will be pleased to communicate any information of value and shall be pleased to have the benefit of your advice."[21]

The student was hungry for knowledge from his preceptor. Wilbur was not a man who asks for things. He was silent and moody, and had a sharp tongue. He did not see others as being smarter than himself, yet here he is playing up to the old engineer. He knew he needed Octave the way a high-wire trapeze artist needs a spotter. Octave would be his closest confidant in all that is aeronautical, and he needed Octave's steadying hand to go where others had not.

"It is my intention to begin shortly the construction of a full-size glider," he wrote in August 1900.[22] There is no "we" in this sentence. Such language would not be inserted until others took the papers of Wilbur and Orville and reinterpreted events. In this letter there is Wilbur stating his intention and not mentioning his brother, who probably did not even know what his plans were. Wilbur wrote, "Hitherto I have used pine in the frames, but for the large machine I wish to use spruce, a wood not obtainable in Dayton yards. It would oblige me greatly if you would give me the name of a Chicago firm of whom I could get the timber I need. Also, I would be glad to have your advice as to a suitable varnish for the cover. I have been using shellac."[23]

So why isn't Wilbur Wright asking his brother Orville where he can get the wood he needs? Why does he ask Octave Chanute about the shellac? Clearly that would be more efficient than waiting weeks for a response. The answer is because at this juncture *Orville is not involved.* And Wilbur seeks another man with the answers over his brother. This flies in the face of the dreary dogma that the brothers were joined at the hip when eating, sleeping, breathing, thinking, and, of course, with all things to do with flying. They were not joined at the hip. In fact, they were not even in the same rooms.

Wilbur commenced working on another glider in the final weeks of August. It had an eighteen-foot wingspan and would cost a whopping $15 in material, whereas Secretary Langley was spending fifty thousand government dollars on his experimental plane. The only thing he did not have were the long spruce spars, but he assumed he could get them when he headed East to Kitty Hawk. Katherine Wright wrote to her father: "we are in an uproar getting Will off. The trip will do him good. I don't think he will be reckless. If they can arrange it, Orv will go down as soon as Will gets the machine ready."[24]

What is interesting to note is that Orville's presence at Kitty Hawk, while expected, was optional at this point. Wilbur was going down to the Outer Banks to fly the glider he built. A final letter to his father then: "I am intending to start in a few days for a trip to the coast of North Carolina in the vicinity of Roanoke Island for the purpose of making some experiments with a flying machine."[25]

There is no mention of Orville going with him or going to meet him. On September 13, 1900, Wilbur Wright boarded the Big Four and C&O and chugged out of Dayton, Ohio. He was going to a remote corner of the eastern seaboard in the first year of the twentieth century. Wilbur Wright had shipped his glider ahead, and now he was going to find the secrets of manned flight.

He was going . . . alone.

PART 2
FLIGHT

"I am intending to start in a few days for a trip to the coast of North Carolina in the vicinity of Roanoke Island, for the purpose of making some experiments with a flying machine."
—Wilbur Wright to his father, Milton Wright,
September 3, 1900

1928

Middle of the Atlantic Ocean

The 1903 *Wright Flyer* had left America, and Orville was not sure whether he would ever bring it back. No one knew what the crates down in the hold of the ship contained. They were lashed down like everything else. There were stenciled letters, but the men who loaded them into the ship didn't read the words *WRIGHT FLYER*. It meant nothing to those men who left the crates in darkness. The Atlantic crossing to London took a week, and the seas were rough. The crates shifted but didn't move as the stormy seas tossed the large ship. Twenty-five years before, the machine in the crates had lifted from the sands of Kitty Hawk and changed the world.

But strange sounds came from below. It happened mostly at night, when the ship was quiet, and the watch reported a hum coming from the dark recesses of the ship. The men on the ship heard the hum several times from below deck and finally tracked it down to the crates marked *WRIGHT FLYER*. They went to the crates and put their ears against the wood. They heard the hum inside and could come up with no good reason about what was making the sound. Eventually, they shrugged and walked away.

That night the hum came again, as if some creature were alive. The men had no way of knowing it, but the strut wires were singing from the vibration of the ship. Wilbur would have recognized the hum instantly. He heard it every time he flew. It was the sound of flight.

THE PILGRIM—1900

Wilbur Wright stepped down into the fetid 100-degree heat of Old Point, Virginia. His suit was wool and melting onto him like a blanket. Most suits were wool in 1900, and his high celluloid collar and black derby were increasing the heat with every second after he left the train, now chugging away. Dayton, Ohio, was a good seven hundred miles behind him. He caught the steamer Pennsylvania for Norfolk, a small, primitive fishing village that was modern in comparison to where he was going.

He checked into the Monticello Hotel and in the morning went looking for some spruce for the spars of his glider. He could find none. Later, Wilbur found some and wrote to his father, "Finally, I bought some white pine and had it sawed up at J. E. Etheridge Co. Mill., the foreman, very accommodating."[1] After securing the pine strips for his glider, which had been crated and shipped to Kitty Hawk, North Carolina, he began inquiring about transportation to the Outer Banks. The weather was near 100 degrees, and Wilbur would later write to his father again, "I nearly collapsed."[2]

Wilbur slept in the uncomfortable hotel and emerged into an even hotter day with his high laced shoes and dark suit reminding him once again that he was not in Dayton, Ohio, anymore. Another train dropped him off sixty miles south at a salty, desolate stop in Elizabeth City. Now he could smell the ocean. Dragonflies clicked in the tall reeds. Blasts of humid, super-heated air wafted up from the sand. From here all transportation stopped. At least trains did. The Outer Banks of North Carolina was a series of islands protecting the coast from the ravages of the Atlantic Ocean. They were also unreachable by horse or car or any other form of ground transportation. The Albemarle Sound had to be forded to get to Kitty Hawk, and Wilbur could find no one who could tell him how this was to be done. "No one seemed to know anything about the place or how to get there," he complained to Milton Wright.[3]

The Civil War had been fought thirty-five years before. The frontier had only been closed for ten years, and parts of the United States were still largely uninhabited. There were no cars to speak of and no radio. Marconi had just pushed wireless to where ships could get updates, but many ships did not use this new technology. The phone was still a new thing for most people, and most of the United States was not electrified.

So, we have the nascent inventor of flight hacking around the desolate town of Elizabeth, in a suit and a tie, unable to get to what would become his laboratory for flight. His high-top leather shoes are muddy, his black derby is an oven, and he can find no transportation to his destination. This should have told him right then and there that Kitty Hawk would be an isolated way-stop on the far peak of the eastern seaboard. If someone had asked him why he was there, then he or she might have thought this overdressed man was insane. "To fly," he would have answered in perfect seriousness. It was a new century. No self-effacement. No self-deprecation. His grey eyes would bore right through you. "I just need someone to get me across the sound. Is there someone who can do that?" There was.

One grizzled Israel Perry answered the call, not caring why this "dude" would want to go to Kitty Hawk, where one could die and no one would even know it for days. Isolation. That was Kitty Hawk. There were some fishermen and some houses. Most everyone was poor as dirt and barely getting by, and some were eating the dirt or trying to grow what they could not in sand. Shipping fish to the east was the only industry, and that didn't pay so much that people didn't have to plant what they could in the sandy loam to survive.

The next morning, Wilbur was there. "I engaged with Israel Perry on his flat bottom boat," he related to his father.[4] "As it was anchored three miles down the river we started in his skiff which was loaded almost to the gunwale with three men, my heavy trunk and lumber." The boat was a skiff that stank of dead fish and leaked like a bathtub full of holes. "The boat leaked very badly and frequently dipped water, but by constant bailing we managed to reach the schooner in safety."[5] Wilbur bailed mechanically, methodically, focused on the task in front of him. He asked only one question between the bailing of the green seawater.

"Is this boat seaworthy?"

"Oh, it's safer than the big boat," Israel sang out, bailing beside him.[6]

The amount of water had Wilbur bailing the whole three-mile trip down the river. The sun was brutal, and Wilbur was weak from dehydration and having nothing more to eat than some jam his sister had packed for him. There was the scent of salt and the smell of dead fish. The sun glared off the brassy green water. The skiff was leaky and barely seaworthy, but the boat they reached at dusk was not much better. "The weather was very fine with a light west wind blowing. When I mounted the deck of the larger boat I discovered at a glance that it was in worse condition if possible than the skiff. The sails were rotten and the ropes badly worn and the rudder post half rotted off," Wilbur later wrote.[7] "And the cabin was so dirty and vermin infested that I kept out of it from the first to the last."

To make matters worse, the weather had changed. The sky had darkened, and spiders of lightning touched down across the sound. This added to the general feeling of impending doom the schooner engendered, silhouetted against the dying light. But they headed out into the sound, into the teeth of warm, wet gusts presaging a coming storm.

Wilbur stared across the sound toward Kitty Hawk. It was an island of trees against the storm light. Wind ruffled his pressed shirt and picked at his tie. He frowned at the time, as it was getting dark quickly. His false teeth hurt. His mouth was dry. Lightning spidered again beyond, and thunder rattled the main sail, then a strong gust caught the jib as they leaned to. He later wrote, "Though we had started immediately after dinner, it was almost dark when we passed out of the mouth of the Pasquotank and headed down the sound. The water was much rougher than the light wind would have led us to expect . . . After a time the breeze shifted to the South and East and gradually became stronger . . . The waves which were now running quite high struck the boat from below with a heavy shock and threw it back as fast as it went forward."[8]

The weather degenerated into a gale after 11 p.m., and Wilbur and a boy who had accompanied Israel bailed for their lives. Leaks appeared in the rotted wood from the constant pitching of the seas, with the boat being driven toward the shore. Any attempt to turn around at this point would invite disaster. Then the foresail suddenly broke loose from the boom and "fluttered to leeward with a terrible roar."[9] There was nothing to do but for Wilbur to go forward with the boy in the dark, in the rain and wind, and secure the sail. He was still in his vest, tie, collar, pressed shirt, and hard shoes.

Wilbur inched out toward the front of the boat, with the monster whipping and snapping in the darkness. He and the boy managed to secure the sail with the boat rolling so badly he thought they might tip.

"By the time we had reached a position even with the end of the point it became doubtful whether we would be able to round the light, which lay at the end of the bar extending out a quarter of a mile from the shore."[10] They could not turn in for safety, and then the main sail tore loose from the boom with the same roar of canvas suddenly unmoored. Wilbur again ascended to the top of the careening ship to secure the sail. The gale was tearing Israel's boat apart. The only chance was to use the jib and sail straight toward the sandbar with the wind behind. It was fitting that the boat leading to the epi-center of flight had now become a kite, and the jib would produce thrust that would either sink them or deliver salvation.

Wilbur Wright wondered then what he had done by finding the most remote spot on the eastern seaboard to fly an experimental glider. The older brother of the two men who had created a printing press and a bicycle shop felt the darkness as something bad, something evil, across the dark, wind-swept bay. He pressed his tongue again against his false teeth. This forty-mile crossing to a place settled by shipwrecked sailors with only some Life-Saving stations and a Weather Bureau station had that same capacity for something going horribly wrong.

In the storied darkness were the Outer Banks of North Carolina, and its people comprised of fishermen and those who had been stranded on the shoals of the barrier islands that protected the coast from the Atlantic. It was a 200-mile strip of sand bent like an elbow at Cape Hatteras. Some fishermen raised corn and beans and kept a few pigs, but the mosquitoes were much better adjusted to the climate than the pigs were. Even the name Kitty Hawk came from a name for the dragonflies that feed on mosquitoes and that the locals called "skeeter hawks."[11] Nags Head was twenty miles to the south, where North Carolinians had been going for a hundred years to escape the heat. Nags Head's only hotel had burned to the ground just a year before Wilbur arrived.

Between Kitty Hawk and Nags Head was four miles of uninterrupted sand that broke for three large dunes known as Kill Devil Hills. It is here that history would be made: a perfect setup for a man with a glider. The only problem was surviving the trip over. There were no bridges in 1900 and of course this was why Wilbur was facing doom in the middle of a gale that was driving the flat-bottomed boat toward a sandbar. The Life-Saving stations and Weather Bureau stations could be of no help, though they had cutting-edge technology with a phone system and a telegraph line that connected the weather station to Norfolk. It was a government line, but telegrams could be sent to the Western Union office. This was a situation that would factor in heavily in 1903.

The problem was that the stations were there to help those whom the Atlantic tossed onto the shoulders of the Outer Banks. Israel Perry's water-laden boat coming from the east and heading toward Kitty Hawk from the Albemarle Sound was not to be rescued. This gave Wilbur no solace as Israel Perry ran his boat up onto a sandbar, with waves breaking over the bow. His high collar had wilted, and his pants were adhered to his long legs. His derby had blown off and wedged in the corner of the bow. He must have questioned the action that had brought him to a leaky boat in a typhoon.

Why had he sent that letter to the Weather Bureau anyway?

We have been doing some experimenting with kites, with a view to con-structing one capable of sustaining a man. We expect to carry the experi-ment further next year. In the meantime, we wish to obtain if possible a report of the wind velocities of Chicago or vicinity for the months of August Sept Oct and November. Do any of the government publications contain such information?[12]

Scouring the *Monthly Weather Reviews*, Wilbur found that the wind was at Kitty Hawk. That is where he would go to fly the glider. Then another letter to the Weather Bureau at Kitty Hawk. Might he know of winds, trans-portation, and lodging? He might. Joseph Dosher, the telegraph operator at the bureau, sealed the deal and described the "mile wide beaches with no trees and clear of high hills for sixty miles to the south."[13] But there were no houses to rent. "So you will have to bring tents . . . you could obtain board." His letter had made the rounds in the fishing village, landing in the hands of William Tate, whose wife ran the post office. It was Tate who told him of Kill Devils Hills and the giant sand dunes that would be perfect for his flying machine.

They dragged the boat up onto the sandbar. Wilbur assisted in anchoring the besieged vessel, watching the wild sea pile into the side of Perry's boat.

Perry's son kept bailing, and what no one knew was that a hurricane had hit Galveston, Texas, where it had whipped up the water of the Gulf of Mexico to a depth of seventeen feet in the streets. This dying storm had descended on the Outer Banks, and it is amazing that Wilbur Wright and the old fisherman and his son had not been drowned.

After finally making landfall that night, the *Curlicue* was tied up to a wharf in the quiet village of Kitty Hawk. The houses were few. Mostly there was the darkness and the sand and the roar of the ocean agitated from the passing hurricane. There were no souls to be seen. No lights on in any home or cottage. What would become a resort town fifty years later was still the lone outpost on the edge of the eastern seaboard.

Wilbur stared toward the ocean and felt the steady wind on his face. There was no choice but to bed down on the deck of the *Curlicue*. Wilbur slept outside with the mosquitoes, quite preferring this to where Israel and his boy slept along with the creatures that had found refuge in the cabin of the old schooner. He lay down on the dried-out wood of the deck. He slapped at a mosquito. He felt the wind and listened to the crash and roar of the ocean. He had traveled eight hundred miles to capture that wind. He loosened his tie. A bicycle mechanic without a high-school degree was lying on the deck of a broken-down ship in the middle of nowhere, having come to solve manned flight. Wilbur Wright sniffed, closed his eyes, then fell fast asleep.

It wasn't three hours later when he woke on the hard deck, feeling pain rippling between his shoulder blades. Israel's snoring from below deck was a throbbing saw that knew no bounds. He and son both had slept in the cabin with the vermin that kept Wilbur outside with the mosquitoes and now facing the blinding-hot sun already baking by 8 a.m. He dug out Katherine's jam and ate some of the sweet strawberries now warmed. It was the only thing he would trust. He looked out from the wharf at Kitty Hawk.

He had seen trees in the distance the night before, but now he saw no trees. He saw sand and a few stumps. Kitty Hawk was composed of a series of houses along the Albemarle Sound, a store, and then the Life-Saving stations along the shore. That was it. The fishing boats headed out from Kitty Hawk or Manateo into the sound and then entered the ocean from the Oregon Inlet. But most people just saw sand stretching forty miles down the coast, broken up by enormous dunes like the three mountains of sand called Kill Devil Hills.

Years later, Orville would describe the area as "like the Sahara or what I imagine the Sahara to be."[14] History abounds in Kitty Hawk. Seventy years later, there would be an outdoor production on the lonely island of Roanoke to commemorate an English colony that mysteriously disappeared. The earliest history goes back to when the explorer Giovanni de Verrazano stumbled upon the Outer Banks and landed at Nags Head woods. He remarked upon the enchantment of the land and kidnapped a native boy to take back to France.

Pirates abounded. The name of a large dune was called Nags Head and Jockey's Ridge, so named for the men who would lead a horse up the giant dune with a lantern tied around its neck. This would trick mariners into thinking that the bobbing light was an inland ship, and they'd run their own ships aground. Cargo and plunder would then be the prize for the land-bound pirates. Blackbeard the pirate had died off the coast of Ocracoke in 1718, and the locals said his decapitated body could be seen swimming around.[15]

William Tate had warned the Ohioan what he would find and said life in Kitty Hawk was one of "Double Barreled Isolation."[16] Clothes were made at home, children went to school for three months a year, and mail came three times a week. The double-barreled isolation must have excited and repelled Wilbur Wright in 1900; he had a laboratory to conduct his experiments with a steady Atlantic wind and an unbroken landscape of sand for soft landings.

Wilbur left the sleeping Israel and his son and set out for the Tates'. The only problem was he didn't have any idea where the Tate home was. He pulled on his derby, which he had found wedged between the sails, and saw a barefoot boy named Baum with a large straw hat and suspenders. It was September 13, 1900. The boy shut one eye against the sun and nodded. Yes, he knew where the Tates lived, and he would lead him there. Wilbur followed his barefoot guide with his own hard shoes squishing in the sand that was already in his socks, his shirt collar, and even in his mouth.

The boy watched the strange, angular man in the high collar, leather shoes, white shirt, and tie now carrying his suit coat over his arm. He didn't look like anyone the boy had ever seen. Nobody in Kitty Hawk dressed like that and truth was nobody had the money to entertain dressing like that. They were hardscrabble, poor, and just hanging on. In the year 1900, the Kitty Hawkers were people who lived by their wits and went from one job to another. Fishing was the only industry and that was spring and summer, and there was some hunting in the fall. The Life-Saving stations were the only option for men along the coast. Fifty dollars a month if they slept in the stations from December to March.[17] It wasn't enough for the risk to their lives when going out into the surf at night in the middle of a gale to rescue men on ships that had run ashore. Between these moments of incredible danger, they walked the beaches with lanterns and shot off flares to warm the ships away from the graveyard of the Atlantic otherwise known as the Outer Banks. But, of course, in this medieval operation of taking a boat into a raging surf, they possessed the only line to the outside world through their phone system and then to the telegraph.

Houses were unpainted, rude structures with leaning porches and floors of unvarnished pine. The Wright home was a palace compared to the Tates', which now appeared at the end of a sandy lane. It had no rugs, no books, and no furniture to speak of. A dilapidated sign hanging above the door read "Kitty Hawk N.C. Post Office." A surviving picture shows the Tates as looking like a family from Appalachia or some Depression-era family out of John Steinbeck's *The Grapes of Wrath*. But the Tates were better off than most.

William Tate was the unofficial mayor of Kitty Hawk. His wife ran the post office, but he was the actual postmaster. Tate sported many hats: notary public, commissioner of Currituck County. His house was two stories and one of the better, if not one of the best, homes in the area. When Elijah Baum knocked on his door and the man behind him doffed his cap and introduced himself as "Wilbur Wright of Dayton, Ohio," Tate was well equipped for the task at hand. It had taken Wilbur a week to travel from Dayton to reach Tate's front door. Wilbur must have hidden his shock at the unplastered walls and bare pine floors with the salty scent of the ocean on the man and the home.[18] "There may be one or two better houses here but his is much above average," he would later write his father.[19] "A few men have saved up a thousand dollars but this is the savings of a long life. Their yearly income is small. I suppose a few of them see two hundred dollars a year. They are friendly and neighborly and I think there is rarely any real suffering among them."

Wilbur asked if he might stay there until Orville arrived and they could stake their tent out on the sand dune. The Tates retired to another room and discussed the man in the white shirt and tie. Tate's wife felt their home would not do for such a man.

"I would be happy with whatever accommodations you can provide,"

Wilbur said, stepping to the door.[20] It was settled. He would stay at the Tates' until his brother came. After a few days' rest, William Tate introduced him around to the Kitty Hawkers and the men at the Life-Saving station who would play a crucial role later, in the early flights. The weekly freight boat eventually arrived with Wilbur's large crates. He went back to the wharf and took delivery of his glider, having it transported a half a mile from the Tates' home to an area overlooking the ocean. He had not been able to find the spruce spars he needed for his glider and had to borrow the Tates' sewing machine and change the size of the fabric, a white French sateen. He erected a canvas shelter in the Tates' front yard under which he could work, but the Tates and others woke many times to find in the yard a man wearing a vest and tie with a sewing machine, pumping away with his foot and with needles in his mouth. Years later, a stone marker would be placed to mark the spot where Wilbur worked on his glider.

Tate and his wife, Addie, were the perfect hosts, and Tate would remember later an awed Wilbur Wright recounting his voyage across Albemarle Sound when he first arrived at the Tates': "His graphic description of the rolling of the boat and his story that the muscles of his arms ached from holding on, were interesting, but when he said he had fasted for 48 hours that was a condition that called for a remedy at once. Therefore, we soon had him seated to a good breakfast of fresh eggs, ham and coffee, and I assure you he did his duty by them."[21]

Wilbur Wright could have been an alien from another planet, and it would have been no different. There were no cars on Kitty Hawk. There was no electricity to speak of. There was the telegraph and the phones of the Life-Saving stations. But most people lived an eighteenth-century existence. Yet here was a man who dressed like someone going to a funeral in New York City and who had come to fly into the sky. The notion that Wilbur Wright had come to this primitive outpost to build a machine to fly was the same as someone landing in our vicinity today and declaring he was from another planet. There was no point of comparison, and some Kitty Hawkers who thought he was crazy would take to the woods and stare at the man fitting spars and running material over the frame of wings. Wilbur Wright was an early celebrity and a curiosity; awe, caution, and respect were just some of the emotions the people cut off from the world at large felt when seeing the man dressed always in his Sunday best.

The seventeen-foot wingspan of Wilbur's glider was not to be hidden from the prying eyes of boys, men, or women who had never even seen an automobile, much less a machine designed to ride the air currents. The Tates' quiet visitor kept to his work and asked for very little, except for a boiled pitcher of water every morning in his bedroom. Orville's near death at the hands of typhoid had forever seared this caution into Wilbur's daily routine. This was the age of typhoid fever, an infection brought on by tainted water. The Tates thought it odd but provided the pitcher every morning. They had no way of knowing Orville Wright had almost died in 1896 from drinking a cup of bad water. Nor that in twelve years Wilbur would be dead from the same strain of salmonella that was behind the hell of Typhoid Mary.

The next day, Wilbur headed out toward the ocean and sat on the sand dunes. The birds held the answers. It was that simple. Understand how a bird flies, and you are almost there. They roll their bodies right or left and then just turn. To bank or lean is the same as a man on a bicycle. But how the birds achieve this is another matter. Only through constant observation could the secret be learned. This had Wilbur sitting on the side of the dune, with the ocean wind ruffling his thin hair that had receded to his crown.

He watched the hawk wheel and look down over the ocean. Still, it did not flap its wings but went even higher, seeing the strip of land that was part of the Outer Banks. The hawk rode in the upward-moving thermals in tight circles. The creature flexed his wings slightly and banked toward the sand dune that spread out into three hills. It was amazing. The hawk glided effortlessly above Wilbur like a god of the air, riding the long, slow, hot drafts of upward-moving air. Wilbur called this soaring.

The hawk saw movement and leaned in and then banked again. It was a man, and the hawk soared above him, passed over, and headed inland. The man scribbled furiously in a notebook as the hawk sailed away, never having to flap his wings. The hawk rode the air as Wilbur wished to do. He rode on what God put there.

Wilbur Wright made a sketch of the hawk. He had to hurry because his brother was coming, and he wanted to meet him at the Tates'. He looked over his notes:

A bird when soaring does not seem to alternately rise and fall as some observers have thought. Any rising and falling is irregular and seems to be due to disturbances of fore and aft equilibrium produced by gusts. In light winds the birds seem to rise constantly without any downward turns.

A bird sailing quartering to the wind seems to always present its wings at a positive angle, although propulsion in such positions seems unaccountable.

No bird soars in a calm.[22]

The object of the tail is to increase the spread of surface in the rear when the wings are moved forward in light winds and thus preserve the center of pressure at about the same spot. It seems to be used as a rudder very little. In high winds it is folded up very narrow.[23]

Hawks are better soarers than buzzards but more often resort to flapping because they wish greater speed.

A damp day is unfavorable for soaring unless there is a high wind.[24]

He had just written Bishop Wright a letter that he wanted to give to Tate to post. "I have my machine nearly finished. It is not to have a motor and is not expected to fly in any true sense of the word. My idea is merely to experiment and practice with a view to solving the problem of equilibrium."[25] Wilbur had already decided that control was everything. While Langley believed in the intrinsic power of the engine to loft a man into the air, Wilbur believed power was secondary: "When once a machine is under proper control under all conditions, the motor problem will quickly be solved. A failure of motor will then mean simply a slow descent and safe landing instead of a disastrous fall."[26]

Wilbur then assures his father that he does not intend to take chances:

I do not expect to rise many feet from the ground, and in case I am upset there is nothing but soft sand to strike on. . . . It is my belief that flight is possible and while I am taking up the investigation for pleasure rather than profit, I think there is a slight possibility of achieving fame and fortune from it. It is almost the only great problem which has not been pursued by a multitude of investigators and therefore carried to a point where further progress is very difficult. I am certain I can reach a point much in advance of any previous person. At any rate, I shall have an outing of several weeks and see a part of the world I have never visited before.[27]

Wilbur points out immediately that his machine will be better constructed than Lilienthal's and will have more control: "The safe and secure construction and management are my main improvements."[28] It is a foregone conclusion that he, not his brother, will be doing the flying in the glider. The glider had a wingspan of 17 feet, 5 inches, with a total weight of 50 pounds. Wilbur would lie "in a cutout section of the lower wing with his feet resting on the T bar controlling wing warping."[29] It would be the father, Milton, who would have the final word. He demanded that the brothers be equal, and this would include the early experiments in Kitty Hawk. But, years later, he would write to Wilbur in France: "I think that aside from the value of your life to yourself and to ourselves you owe it to the world that you should avoid all unnecessary personal risks. Your death or even becoming an invalid would seriously affect the progress of aeronautical science. Outside of your contacts and your aviations, you have much that no one else can do as well. And, alone, Orville would be crippled and burdened."[30]

When his father wrote these words, it was at a time when Wilbur and Orville were at their pinnacle of fame. They were the *Wright Brothers*, equal before the world, yet Milton knew that Wilbur was the one who broke the code of flight. Orville would receive no such letter, and the bishop followed up with a letter to Katherine during this period that was somewhat cruel but showed his true feelings toward his sons: "It does not make much difference with you, but Wilbur ought to keep out of all balloon rides. Success seems to hang upon him."[31] The best he could say of Orville was that "his mind grew steadily."[32]

This may be damning with faint praise, but the reason to bring it up is that with Orville's arrival in Kitty Hawk the grand plurality began. The "I" would be replaced with "we" from now on in Wilbur's letters to both his father and Chanute. The other Wright brother knocked on William Tate's door on September 28, 1900. Tate must have thought he was seeing double. Here was another man in a high collar, tie, dark coat, cap, and mustache, looking like he just stepped out of an office in the city. He wore the same shined, hard-sole shoes and spoke with the same Dayton twang that came through the nose when the voice came through at all.

Tate opened the door wide and admitted the man, who was "equipped with a tent and cots, as well as coffee, tea, sugar, and a few other items unavailable in Kitty Hawk."[33] Wilbur met his brother, and who knows what Tate thought of the two men who said little but shook hands affectionately. Wilbur had been gone a good deal of the time working on his flying machine out by the camp he had established that would have a tent and cots and food and would become their home. Orville did stay with Wilbur at the Tates' a few days until the glider was completed. While they worked, Wilbur and Orville observed the local birds and had made many notes. A local man named John T. Daniels would later write, "They would watch the gannets and imitate the movements of their wings with their arms and hands. . . . We thought they were crazy."[34]

Their camp on the edge of the dunes began on October 3. Orville's letters then began, and many were to their sister, Katherine, concerning the conditions of the camp. They suffered through several storms: "When one of these 45-mile Northeasters strikes us, you can depend on it, there is little sleep in our camp. We have just passed through one which took two or three wagonloads of sand from the NE end of our tent and piled it up eight inches on the flying machine, which we had anchored about fifty feet southwest. The wind shaking the roof and sides of the tent sounds exactly like thunder. When we crawl out to fix things the sand fairly blinds us."[35]

Kitty Hawk was a desolate outpost and, like all remote areas in 1900, there was a lack of items the Wrights took for granted in Dayton. Besides being out of communication with the world except by mail that went out only three times a week, basic foodstuffs were lacking as well—to say nothing of getting parts for a flying machine. The Wrights were pushing known technology to its very limit in an area of the country that resembled America in the early nineteenth century. This was confirmed by Orville in a letter sent later to his sister: "There is no store in Kitty Hawk, that is, not anything you would call a store. Our pantry in its most depleted state would be a mammoth affair compared with our Kitty Hawk stores. Our camp alone exhausts the output of all the henneries within a mile . . . they [residents] never had anything good in their lives and consequently are satisfied with what they have. In all other things they are the same way, satisfied with keeping soul and body together."[36]

Orville then makes an interesting observation, connecting their quest to fly with the age of exploration: "Trying to camp down here reminds me constantly of those poor Artic explorers. We are living nearly the whole time on reduced rations. . . . We have appointed the Kitty Hawk storekeeper our agent to buy us anything he can get hold for, in any quantities he can get in the line of fish, eggs, wild geese or ducks. We have had biscuits [with] molasses, coffee and rice today. Tomorrow morning, we will have biscuits, coffee, and rice."[37]

Tommy Tate, the sixteen-year-old nephew of William Tate, took to hanging around the camp while the brothers readied their glider. He told the brothers that the richest man in town was the druggist, Doc Cogswell, a man owed $15,000 by his brother. The arrival of the freight ship from Elizabeth City was eagerly looked for by Kitty Hawkers, and the Wright brothers, as they could then "have a blowout" with "canned tomatoes, peaches, condensed milk, flour and bacon and butter."[38] But it would usually only last a day, and they were back to existing on subsistence fare. "Will is most starved," Orville would write their sister when rations were low.[39]

The mosquitoes, chiggers, and ticks, and the sand blowing constantly, did not diminish their love for their newfound oasis. Both Wrights came to believe in time that the fresh air, beauty, and stress-free environment of Kitty Hawk could cure all ills. Orville would write Katherine, "The sunsets here are the prettiest I have seen. The clouds light up in all colors in the background, with deep blue clouds of various shapes fringed with gold before. The moon rises in much the same style and lights up this pile of sand almost like day."[40]

Wilbur, on the other hand, also saw Kitty Hawk as nothing short of his laboratory, an unencumbered space where he would not be bothered by the world to get his work done. This was harder and harder in Dayton, where the bicycle business demanded attention and, increasingly, so did his father. Milton was in a legal tussle with his church that would require Wilbur to veer away from his work on aeronautics and all things related to flying. But in Kitty Hawk all cares were distant. The isolation provided a wall that would later be recognized by people who would make it their once-a-year vacation spot and would swear to the beauty, the climate, and the wide-open beaches.

But it was roughing it for the two men in high collars and ties in a tent at the bottom of a giant sand dune. As Orville would write his sister, "The sand is the greatest thing in Kitty Hawk and soon will be the only thing."[41] The days were brutally hot, and the nights cold. "A cold nor'easter is blowing tonight and I have seen warmer places than it is in this tent. We each of us have two blankets, but almost freeze every night," Orville wrote his sister.[42] "The wind blows in on my head, and I pull the blankets up over my head, when my feet freeze and I reverse the process. I keep this up all night and in the morning am hardly able to tell where I'm at in the bedclothes."

One month after arriving in Kitty Hawk, the glider was finally ready and the storms had abated. "With everything in place, it consisted of two fixed wings, one above the other, each measuring 5 feet by 17 feet. In addition, it had warping controls and a movable forward rudder—the horizontal rudder or elevator—of twelve square feet. There were no wheels for takeoffs or landings. Later models would have wooden skids, far better suited for sand. . . . The whole apparatus weight slightly less than 50 pounds. . . . With Wilbur aboard as 'operator' it would total approximately 190 pounds. . . . He would lie flat on his stomach, head first, in the middle of the lower wing and maintain fore-and-aft balance by means of the forward rudder."[43]

The problem was even though the storms had passed, the winds still clocked in around 30 miles per hour. Orville wrote his sister, Katherine, "Monday night and all-day Tuesday we had a terrific wind blowing 36 miles an hour. Wednesday morning the Kitty Hawkers were out early peering around the edge of the woods and out their upstairs windows to see whether our camp was still in existence."[44] Wilbur decided then to fly the machine like a kite and steer it by remote control with strings to the ground. He put chains on the kite to see how it would perform with an operator. Orville reported to Katherine: "Well after erecting a derrick from which to swing our rope with which we fly the machine, we sent it up about 20 feet, at which height we attempt to keep it up by the manipulation of the strings to the rudder. The greatest difficulty is in keeping it down. It naturally wants to go higher and higher. When it gets too high we give it a strong pull on the ducking string, to which it responds by making a terrific dart to the ground."[45]

They then sent it back up and took some pictures. The kite experiments came to a stop with a wind that "quicker than thought"[46] caught the kite on the ground and lifted it in to the air, sending it cartwheeling for twenty feet. The damage was extensive, and at first glance Wilbur deduced that the experiments at Kitty Hawk had come to an end; then he decided it might be repairable. They photographed the wreckage and then dragged it back to camp, where for three days they repaired the damage.

Wilbur wanted to fly now. He had heard of a place where the wind was strong and the dunes even larger. Orville, in the close of one his letters, tipped his sister off to the name of some hills that would live in history: "We will probably go down to the Kill Devil Hills tomorrow, where we will try gliding on the machine."[47]

THE WRIGHT SISTER—1900

W ilbur left behind a pressure cooker of work and family obligations. Katherine was twenty-six in 1900. The sister of the Wright family would be the primary female relationship in Orville's and Wilbur's lives. Her mother had died when she was fifteen, and she stepped into the role of mother with Milton's approval, if not his demand. She had an offer of marriage while in college, but that never came to fruition. When she was in college, a friend gave her a book titled *Middle Aged Love Stories*. With her bun, pince-nez, and plain demeanor, she was already the spinster in waiting.

Wilbur and Orville, as well as their father, were in Katherine's charge. The bishop was already a task master of feminine decorum: "I am especially anxious that you cultivate modest feminine manners and control your temper, for temper is a hard master."[1] This was written while Milton was out on the circuit, gone as he habitually was. He had entered a fight with his own church, United Brethren, that was perfectly suited for the old reprobate. The younger members or the more progressive ones wanted to allow members to join secret societies such as the Masons. Milton saw this as dangerous and thought it smacked of exclusion. He put it in the same well as vanity, drinking, and smoking, all of which was the work of the devil. The church split over the issue in 1899, with Milton starting a new sect in alliance with the old policies of the church. He was a holy warrior, and the fight was one that eventually would drag in Wilbur, with lawsuits and recrimination.[2]

But the bishop needed a stable home warm with people, food, and beds still folded back from a woman's hand. He needed his daughter to step into the role of his dead wife: "Home . . . seems lonesome without you," he wrote when Katherine dared to go see some relatives.[3] "But for you, we should feel like we had no home." Guilt upon guilt, it would be thirty years before his daughter could escape the home of men.

But she had escaped once before, to Oberlin College. Between caring for Milton, her brothers, and her brother's wife who just had a new baby, she did not have time to graduate from high school. The younger Wright children just couldn't seem to get a diploma. Oberlin required her to take a preparatory program to compensate for lack of a degree. The college was not segregated; men and women were in the same classes. Few people attended college in the 1890s, and fewer women. Bishop Wright saw Katherine as a teacher, and Oberlin was well suited for the avocation and had a strict code of discipline. Students were up at six, went to bed at ten, and had daily prayers, and wrote reports on their moral conduct. Professor Woodrow Wilson visited the college from Princeton and gave a lecture on democracy. Jane Addams also spoke on the plight of the poor in Chicago. It was, despite the asceticism of a daily life, a liberal education.

Katherine Wright went from a house full of men to a house full of women. Her roommate, Margaret Goodwin, became her best friend for life. In a picture of the time, Margaret and Katherine look like a modern couple in Victorian garb. Margaret was a minister's daughter from Chicago, and she had the same sense of release Katherine felt. They spent all their time together and sometimes ditched their studies to go ice-skating. "Margaret was such good company always—never a bore," Katherine later wrote.[4] A teacher once asked her why she and Margaret always had so much to talk about, and Margaret replied quickly that "they just covered the same subjects over and over without realizing it."[5]

Clearly the pleasure of each other's company was enough, and they joined the Ladies Literary Society together. The LLS sounded too formal to Katherine, so they changed it to *Litterae Laborum Solamine* in Latin.[6] The translation was "literature is solace from troubles." It was basically a club for public speaking. Margaret apparently was a charismatic speaker. She was asked to speak on peace, and "at first there was a frown and a look of dismay on Miss. Goodwins' face ... then a vacant expression followed by a smile, which finally developed into a giggle. Having thus relieved herself, the ideas came readily and she discoursed at some length on peace among nations, parties, and individuals."[7]

Debates were also held, and Katherine triumphed in a debate on deception. Richard Maurer, in *The Wright Sister*, explains that "her assignment was to argue that deception is sometimes justified. She won by citing examples, probably the white lie variety from her own experience."[8] Of course, she would take this to high art when Arthur Cunningham, captain of the baseball team and a young scholar, proposed to her. Their engagement drifted for two years until Katherine broke it off. Arthur was apparently relieved, and Katherine was, too, as she had not told her father. The fact that she didn't tell her own father speaks volumes about their relationship. To marry would betray the bishop, who had made her his own unofficial housekeeper, if not wife. He would never know, and Katherine would later refer to her "narrow escape,"[9] but she said she was "unhappy for several years all the time glad [at] what I had done but brokenhearted over a great ideal with me."[10]

Marriage was an ideal she carried, but the reality was not for her. Upon graduation, Margaret took a teaching position in Canal Dover, Ohio, while Katherine began substitute teaching at Steele High School and moved back in the family home. The two friends would keep up with each other through letters, and in 1904 Katherine would travel to the World's Fair and stay several weeks with Margaret. Margaret's husband seems to have not been around. Outside of her father and brothers, Katherine Wright's primary relationships were with women, and one cannot help but think that Margaret might have been more than a friend.

The account of this trip is one of weeks of exploration: "We walked through the Transportation and Machinery buildings and through one corner of the varied industries," Katherine wrote her father.[11] They sampled "German, Italian, and other foreign foods along with several new dishes developed especially for the fair: iced tea, ice cream cones, hot dogs, and a spun sugar confection called fairy floss later known as cotton candy."[12]

Katherine eventually returned to Dayton and her part-time teaching duties. This intrigued Wilbur and filled him with more angst at the time. Katherine had taken the road he had missed in his three-year depression, and now she was going to take up the vocation he had held out for himself. This must have made the drifting young man more unsure of himself. His younger sister had eclipsed him while he worked on bicycles and mooned about building a flying machine. Wilbur desperately wanted to make his way in the world, and getting on the train to Kitty Hawk must have been a great relief in one sense. At the very least, he had a sense of purpose.

Even at the juncture where Wilbur had left for Kitty Hawk, one could make a case that he was still drifting. Here was a man who had gone into business with his brother, built a glider over their store, and then went down to a godforsaken stretch of land on the coast to fly it. This would be akin to someone building a rocket today to fly to the moon. It was a fantastical ambition to which few, if anyone, could relate. Only a true loner, a misanthrope with extraordinary powers of concentration, could wall out the dissenting voices. Was he not just wasting his time? He still lived at home in his thirties with his father, and he had not even graduated high school. He had no formal training in anything except for being able to build a bicycle. He did not date and didn't look to have any interest in women. From the outside, it would look like Wilbur Wright was on the verge of becoming a failure in the basic game of life. If he did not solve the problem of flight, it would be another failure in a list of failures. And though the bicycle business was still going along, Wilbur had already moved on intellectually. For him there was only one way out, and that was to crack the code of flight down in the hot sands of Kitty Hawk. Orville would happily return to the bike shop and be satisfied if their experiment failed. Wilbur would return to intellectual exile and face the fate of a man who could not find his place in the world. The only way out for Wilbur Wright was to fly.

But to Katherine they were her brothers to serve, and even as she took a job at the Steele High School, she also had to run the bicycle business and act as intermediary between the brothers and their father. Later historians would refer to her as "the third Wright brother" for her support function. It is hard to know to what degree she was a third Wright brother, but she did serve as a conduit between Milton and his sons, keeping him up on what they were doing. "Orv went south Monday evening to join Will," she wrote Milton on September 26, 1900.[13] "They got a tent and will camp after Orv gets there which will be tomorrow morning. They can't even buy tea or sugar at Kitty Hawk, so Orv took a supply along. They also took cots and Orv took your trunk. We put your things all in the old trunk. I loaned my trunk to Will. I was glad to get Orv off. He had worked so hard was so run down. They never had a trip since the World's Fair. . . . They had a hard time getting anyone to look after the shop and do the repairing. . . . Lorin and I are the managers."

So, while starting out in her first job as a teacher, Katherine now had to run her brothers' bicycle business and navigate a garrulous father who had just learned that his two sons had gone down to the ends of the earth to fly a machine Wilbur built over the bicycle shop. Milton was just enough of a misanthrope himself to take it all in stride. Nineteenth-century people were used to the paradigm of starting businesses and failing. It was part of a growing economy, and, besides, he was not home to tell his sons they were crazy. He received letters from Wilbur and little reports from Katherine: "I have not heard from the boys since last Friday which was before Orv had got to Kitty Hawk. Probably the mail goes out but once a week. I never did hear of such an out of the way place."[14]

These were the letters Milton was getting as he warred with his own church while his daughter ran his sons' business, taught school, and fulfilled her role as matriarch of the household. Orville instructed her from afar in Kitty Hawk: "I got your telegram yesterday announcing the dismissal of Dillon. I rather expected he would not do. I telegraphed you in reply to the sundries of the E. H. Hall Co., Rochester, N.Y. The catalogue is at the store and the price list at home in the bureau drawer. When you get the bill of goods you order, remit at once by draft, deducting 5% for cash. . . . If there is anything needed which you cannot wait for, go to Forrer and Schaeffer 22 E. Second."[15]

Katherine had her hands full. In time, people would point to the Wright sister as a support person who made the invention of flight possible by taking care of the home, running their business, and keeping their father occupied. Orville Wright in 1924 would nip that one in the bud as well: "Katherine was a loyal sister who had great confidence in her brothers, and [when] we said we would fly she believed we would. But she never contributed anything either in money or mathematics."[16]

Orville was a man of his time, and he had the view that women could not do much more than teach or nurse. Complicating this was his own bizarre, complex relationship with the opposite sex, which at the time, in public at least, did not seem to exist. It is still curious that historians have taken the absolute lack of a sex life for either brother as perfectly normal. But certainly, they were men with normal sex drives, and the total lack of relationships of any kind is odd, if not improbable.

Add to this Orville's rage at his sister marrying twenty years down the line, and there are more questions than answers. To even hint that the Wright brothers or their sister were gay seems blasphemous against the biblical account of three individuals who seemed to operate in an asexual world deemed by their father as the only type of existence worth having. Of course, the bishop enjoyed a sex life with his own wife, but what was good for the bishop was not good for his children.

And so, we circle back around to Orville's reply to people who saw Katherine as having a role in the development of flight, if only a supporting one. Some even suggested she had funded the brothers. Orville was firm in saying that they never took any funds from their sister and she had nothing to do with the science of flying. One could make the case in 1900 that neither did Orville.

KILL DEVIL HILLS—OCTOBER 18, 1900

I t was damn hot walking along the beach road with their glider. Almost 100 degrees, with high humidity. Two men in dark wool coats sweated silently, making their way down the sandy road toward the large dunes. They had to get their kite to a higher point, and that meant walking the four miles to Kill Devil Hills with their glider in tow, along with William Tate. Wilbur Wright was suffering for his dream, but it had been that way ever since he boarded Israel Perry's schooner and headed into the unknown.

So now the brothers were together. Two young men from Dayton, Ohio, in a tent at the bottom of a sand dune in the middle of nowhere. Orville's correspondence with his sister spoke of a man who was on a vacation: "This is a great country for fishing and hunting. The fish are so thick you can see dozens of them whenever you look down into the water. The woods are filled with wild game, they say even a few 'bars' are prowling about the woods not far away."[1]

He goes on to describe several storms for his sister and then sums up their flying this way:

> We spent half the morning yesterday in getting the machine out of the sand.
> When we finally did get it free, we took it up a hill and made a number of
> experiments in a 25 mile an hour wind. We have not been on the thing since
> the first time we had it out, but merely experiment with the machine alone,
> sometimes loaded with 75 pounds of chains. We tried it with tail in front,
> behind, and every other way. When we got through Will was so mixed up
> he couldn't even theorize. It has been with considerable effort that I have
> succeeded in keeping him in the flying business at all. He likes to chase buz-
> zards, thinking they are eagles, and chicken hawks, much better. . . .[2]

What can we take away from this letter from Orville in 1900? Orville never flew on the glider in 1900, yet he wrote, "we have not been on the thing."[3] Not exactly the scientist. But he goes on to say that Wilbur is so frustrated or mixed up that he has to keep him in "the flying business"[4] and keep him from killing time to "chase buzzards, thinking they are eagles and chicken hawk."[5] Orville paints a picture of himself as the man who is really interested in flight while Wilbur is in danger of giving it up.

We see early on that Orville is very concerned with making sure he has weight in the "flying business" equal to his brother. The letter to Chanute from Wilbur after returning to Kitty Hawk tells a different tale: "The machine had neither horizontal nor vertical tail. Longitudinal balancing and steering were affected by means of a horizontal rudder projecting in front of the planes. Lateral balancing and right and left steering were obtained by increasing the inclination of the wings at one end and decreasing their inclination at the other. The short time at our disposal for practice prevented as thorough tests of these features as we desired, but the results obtained were very favorable and experiments will be continued along the same lines next year."[6]

The scientist working out his experiments comes though with a firm declaration to continue. This is at odds with the almost-comical scene Orville paints of a man who would rather be chasing chickens. So what did happen in Kitty Hawk? The truth of the time in North Carolina in 1900 was theory meeting reality. What had begun in the dark years of Wilbur's depression was now coming to fruition in the sands of Kitty Hawk. Orville did write to his sister that they were ready to try the glider. The first time they took it to the beach, a thirty-mile-an-hour wind took hold of the glider and with Orville and Wilbur holding onto it the double-winged creature tugged to go higher. "It naturally wants to go higher and higher. . . . When it gets too high, we give it a pretty strong pull . . . to which it responds by making a terrific dart to the ground."[7]

Wilbur recorded none of these first glides, but one time the glider took control and was caught by a wind and threw Orville, who had been hanging on to the rear spar, twenty feet away. He was unharmed, but the glider was badly damaged: "The right side of the machine was completely smashed. The front and rear struts were broken in several places, the ribs were crushed and the wires snapped."[8] They dragged it back to camp and considered leaving but then decided they could fix it and try again. Wilbur had not ascended in the glider at this point, and we can only imagine the angst he was feeling. Nearly six weeks in Kitty Hawk with nothing but a few kite glides and a freak accident to attest for his grand experiment. He had to come back with something tangible in order to continue. He was not unlike the artist who needs some sort of success to continue pursuing what many think is plainly crazy.

Orville did not feel this angst. If things didn't work out and the flying machine didn't leave the ground, then he would simply return and continue manufacturing bicycles. It is the difference between the assistant and the doctor. Wilbur must solve his itch, his desire that was born in flying the kite in Dayton; and he must do it before they leave.

For three days, they worked on the glider while trying to keep warm at night. Two men freezing in a canvas tent on the edge of a sand dune with a glider tied up nearby. This was the cutting edge and the beginning of manned flight in the first year of the twentieth century. The unintended consequence was the therapeutic value of their trip into the wilds of the Outer Banks. Their laboratory was beautiful. Wilbur had found a prime location to bend the elements and decipher the invisible air currents. It was such a primitive place for humans to conquer the final obstacle to traveling about the earth. A spiritual presence did seem to be in Kitty Hawk with the two men. Like any great scientist, the inventor needs a shield from the world to tackle and solve what others cannot. Kitty Hawk proved to be this shield for Wilbur Wright.

What he needed, though, was a better launching pad, a place where the wind could take hold of the glider and they could get a running start. Wilbur was going with his glider based on the Lilienthal model, with a cambered wing (curved for better lift) and a double-decker design based on the 1896 Chanute Herring experiments near Chicago. He was basing the design of his wing on the aeronautical data on lift published by Lilienthal.[9] It was as if he was baking the perfect cake—a little salt from here, a partial recipe from there, some flour from somewhere else. Even the trusses on the wings were braced by wires in their own version of Chanute's modified Pratt truss.[10] The forward rudder was mounted in front of the wings as a means of protection against a nose dive, much like the kind that had killed Lilienthal.

All Wilbur now had to do was take a run into the wind and jump off the side of a hill. They would take the glider to Kill Devil Hills: "A cluster of three prominent sand dunes that Tate in his letter of August 18 had described as 'not a tree or bush anywhere.' . . . The view from the Big Hill was spectacular in all directions. Three quarters of a mile to the east beyond the beach was the great sweep of the blue green Atlantic Ocean."[11] It was where Wilbur would make his first flight, but first they had to get there.

William Tate secured a horse and a wagon, and on October 3 they began the four-mile trek with the glider to Kill Devil Hills. It was sunny with a light wind and perfect for flight. Anyone passing the men on the sandy road would have stared at the two men in high collars and ties, with the giant glider resting across the wagon, and sunburned William Tate in his large straw hat at the reins next to the men who were sweating in the high heat of midday. *What in the hell . . . ?* would be a typical response to someone seeing a flying machine in the remote shoals of the Outer Banks in Kitty Hawk. The proverbial flying saucer would elicit no different reaction in the year 1900.

Once the small caravan reached Kill Devil Hills, they trekked up the giant sand dune, huffing and puffing and fighting the increasing wind. The dune gives a bird's-eye view of Kitty Hawk, the ocean, and the sky. There was a strong wind, and Wilbur tried the glider as a kite again and was satisfied with the control. Wilbur then turned around and looked out from the Big Hill and could see Albemarle Sound, where he had crossed with Israel Perry six weeks before. He turned around, and there was the rich blue of the Atlantic. The salty ocean breeze fairly slapped his cheek with a fine grit of sand that lifted from the giant dune. A man could bound down the dune in great leaps, but he would have to trudge back up. Wilbur had come all this way to prove that he could make an advancement in manned flight and that he wasn't some floundering bicycle mechanic with grand dreams. Now was the time to prove to himself that he was more than the world had given back to him. He would fly.

They positioned the glider on the hill. Orville and William Tate held on to each wing with two fifteen-foot ropes that were attached to both sides of the wings for control. Wilbur climbed inside the cutout of the lower wing, with his feet on the ground. He was the airplane's wheels. He grasped the spars in front of him and stared into the wind. Now was the moment. Wilbur paused, then looked at his brother and William Tate and nodded. The three men trotted forward into the stiff wind until the wings began to lift.

Wilbur then ran in the sand, staring straight ahead, and felt the craft rising around him like a creature rising from the dead. The wind lifted the wings further, and he was lifted from the earth by his arms. He quickly scrambled onto the wing and stretched his feet out to the T bar below and grabbed the elevator control. The glider lifted higher as the hill fell away, with the men playing out the lines rapidly. Wilbur Wright felt the wind against his cheeks, blurring his eyes, and heard only the musical pitch of wires. The silence of flight was transforming, a mystical quiet with only the wind, and Wilbur felt himself suspended above terrestrial cares. The ocean was in the distance, the land flattened out, and he heard a strange whistling in the air as a feeling of absolute peace settled on him. Simply, he was flying.

Then the plane began to bob up and down as Wilbur moved the elevator control to no effect. "Let me down!"[12] The two men pulled on the ropes, and "the craft settled gently back into the sand."[13] Orville ran to him, his hard shoes digging into the dune, and asked why he had come down when he was just beginning to fly. Wilbur looked at his brother. "I promised Pop I'd take care of myself."[14] Was this true? Milton ruled absolutely, and Wilbur was caught between his father's world and a yearning to go his own way. The bishop was all about restraint, about controlling emotions, desires, feelings. The world was evil, and to be out there was to possibly fall and fail like his two older sons. Could flying, with all it promised, be an escape from the ecclesiastical cage of father Milton and the great evil of the world?

Though Wilbur had denied fame and fortune as motivating factors, they had crossed his mind and would certainly set him free. He would have proven to Milton, to the world, and to himself that he was not crazy. He would fly away from himself into a freedom few dared to dream about. But just when he was lifting off, the long arm of the father knocked him back to Earth. He would have to fly higher than fifteen feet to get away from the bishop.

But this was the first of a series of flights that Wilbur made on that day, with some going 300 to 400 feet in length and speeds on landing of nearly 30 or 40 miles an hour.[15] Interspersed with these flights were tests with chains loaded on the glide, and a small derrick was erected and the plane tethered to it to test the wing warping. They then took the fifty-pound glider and literally threw it into the air several times to see what would happen. Patching and splinting the glider back together over a series of days kept them testing. Orville described these thrown glides this way to his sister: "It would glide out over the side of the dune at a height of 15 or twenty feet for about 30 feet, gaining, we think, in altitude all the while. After going about 30 feet out, it would sometimes turn up a little too much in front, when it would start back, increasing in speed as it came, and whack the side of the hill with terrific force."[16]

Wilbur was able to run down the giant dune and lift himself into the glider and fly twice as fast as he ran. He was flying, and no amount of testing or data could compare with the sensation. As Fred Howard wrote in *Wilbur and Orville*, "It was one thing to dangle by the forearms from a pair of wing-supported horizontal bars like Lilienthal. It was another thing altogether to lie motionless between a pair of seventeen-foot wings on a sea-scented updraft, using hands and brains to maintain an equilibrium rather than instinctive body movements. For the first time outside of dreams, a man had been carried through the air in a prone position on a pair of wide white wings just as surely as the squeaking gulls—and had survived."[17]

Years of thinking, theorizing, and building had come together in the form of a machine that could leave the ground; and, while not completely controllable, it had the seeds that would blossom into the 1903 *Flyer*. The tall, angular man who spoke little had pushed flight along unknowingly, with a simple theory that balance and control were the keys to man taming the air currents and being able to soar like the hawks he observed for hours on end. A year later, he would summarize it this way: "Although the hours and hours we had hoped to obtain finally dwindled down to two minutes . . . we considered it quite a point to be able to return without having our pet theories completely knocked in the head by the hard logic of experience, and our own brains dashed out in the bargain."[18]

Wilbur wrote using the plural "we," but it was he who flew. Orville did not. Orville was helping his older brother mount a glider and take off. The question is then: Why didn't Orville fly at least once in the glider? Some might say it was a promise to their father to keep Orville safe, though there is no evidence such promise was ever made. The real reason Orville did not fly is that flight was *Wilbur's* domain in the same way that the printing business was Orville's and to a large degree the bike business was as well. Wilbur had initiated the foray into manned flight, and he had pursued it all the way to Kitty Hawk.

It was Wilbur who wrote to the Smithsonian to inquire about current literature on flight and to the US Weather Bureau to inquire about the wind conditions across the country; and then he consulted with the Smithsonian Institution in search of a testing ground. It was Wilbur who reached out to Octave Chanute and then decided Kitty Hawk would be the best place to try out his glider that he had designed and primarily built. It was Wilbur who went down to Kitty Hawk alone.

Once in Kitty Hawk, the brothers' relationship was clear. Orville joined Wilbur there later in a support mode, but from his letters to Katherine one can see he was more interested in the domestics of camp life at this point. Orville and William Tate helped Wilbur fly by holding onto the plane and making sure they could pull him back down if he got in trouble. Wilbur was clearly the pilot, and if there was any role for Orville, it was one of mechanic at this point. It may not have stayed this way, but in 1900 it was all Wilbur's show before Kitty Hawk and at Kitty Hawk.

As Larry Tise wrote in *Conquering the Skies*, "Of the inseparable pair, Wilbur was the adventurer, the explorer, the pathfinder. . . . He framed the challenges they faced and established their goals. . . . Unlike Orville, who thrived on mechanics, applied mathematics, drafting and the sciences of materials, Wilbur was a man of ideas and ideals, of dreams and drama."[19]

One thing Wilbur did find was that the most efficient and comfortable way to fly the glider was to lie down, putting the final nail in the coffin of the Lilienthal method of using body weight to navigate. The pilot was born here, a man who would *ride in* the machine rather than *be part of* the machine. He would later write, "we found the position far more comfortable than hanging by the arms; the action of the machine was much steadier and landing was effected in the soft sand at speeds of twenty to thirty miles an hour, without any injury whatever to operator, or breakage of the machine."[20]

Before they left for Israel Perry's boat, the Wrights took the plane back to the dune and gave it one last toss off the top. It came to a landing in hollow of sand, and there it stayed. Wilbur stripped off the sateen covering and gave it to William Tate's wife, who made two dresses out of it. When he would return in 1901, the struts of one wing would still be protruding from the sand. A gale would later obliterate the last remains of man's first attempt at controlled flight.

THE MENTOR—1901

ilbur Wright returned from Kitty Hawk, North Carolina, where he had flown tethered, with Orville and William Tate holding ropes to keep the wings stable, and then had flown untethered. Wilbur had now joined Lilienthal as one of the few men to know the feeling of leaving the earth and floating on the air. The German Lilienthal must have had magical moments of elation as he soared in his glider, kicking his legs one way and then the other to make turns and to remain stable. Wilbur, Lilienthal, and a few others had managed to fly—if only for seconds. The man who had returned to a bicycle business in need of attention, a frazzled sister, and a demanding father, now had a bigger problem. He had left the earth and flown . . . but he wanted to do it again.

If Wilbur had failed, then there might have been a turning away, although like Teddy Roosevelt who would become president that year, Wilbur Wright seemed destined for something greater. The taste of flight was too much to put the genie back in the bottle. Like the addict who has had just a taste, Wilbur wanted to return as quickly as possible to Kitty Hawk. But first he had to understand what had happened in the hot sands of the Outer Banks. He needed to go back to the school of one, and that did not involve his brother Orville.

Wilbur did not sit down with Orville and theorize. Orville was a mechanic, but Wilbur needed to understand how the gilder flew, how he could control it, and how he could improve on it. He was the visionary, the savant who had to get to the top of the mountain, and he could not find that path by talking with his brother. He needed someone else, an intellect equal to his in knowledge, inquisitive reasoning, and logic—and at least as up to date on the latest aeronautical data.

What exactly had happened on the sand dunes of Kitty Hawk? Wilbur had loaded the glider with a fifty-pound chain and flown it. He had flown off of Kill Devil Hills. They had run around in the sand and chased the glider thrown off the edge of the dune. He had built a glider above his bicycle shop, and then he had lain down on the wings and flown for several minutes combined. Now he was sunburned and tired, and the regular world demanded attention. Wilbur was not unlike an astronaut returning from a trip into space.

So he had returned and taken the bicycle business in hand and suffered through Milton's admonishments to keep a warm and happy home for him. Katherine was relieved of her duties and could focus on teaching, and Orville was once more engaged as the bicycle entrepreneur; now Wilbur could sit in the parlor with the Gibson clock and pick up pen and paper and write to the one man who could help him, Octave Chanute:

> In October my brother and myself spent a vacation of several weeks at Kitty Hawk, North Carolina, experimenting with a soaring machine. We located on the bar which separates Albemarle Sound from the ocean. South of Kitty Hawk the bar is absolutely bare of vegetation and flat as a floor, from sound to ocean, for a distance of nearly five miles, except a sand hill one hundred and five feet high. . . . It is an ideal place for gliding experiments except of its inaccessibility. The person who goes there must take everything he will possibly need, for he cannot depend on getting any needed article from the outside world in less than three weeks.[1]

What is the significance of this correspondence between the seventy-year-old engineer and the thirty-two-year-old bicycle mechanic? It is the school of one. As Tom Crouch summarizes in *The Bishop's Boys*, "From the time of Wilbur's first note of May 13, 1900, to Chanute's last on May 14, 1910, a total of 435 letters would pass between them. The sheer bulk of the exchange was extraordinary, averaging one letter every eight or nine days over an entire decade."[2] And these letters were not between Chanute and the Wright brothers. These letters were between Wilbur Wright and Octave Chanute. The *Papers of the Wright Brothers* include many of them, and they are striking in their length, their breadth, and the density of the discussion. It was a seminar of early aeronautics, and the pupil in the beginning was Wilbur; and then it became a seminar of two equals trying to find the answer to a riddle in a dark coal mine. In all the Wright–Chanute correspondence, there is but one letter between Octave Chanute and Orville Wright, and it centers on travel logistics. The rest are all between Wilbur and Octave. Historians have treated this by saying that Wilbur was a better writer than the profoundly shy Orville. This is ridiculous since Orville was the primary letter writer from Kitty Hawk on all matters to his sister, Katherine. The truth is, Wilbur had his hand on the pulse of his quest to fly, and he is the one who had the questions, the data, and the theories that would fly back and forth between the two men. Wilbur possessed the hot light of invention that demanded some kindred spirit to talk with, compare, inquire, and at times empathize with on the head-numbing audacity that would push a man with no degrees, no credentials, and no real successes to think he could be the one to solve what others could not.

And so, Wilbur sat down and wrote his letter on November 16, 1900: "We began experiments by testing the machine as a kite and found that a wind of twenty-five miles would more than support it with an operator on it." Wilbur then described his glider and gave the results of their gliding tests. He explained the logic behind the operator lying down: "We had intended to have the operator turn his body to an upright position before landing but a few preliminary tests having shown that it was feasible to let the machine settle down upon its lower surface with the operator maintaining his recumbent position, we used this method of landing entirely."[3]

Everything was new. No one knew how a man should *even sit* in a flying machine. Should someone sit up as if in a parlor or a car, or should someone lie down and decrease the drag upon the body? What was safer and more efficient? Wilbur was convinced that the correct way to fly was to lie down: "And although in appearance it was a dangerous practice we found it perfectly safe and comfortable except for flying in sand."[4] Who else but Chanute could he tell this to and get approval or disapproval? Wilbur needed a sounding board with someone who could show him the way and then set him free to find the answers. He described for the old scientist his method of experimentation:

> Our plan of operation was for the aeronaut to lie down on the lower plane while two assistants grabbed the ends of the machine and ran forward till the machine was supported on the air. The fore and aft equilibrium was in entire control of the rider, but the assistants ran beside the machine

and pressed down the end which attempted to rise. . . . The speed rapidly increased until the runners could no longer keep up.[5]

The aeronaut was Wilbur, of course, with Orville and William Tate running alongside. Chanute wrote back immediately: "I thank you much for your letter of 16th which I have found deeply interesting and I congratulate you heartily upon your success in diminishing the resistance of the framing and demonstrating that the horizontal position for the operator is not as unsafe as I believed."[6] Then Chanute asked for permission to include the results of the Kitty Hawk trip in an article in *Cassier's Magazine*. This was quite a validation for Wilbur, yet we see in his reply his quest for secrecy and to some degree paranoia. This was the self-knowledge that he possessed, the ability to discover the secrets of flight: "We will gladly give you your own information or anything you may wish to know, but for the present would not wish any publication in detail of the methods of operation or construction of the machine."[7]

Octave Chanute then proposed a visit to Dayton and included the article he intended to publish for Wilbur's approval. "I have lately been asked to prepare an article for *Cassiers Magazine* and I should like your permission to allude to your experiments in such brief and guarded way as you may indicate."[8] There followed two letters about load and lift coefficients. Wilbur sent him several photos of flying the glider as a kite to use in the article, and Chanute promised an anemometer (to measure wind speed) for Wilbur to use in his next trip to Kitty Hawk.

Wilbur then wrote him about a return to Kitty Hawk with a new glider: "Our plans call for a trip of about six or eight weeks in September and October at the same locality we visited last year on the North Carolina Coast. We will erect a frame building 16 ft by 25 ft to house the machine in. The glider itself will be built on exactly the same general plan as our last years [sic] machine but will be larger and of improved construction in its detail."[9] Wilbur then invited Chanute to Kitty Hawk: "It is scarcely necessary to say that it would give us the greatest pleasure to have you visit us while in camp if you should find it possible to do so."[10]

For an intensely private man like Wilbur, this showed the amount of respect he had for Chanute and his desire to keep their relationship strong and the information flowing back and forth. Wilbur Wright needed Octave

Chanute, and some could argue that Octave Chanute needed Wilbur, but this would come later in the relationship. Wilbur then did something very singular. He published two articles of his own in June 1901, the first under the title "Angle of Incidence."[11] He wrote the article and sent it to the editor of the *Aeronautical Journal*, who quickly published it. Wilbur wrote, "If the term 'angle of incidence,' so frequently used in aeronautical discussions, could be confined to a single definite meaning, viz the angle at which the airplane and wind actually meet, much error and confusion would be averted."[12] It is a highly technical article on aeronautics by a newcomer to the game but who is instantly taken seriously. This was Wilbur Wright's first notice to the world of his experiments at Kitty Hawk.

The second article, "The Horizontal Position During Gliding Flight," was published in a German magazine.[13] He included a photograph of the 1900 glider being flown as a kite.

> All who are concerned with aerial navigation agree that the safety of the operator is more important to successful experimentation than any other point. The history of past investigations demonstrates that greater prudence is needed rather than greater skill. Only a madman would propose taking greater risks than the great constructors of earlier times. . . . The principal advantages of the upright position are obviously in starting and landing. Once in the air, many disadvantages become evident. . . . The experiments which my brother and I conducted were carried out at the seashore where sand hills rise on the sloping plain.[14]

The article wades into the debate on pilot position, with Wilbur arguing against the Lilienthal model again and advocating for the recumbent position as the best position of control. The point is Orville did not write these first two articles on what happened in Kitty Hawk. Wilbur wrote the articles and announced to the world *that he* was doing flying experiments. He does mention his brother, but the fact is Wilbur published these articles that put forth *his thesis* on flying. There can only be one author even though the plural "we" is now being used; the thrust of a letter to Octave Chanute is that of an inventor relaying his discoveries:

> Our final estimate of its soaring speed was twenty-two miles. We soon found that our arrangements for working the front rudder and twisting the

planes were such that it was very difficult to operate them simultaneously
... two minutes [*sic*] trial was sufficient to prove the efficiency of twisting
the planes to achieve lateral balance. ... Our rudder had an area of twelve
square feet, and it was our sole means of guiding and balancing longitudi-
nally. We never found it necessary to shift the body.[15]

One thing to note here: Wilbur was announcing that his discovery of
wing warping as a means of controlling the airplane was a success. It would
be the first time wing warping is mentioned, and Chanute lost no time in
responding and suggesting a meeting: "I shall hope to meet you either here
or in Dayton to obtain further details and to compare calculations of lift and
resistances. If your machine is not irretrievable I would much like to see it."[16]

Clearly Octave Chanute saw something in Wilbur Wright, who had just
gone down and flown a glider kite at Kitty Hawk. He saw a kindred spirit
and an intellectual equal. Chanute then wrote that he was coming to Dayton
that summer; Chanute, the renowned engineer, was not coming to visit
Orville Wright. He was coming to see the man with whom he had been corresponding about the best way to crack the Gordian knot of flight. He was
coming to see Wilbur Wright.

DANGEROUS TIMES—1901

During the same time that Octave Chanute was preparing to meet with Wilbur Wright, the assassin Leon Czolgosz had been living on his parents' farm and had been converted to the new radical movement, anarchism. He might have had a nervous breakdown, but he emerged determined to go see charismatic speaker and writer Emma Goldman and learn more about being an anarchist. Then he left to go kill the president. President William McKinley was walking the grounds of the Pan American Exposition in Buffalo, New York. A young man was walking toward him, and McKinley raised his arm to shake the man's hand. Czolgosz's concealed revolver fired twice, with one bullet grazing the president and the second burrowing into his abdomen.[1] McKinley would be dead three days later from gangrene, and, at the age of forty-two, Vice President Teddy Roosevelt would become the youngest president in history. He matched the mood of the young nation: cocky and assured, a cowboy looking for the next great moment that was sure to come in the new century.

Change was in the air.

Secretary Samuel Charles Pierpont Langley had emerged as the king of flight, at least in his mind. His steam-powered model had flown, and the coffers of the Smithsonian Institute had been opened to him. He would produce the most expensive plane so far in man's attempt to fly. He was convinced that now it was all just propulsion. His model had flown well enough and circled the boat and landed on the water just fine. Control had been conquered. Just build a bigger model and put a man inside of it. The problem was that steam was out as an engine. He needed something more powerful.

"All sorts of contrivances have been proposed," Octave Chanute wrote in the *Journal of Western Engineers* as far back as 1897, "reaction jets of steam or compressed air, the explosion of gunpowder or even nitro glycerin, feathering paddle wheels of varied design, oscillating fins acting like the tails of fish, wings like the pinions of birds, and the rotating screw."[2] Langley had settled on the screw, and he determined that a gasoline engine would be powerful enough to drive it and put his craft in the air. He soon had Charles Manley building the most powerful engine in the world.

Meanwhile, Glenn Curtiss was working on that very problem. Glenn liked to draw in the dirt. That was how he worked out problems a lot of the time. His brow would come down, his bushy eyebrows would move forward, and his mouth would be slightly pursed, like some old character out of a William Faulkner novel. The lanky mechanic of the homespun variety would then work out the bugs of his latest engine. His company couldn't build the engines fast enough for his motorcycles, and now he had just discovered that there was another customer base that needed his lightweight, powerful engines—dirigible pilots.

Take Captain Thomas S. Baldwin, who was the perfect example of how one thing leads to another. Glenn would tell this story many times because it helped show that if you did a good job, then one thing *did* lead to something else. Baldwin was at his California ranch, trying to get his dirigible off the ground, but the engine kept quitting. The cowhands were having a field day. The lawnmower engine was underpowered and, worse, it would sputter out every time he tried to lift off. And then came the mythical part. Just as he was about to give up, a dust cloud appeared on the road and was coming closer and closer. It turned into a tornado, with a bug-eyed man in front, gunning down the road on a Curtiss motorcycle. "It's Harry White," a bystander drawled, "on his newfangled motorcycle he just got from the East."[3]

Like a character out of an old *Saturday Evening Post* story, Harry swung off, and Captain Baldwin had a close look at the puttering engine. Then Harry produced a dog-eared catalog for G. H. Curtiss Manufacturing Company in Hammondsport, New York. Baldwin thumbed through the catalog of Curtiss motorcycles and engines and hollered out, "Boys, dump the gas out of the bag and chuck that old junk pile of a motor. . . . I've found the motor we need."[4]

The telegram that came into Glenn Curtiss's office wanted a two-cycled motorcycle engine shipped as soon as possible. Curtiss never had enough engines, so he ripped one out of a motorcycle and sent it off to Captain Baldwin. The motor reached Baldwin, and he promptly "installed the engine toward the rear of the spruce keel which was suspended, like a catwalk by cords from a net surrounding the bag of his newest hopeful dirigible."[5] As Cecil Roseberry describes the airship in *Glenn Curtiss: Pioneer of Flight*, "The rather shapeless non-rigid bag 52 feet long by 17 feet in diameter when inflated with hydrogen, was made of varnished Japanese silk. By means of a long shaft of steel tubing, the engine drove an 8-foot propeller mounted at the front to drag the craft through the air." The pilot sat with a vertical rudder and guided the airship not unlike a boat. "The *California Arrow* was the first successful dirigible to fly in the United States."[6] And it had a Glenn Curtiss engine.

It would seem natural that Glenn would follow his engines. Captain Baldwin went to Hammondsport after winning the grand prize at the St. Louis World's Fair for flying the longest and returning to the same starting point. Baldwin thought the Curtiss factory to be small and unassuming, as was the man. Glenn Curtiss was very young and dressed more like a mechanic than the owner of a motorcycle factory: "[Baldwin] found himself face to face with a disarmingly young man, reticent almost to the point of shyness, informal, working alongside his employees in shop clothes."[7]

Baldwin was jovial and corpulent, with a loud voice and a backslapping manner. The captain was later quoted in the local paper as saying, "Navigation of the air is as practicable as navigation of the water. . . . The Curtiss motor is absolutely perfect."[8] He ordered two more motors and entered into a long-term contract for a line of *California Arrow*s. Baldwin couldn't help but notice the pencil drawings of engines that Curtiss had sketched out on the walls. They were almost like fine etchings, but Glenn wouldn't bother with paper when showing an innovation to the workmen. Curtiss had found his niche in the construction of engines, but he didn't take the conquest of air too seriously. "I get twice as much money for my motors from those aviation cranks," he would later boast.[9] However, Curtiss would later find two aviation cranks who would change his life. Baldwin had found the man to power his airships and had pointed Glenn Curtiss on a collision course with the Wright brothers.

Langley didn't know of Curtiss at this point and had found Charles Manley, his senior engineering student, at Cornell University. He was just what Langley was looking for in an assistant, a "young man who is morally trustworthy with some gumption and professional training."[10] Manley would oversee the design of the new flying machine and eventually fly it. He would spend two years developing the power plant that would generate 50 horse-power to drive the aerodrome. Money was no object, and everyone expected

Langley to be the man who would crack the code of being able to ascend to the heavens. People would have laughed at the suggestion that a bicycle mechanic was already further along than the great scientist who headed the Smithsonian Institute, Secretary Langley. Money, government support, and the best minds of science were required to tackle flight. Not some man in a tent in the sands of Kitty Hawk, North Carolina. That was laughable.

But Octave Chanute would not have laughed as he knocked on the door of the house on Hawthorne Street. Wilbur had taken a walk and when he returned, the professorial Chanute was in his parlor. On his stroll around the neighborhood, Wilbur might have passed Oliver Crook Haugh's old home. Maybe he pushed his tongue against the bridge in his mouth and thought of that day of ice-skating that changed the course of his life. In five years, an electric chair would end Haugh's life.

Sprouting a white goatee and a cane, Chanute lit up the Wright home with his wit, insight, and, much more than all that, his knowledge of the science of aeronautics. Katherine Wright had let in the distinguished man with the snow-white hair, and Milton must have met the dapper, world-famous engineer with mixed emotions. "O. Chanute spent the evening with our boys. . . . Mr. O. Chanute spent most of the forenoon and till after 2:00 with us. He is an authority on aerial navigation."[11] These short entries in his diary could have been the same if another boy from the neighborhood had dropped in.

Milton was the star of the household, the fount of knowledge and morality, if not God, and here was this secular man who really was a player on the world stage. Milton liked to think his travels and his importance required and deserved the support of his grown children. But here was a man from the outside, an important man who took the lark to Kitty Hawk to fly a crazy contraption to another level. Could his son Wilbur really be onto something? This man seemed to think so.

There is very little written about this encounter but, it may be speculated, however, that Wilbur Wright took this occasion to tell Chanute of his two articles, "Angle of Incidence" and "The Horizontal Position During Flight."[12] As the editor of *The Papers of Wilbur and Orville Wright* speculated, Chanute probably encouraged Wilbur to "publish more details of their experimental work, and especially the results of the 1901 season, then about to begin and the germ of the idea probably started here of having Wilbur Wright address the *Western Society of Engineers*."[13] This would come to pass later in the year.

The importance given to Chanute's visit by Wilbur is really shown by the Wright housekeeper Carrie Kaylor Grumbach's recollection fifty years later of an incident involving dessert. Katherine Wright had "decided on melons for dessert and gave instructions that if one melon on cutting proved to be better than the other, Carrie was to make sure Mr. Chanute got a piece of the better one."[14] Carrie saw only partially ripe melon and decided to parse it up into bite-sized portions for everyone. So, Chanute ended up with a grape-sized piece. Katherine was not happy, as she knew how much for Wilbur was riding on this visit.

Milton saw outsiders as invaders, and already others were entering their lives. The boys had hired Charlie Taylor to run their business because they were heading back to Kitty Hawk again. Milton didn't like this. People were leaving. He was leaving, and that was fine; but others should remain home to keep the hearth fires burning. He was doing God's work. He was doing important work. He was not trying to fly, which God did not intend man to do. And now they were bringing in this farm boy to run the bicycle business.

What Milton didn't know, but the Wrights recognized, was that Charlie Taylor was a crack mechanic with an intuitive sense of how things worked, and he could make up something on the spot to fix a problem. Wilbur valued this ability above all else. Charlie smoked cigars one after another and irritated their sister with his braggadocio, but he could work like hell and was fully capable of handling the business, though he and Katherine would clash.

In the history of flight, the hiring of this man—who had quit school in seventh grade, owned his own machine shop, fathered two children, and had worked at several places before doing freelance jobs for the Wrights—would be almost as important as Wilbur's first letter to the Weather Bureau. He was to the Wrights as Charles Manley was to Langley or Glenn Curtiss was to Baldwin, though they didn't know it. Charlie would eventually be put to task building a motor that could go on the Wrights' airplane, and he would have to do it from scratch. He would not spend the thousands that would be used in the pursuit of the latest technology to power Secretary Langley's machine. He would build the machine for less than a hundred dollars.

Years later, Charlie Taylor would look back on his entry into the world of aeronautics, and it was not the story of Langley searching out the best and the brightest among the top schools that he remembered: "There were just the two of them in the shop and they said they needed another hand. They offered me 18 a week. That was pretty good money; it figured up to 30 cents an hour. I was making 25 cents at the Dayton electric company, which was about the same all skilled machinists were getting. The Wright shop was only six blocks from where I lived."[15]

American ingenuity and resourcefulness seemed to be rich commodities in the early years of the century. Ford, Edison, Westinghouse, and Wright, but now Wilbur had Octave Chanute sitting at his kitchen table at 7 Hawthorne Street. It was June 26, 1900, and Milton, Wilbur, Orville, and Katherine were eating lunch. Chanute was impressed with the two young men in front of him. There are no records of the conversation, but Chanute's view that flying would be solved by a team of men came through. He believed young, enthusiastic men who were bright and innovative could *collectively* solve the riddle of flight. He did not believe a lone individual like Wilbur could do it on his own.

It was during his two-day visit that he told them about Edward Chambers Huffaker. A devotee of Langley's, he had worked for the Smithsonian before feeling that he had to go out on his own. Huffaker was no slouch; as Tom Crouch cited in *The Bishop's Boys*, he was "one of the most experienced and best educated aeronautical engineers in the United States."[16] He continued, "Huffaker was a graduate of Emory and Henry College and held an MS in physics from the University of Virginia." The total of degrees between Huffaker and Chanute was easily four or five. The Wrights had not even graduated high school, and yet Chanute had latched onto Wilbur's letters and was now sitting in his home. What had he seen in the short correspondence that led him to bother with a man who could be another crank trying to ascend to the sky?

Huffaker was building Chanute a glider, and the Frenchman wanted him to bring it to Kitty Hawk to join the Wrights. It is amazing that Wilbur did not reject this out of hand, and it shows that he was very careful not to antagonize Octave Chanute. What was coming together at the table in Dayton was the hub of a wheel, and on each spoke were men working toward a common goal. Wilbur needed to be on that wheel to get the cross-pollination he required. Another man working with Chanute was George Alexander Spratt, who had written to Chanute and professed his desire to fly. He was a young physician with absolutely no experience in gliders, but Chanute saw something in him.

Chanute believed in his intuition regarding the men who would solve the problem of flight. He felt that Wilbur Wright was onto something, and Huffaker, through his guidance, might produce a flyable airplane. Who knows, even Spratt might hold the magic key. Wilbur took all of this in and did not say no to either man coming to Kitty Hawk. Chanute was a bit like a gambler betting on a lot of different horses but not sure which one could really cross the line. The Huffaker glider did not work out; Chanute recognized the faulty design and suggested that Wilbur fly it at Kitty Hawk as a kite. He offered to send Spratt and Huffaker to assist the Wrights in flying the glider.

Wilbur Wright did not need assistance, but he did need Chanute. And so, he managed a diplomatic letter after Chanute had left. "As to Mr. Huffakers [sic] trip to Kitty Hawk I do not feel competent to advise you. . . . If however, you wish to get a line on his capacity and attitude and give him a little experience with a view to utilizing him in your own work later, we will be very glad to have him with us."[17]

In other words, Spratt and Huffaker could come if this would ensure the relationship with Chanute, which Wilbur desperately needed. The truth was that Wilbur had latched onto a group of men who were in the forefront of aeronautics. He would surpass them all, but on the eve of the second trip to Kitty Hawk he needed to be in the loop before he left them all behind. In a letter to Octave, he explored the idea that someone coming to their camp might appropriate their ideas if not their technology. This was after Chanute assured him that the men would be discreet. Wilbur immediately wrote back that "we [he and Orville] do not think the class of people interested in aeronautics would naturally be of a character to act unfairly. . . . The labors of others have been of a great benefit to us in obtaining an understanding of the subject and have been suggestive and stimulating. We would be pleased if our labors should be of similar benefit to others."[18]

This is just a glimmer of what would later become a full-blown obsession with keeping their invention secret. Wilbur was willing to risk someone taking his ideas on wing warping or the position of the pilot or the angle of incidence if it meant keeping the door open. His mind was still hungry for what others knew in a field that was entirely new. At this point, the relationship between Wilbur and Chanute bordered on teacher/mentor/student. Lilienthal, Spratt, Huffaker, Chanute, and even Langley and Charlie Taylor all were faculty at the university of Wilbur Wright with its one student. This would change after the third trip to Kitty Hawk, but for now the letters would flow between them even more furiously. The school of one was in full session and would convene in the sands of Kitty Hawk.

RETURN TO KITTY HAWK — 1901

13

Wilbur was eager to get back to Kitty Hawk. "Owing to changes in our business arrangements we shall start on our trip much earlier than we had expected, probably not later than July 10th," he wrote to Octave Chanute, who planned to join them.[1] He wanted to get back on the hot sand. The dragonflies crackled in the weeds along with the smell of dead fish and sand crabs skittered by, then disappeared into holes. The ocean rose and fell. Here was the edge of the country, and beyond the ocean was Europe. In 1901, there was just the sand, the ocean, the silence, the heat, and the rain.

Chanute quickly wrote back promising to bring the anemometer Wilbur had requested. The Wrights left for Kitty Hawk on July 7, 1901. They arrived in Elizabeth City in the middle of a hurricane with 93 mph winds. "We reached Kitty Hawk several days later than we expected owing to the greatest storm in the history of the place," Wilbur wrote Chanute.[2] Octave Chanute, Edward Huffaker, and George Spratt were to join them at their camp. Their camp would be not in Kitty Hawk but in Kill Devil Hills, where Wilbur had flown the year before. "The practice ground at the Kill Devil Hills consists of a level plain of bare sand from which rises a group of detached hills. . . . The three which we use for gliding experiments are known as the Big Hill, the Little Hill and the West Hill," Wilbur would write later.[3]

Four miles from Kitty Hawk, Kill Devil Hills was where Wilbur would crack the code of manned flight in 1903, but "Kitty Hawk" rolled off the tongue easier, and it stuck. The memorial to flight is in Kill Devil Hills and not Kitty Hawk. This is one of many misnomers regarding the Wright brothers. But they had to get there still. For two days they waited out the storm and then started across the sound, but not before Wilbur wired instructions to the three men who were to join them: "Leave Norfolk at 10 AM Monday,

Wed or Saturday arriving at Nags Head the same day. . . . Nags Head is eight miles South of Kill Devil Hills where we camp. If notified in time we can meet you at Nags Head if weather is favorable, otherwise you can get conveyance there. Our freight arrived in Elizabeth City this morning and will go down to Kitty Hawk with us."[4]

The Wrights spent the first night at the Tates', then loaded all their lumber and equipment into a beach cart and began the long, wet trek to Kill Devil Hills. The rain was incessant and lasted for seven days. They could do little but wait. They were two men in wool pants, vests, high-collar shirts, and hard shoes. There were no tennis shoes or shorts or t-shirts or floppy hats. They were cut off from civilization and could only wait out the rain in their tent. Orville later wrote to his sister:

> After fooling around all day inside the tent, excepting on a few occasions when we rushed out to drive a few more tent pegs our thirst became unbearable, and we decided upon driving the Webbert pump, no well where we could get water being within a mile! Well we got no well, the point came loose down in the sand and we lost it! Oh misery! Most dead for water and none within a mile excepting what was coming from the skies. However, we decided to catch a little of this and placed the dish pan where the water dripped down from the tent roof; and though it tastes somewhat of the soap we had rubbed on the canvas to keep it from mildewing, it pretty well filled a long felt want.[5]

Finally, they could begin work on their hangar on Monday, July 15. Work proceeded for three days: "The building is a grand institution with awnings at both ends; that is, with big doors hinged at the top, which we swing open and prop up, making an awning the full length of the building at each end. . . . We keep both ends open almost all the time and let the breezes have full sway."[6] And then Edward Huffaker arrived. They watched the heavily bearded man huff across the sand dunes like a lonesome traveler cross the Sierra. Huffaker immediately took shelter in their tent, not offering to lend a hand on the construction of the shed. The author of the pamphlet *On Soaring Flight* had been a protégé of Langley at the Smithsonian.[7] His epiphanic moment was when he took strands of Chinese silk and waved it in to the wind to prove that "birds soared on currents of rising sun-heated air."[8]

After this high point, Huffaker was a man who spat tobacco juice in a spittoon with his feet on his desk while reading documents. When he came to work for Chanute, Langley had given him high praise but was probably glad to be rid of the chewing, spitting scientist. But Huffaker did write in his diary to record his observations upon arrival: "The Wrights reached here about the 10th of July and proceeded to erect a tent and workshop. The latter is 16 × 25 in horizontal dimensions and 6 1/2 feet in height, with low pitched roof, covered with tar paper. The ends are closed with falling doors, hinged on a level with the eaves, and both can be closed and opened at will. . . . In this building the machine is to be put together and housed in bad weather."[9]

While the Wrights finished up their hangar, Huffaker gave them lectures on morality while using their box camera for a stool. Wilbur detested the man but said little, later writing, "He is intelligent and has good ideas but little execution. His machine, which he built at Mr. Chanute's expense, is a total failure mechanically."[10]

Huffaker worked on Chanute's glider and complained about the weather in his diary: "The weather has been so warm that work in the afternoon has been out of the question."[11] With Huffaker came a black plague swarming down from the skies. They had just finished the hangar, and the construction of the glider was next, but the sun was suddenly blotted out by a mighty swarm of mosquitoes fueled by the recent rains. In the Outer Banks, the mosquitoes were only supposed to strike en masse once every ten years. This time they came in 1901. Orville would later say it was the worst experience of his life, and that included fighting off typhoid fever:

> The agonies of typhoid fever with its attending starvation are as nothing in comparison. But there was no escape. The sand and grass and trees and hills and everything were crawling with them. They chewed us clean through our underwear and socks. Lumps began swelling up all over my body like hens' eggs. We attempted to escape by going to bed, which we did at a little after five o'clock. We put our cots under the awnings and wrapped up in our blankets with only our noses protruding. . . . The wind which until now has been blowing over twenty miles an hour, dropped off entirely. Our blankets then became unbearable. The perspiration would roll off us in torrents.[12]

The three men then set up their cots beneath mosquito netting out in the open. "We put our cots out on the sand twenty or thirty feet from the tent and the house and crawled in under the netting and bedclothes, Glen Osborne fashion, and lay there on our backs smiling at the way we got the best of them. The tops of the canopies were covered with mosquitoes," Orville later described to Katherine, "until there was hardly standing room for another one, the buzzing was like the buzzing of a mighty buzz saw. But what was our astonishment when in a few minutes we heard a terrific slap and a cry from Mr. Huffaker announcing that the enemy had gained the outer works."[13]

They abandoned their cots and "fled from them, rushing all about the sand for several hundred feet around trying to find some place of safety."[14] The men then tried to find refuge again and were forced back to their wool blankets. They considered that they might have to abandon camp until they began to burn old stumps to drive the mosquitoes away. "We proceeded to build big fires about camp, dragging in old tree stumps which are scattered out over the sands at about a quarter mile from the camp, and keeping up such smoke that the enemy could not find us."[15]

During this siege, Chanute's second protégé, George Spratt, arrived. Not able to handle the smoke the other men were sleeping in, he set his cot out in the open air: "Mr. Spratt after getting in bed with the smoke blowing over him before long announced that he could no longer stand the fire and dragged his cot out in the clean air. A few minutes later he returned, saying the mosquitoes were worse than the smoke."[16]

Spratt, while much more amenable to the Wrights, had no real credentials other than a desire to fly. He turned out to be a hard worker who had studied the problem of flight. Chanute had billed him as a man who had a medical background, but this turned out not to be true. He was one of many men of the time who dreamed of flying but had no real methodology or science to work toward the goal. Aviation attracted drifters in 1901. It was an unreal science that promised man the ability to leave the earth, and for this there was no shortage of fabulists who glommed onto men like the Wright brothers or Octave Chanute. In this new field, the lack of structure, the roll of the dice, and the very absurdity of flight were the lights for the moths of discontent. Octave Chanute had probably taken on Spratt based on his youthful zeal, which the old man felt he needed in order to get a plane off the ground. Spratt also had a streak of melancholia that Wilbur tried to help him with since he had his own three years of depression. Even with his lack of credentials and psychological deficiencies, Spratt was much preferable to Huffaker, whom the Wrights identified as a shirker and a poser.

There were four men now living in the hangar, and Orville did a lot of the cooking. They created a gas stove out of metal barrel, "and shelves lined with canned goods, Arm and Hammer Baking Soda, Chase Sanborn Coffee, Royal Purple Hand Picked Tomatoes, Gold Dust Green Gage Plums. Fresh butter, eggs, bacon and watermelon had to be carried on foot from Kitty Hawk."[17] Huffaker made a habit of using other people's personal items and probably took more than his share of the food. He had abandoned his own plans to fly Octave Chanute's glider, which was slowly being covered with sand. Still, he was no help at doing dishes or pitching in on the general duties of camp. It is a testament to Wilbur Wright's respect for Octave Chanute and his desire to keep that relationship steady that he allowed someone like Huffaker to camp with them in the wilds of the Outer Banks.

Between dissertations on character building, the slovenly Huffaker dimly realized that he was out of his league. He saw how far Wilbur Wright had come, and he was ready to watch history in the making. On July 27, the glider was ready and the day was clear. Wilbur stood in the cradle on the glider, breathing the heat just below. Sand stung his eyes and peppered his cheeks. He faced the edge of the Big Hill, with Orville holding one wing and Spratt holding the other. Huffaker, William Tate, and Tate's half brother, Dan, were there to help. The wind was blowing at 25 miles per hour, with the ocean blue in the distance. The beach road beyond the dunes was a long, slim gray line, and the cloudless sky was a stunning cerulean expanse. It was a perfect day to fly.

The men began to run with Wilbur. He was heading toward the cliff of the dune and felt the lift pushing up under his arms. He reached the edge of the Big Hill and felt the glider lift him off the ground. Wilbur pulled himself up and lay down inside the wing. The wind whistled through the wired struts as the rising air floated the glider up toward the sky. Wilbur moved his hips and took the handles as the sand dunes became small and suddenly the ocean appeared. It was just the wind now. Silence for a few seconds. Flying now. Wilbur moved the elevator when the glider nosed down, and he rushed toward the yellow, glaring plane as the sand rose up to meet him.

Wilbur bashed his nose on the elevator and felt the wind go out of his lungs. He could have been killed if he had gone higher. The glider had nosed down into the sand after a few yards. The elevator was not working the way it should. "The operator having taken a position where the center of gravity was supposed to be, an attempt at gliding was made," Wilbur later wrote in his article "Experiments in Gliding."[18] "But the machine turned downward and landed after only going a few yards. This indicated the center of gravity was too far in front of the center of pressure. In the second attempt the operator took a position several inches further back but the result was much the same."[19]

Wilbur kept moving back on the wing, not unlike a man on a teeter-totter, trying to compensate for the glider's continued nosing toward the ground. Finally, he was almost on the very back of the wing when "the machine sailed off and made an undulating flight of little more than 300 feet. To the onlookers this flight seemed very successful but to the operator it was known that the full power of the rudder [elevator] had been required to keep the machine from running into the ground."[20] As Wilbur would later write to Chanute, "In the 1900 machine one fourth as much elevator has been sufficient to give much better control. It was apparent that something was radically wrong."

Huffaker later recorded in his diary the flights made on that day in August:

A number of excellent glides were made, Mr. Wilbur Wright showing good control of the machine in the winds as high as 25 miles an hour. In two instances he made flights curving sharply to the left, still keeping the machine under good control—length of flight in each case 280 feet. Longest flight 335. . . . On the occasion of the last flight made while skimming along about a foot above the ground, the left wing became depressed and in shifting his body to right to bring it up again he neglected the fore and aft control and plunged suddenly into the ground. He was thrown forward into the elevator, breaking a number of the rudders ribs and bruising his eye and nose.[21]

Wilbur had decided it was all his fault. And once the glider fell backward to the ground. "Screams from the ground sent the pilot scooting rapidly forward toward the leading edge. To everyone's relief, the glider pancaked straight down from an altitude of twenty feet, landing without injury to pilot or machine."[22] Each time, Wilbur had a sinking feeling of loss of control and a panicky thought that he might be in danger. The sands of the Outer

Banks saved his life more than once that day. Nothing was working the way it should. "In one glide the machine rose higher and higher till it lost all its headway. This was the position from which Lilienthal had always found difficult to extricate himself," Wilbur later wrote.[23]

These stalls were the death zone in 1901 and are still a pilot's nightmare. Lift ceases and the plane falls like a stone. Even large, modern airliners, with all their electronic equipment to detect stall conditions, have stalled. The nose goes high, and the airflow across the wings ceases. For the first time, there was real fear that Wilbur might kill himself. The front elevator took the brunt of the nose dives and possibly saved his life, but the 1901 glider was much less controllable than the 1900 glider. And it was much more dangerous. Huffaker was clueless and wrote later that a glide by Wilbur of 315 feet was the best he had ever seen. Wilbur knew something was terribly wrong. The lift coefficients were all wrong. "The adjustments of the machine were way off," Orville explained in a letter.[24] Essentially, the curve of the wing—the camber or lift—was wrong. As the Smithsonian National Air and Space Museum explains it, "a key term in the lift and drag equations was Smeaton's coefficient, which accounted for the density of air. A value for the coefficient of 0.005 had been widely used since the 18th century. Using measurements obtained from their glider tests at Kitty Hawk and the lift equation, the Wright brothers calculated a new average value of 0.0033. Modern aerodynamicists have confirmed this figure to be accurate within a few percent."[25] Essentially they had adopted Lilienthal's equations, but Wilbur began to suspect the numbers were wrong.

Wilbur went back to the drawing board and reshaped the wings in the shed. Author Tom Crouch wrote of this period, "As in 1900 they decided to pause and gather a full range of data while flying the glider as an unmanned kite before risking any further damage to craft or pilot."[26] Wilbur then took off again, with much better results. He wrote later of his glides, "The operator could cause it to almost skim the ground, following the undulations of its surface, or he could cause it to sail out almost on a level with the starting point, and passing high above the foot of the hill, gradually settle down to the ground."[27]

Huffaker speculated that history would soon be made. Wilbur wrote to his father that there was much more work to be done: "Mr. Huffaker remarked that he would not be surprised to see history made here in the next six weeks. Our opinion is not so flattering. He is astonished at our mechanical facility and as he has attributed his own failures to the lack of this, he thinks the problem solved when those difficulties . . . are overcome, while we expect to find further difficulties of a theoretic nature which must be met by mechanical designs."[28]

In other words, Wilbur knew instinctively the complex problems that were presented by flying a glider under control. Huffaker and other men were thrilled to see anything resembling manned flight since their own experiments had yielded dismal results. But like the painter or the writer or the scientist who is bent on the completion of the project, Wilbur knew how far they must go: "As we had expected to devote a major portion of our time to experimenting in an 18 mile an hour wind without much motion of the machine, we find that our hopes of obtaining actual practice in the air reduced to about one fifth of what we hoped."[29]

Out of all the men present in Kitty Hawk in 1901, Wilbur alone was flying the gliders, and he alone was risking his very life in a field that few knew anything about. They installed a hip cradle to try out the wing warping and immediately stumbled into a fundamental problem of control. "We found [ourselves] completely nonplussed."[30] When the warping was applied for a short time, the plane could be righted quickly, but when a turn was sustained, "things began to fall rapidly apart . . . [as] Wilbur sensed the machine was turning, skidding, really, to the wing that presented the most surface to the air."[31] Flying was proving to be more hazardous than he initially thought. "It was a very difficult thing to put your finger on," he later explained. "To the person who has never attempted to control an uncontrollable flying machine in the air, this may seem somewhat strange, but the operator on the machine is so busy manipulating the rudder and looking for a soft place to alight, that his ideas of what actually happens are very hazy . . . a peculiar feeling of instability."[32]

Wilbur's own glider experiments had given him the suspicion that aeronautical science might all be founded on flawed data that he must correct, or quite possibly it would kill him. Necessity was the mother of invention, or at least survival. Chanute soon arrived at their camp and was impressed with Wilbur's long-sustained glides. One gets the feeling that these men, while well-schooled in the science of flying, were not sure man *could* fly. Certainly, Chanute thought he might not see it in his lifetime. It was as if the true reality of flying was not to be taken seriously. Progress toward the goal was acceptable, but to solve the problem of flight, well, that was still a fantastical idea.

But to see Wilbur Wright soaring over the dunes and breaking the wide blue sky and blazing white sand, with the figure of his glider and his prone body soaring toward the heavens, it must have seemed like so much magic. Wilbur was really the one who thought man *could* fly and control the air. It is a bit like the one person who sees success as not a hope but as a realized dream. Theory is one thing, but to see a man fly was, in 1901, still quite astounding. The men who watched Wilbur lift into the sky were stupefied that someone—who was not on a bobbing contraption or in a rocket—was flying in a controlled way that was unseen on Earth up to that moment.

The pictures of these glides are still as amazing as Wilbur had found them when he returned home to his darkroom. He would later tell the Western Society of Engineers.

> In looking at this picture you will readily understand that the excitement of gliding experiments does not entirely cease with the breakup of camp. In the photographic darkrooms at home we pass moments of as thrilling interest as any in the field when the image begins to appear on the plate and it is yet an open question whether we have a picture of a flying machine or merely a patch of open sky.[33]

But Wilbur had detected another severe problem while careening across the sky. The wing-warping system, the gold nugget of their aeronautical discoveries, did not seem to be working at all. Another crash illustrated the problem. While skimming close to the ground, the left wing dipped unexpectedly, and Wilbur pulled hard on the elevator to get some altitude, but it was too late. The glider nosed down, and Wilbur felt himself catapulted forward like a human missile. He went crashing into the elevator, bruising his ribs, blackening his eye, and nearly breaking his nose. If it were not for the sand, the crash would have been far worse. But Wilbur was back to thinking that nothing was behaving as it should, and he had a nagging feeling that "there was a fundamental problem with the information they had inherited from Lilienthal and others."[34]

Still, Chanute was impressed, and he wrote in his diary on August 9, "A number of excellent glides were made, Mr. Wilbur Wright showing good control of the machine in winds as high as 25 miles an hour. In two instances he made flights curving sharply to the left, still keeping the machine under good control."[35] Clearly Chanute was impressed and left Kitty Hawk two days later feeling that Wilbur was on the right track. To Wilbur, though, he saw the "new difficulty with lateral control was even more disturbing. . . . The realization that there was some mysterious problem with the warping mechanism was the worst blow."[36]

The rain came for four days, and the Wrights felt it was time to go home. Wilbur got a cold. Spratt left, and then Huffaker—but not before helping himself to one of Wilbur's blankets: "When we came to pack up I made the unpleasant discovery that one of my blankets that had lived with me for years on terms of closest intimacy . . . had abandoned me for another."[37] Wilbur and Orville left on August 20. Once home, Wilbur wrote Chanute of his disappointment in being able to control the glider:

> We left Kitty Hawk at daybreak Tuesday morning and reached home this [Thursday] morning. It rained four days in succession after you left and then blew straight from the South till our departure. . . . The last week was without very great results though we proved that our machine does not turn toward the lowest wing under all circumstances, a very unlooked for result and one which completely upsets our theories as to the causes which produce the turning to right or left.[38]

Orville would later say that Wilbur groused on the train, "man would not fly for a thousand years."[39] Actually, he said fifty years. Either Fred Kelly changed it or Orville exaggerated.[40] So why would Wilbur say such a thing, and what was it he saw that his brother and others did not? The answer is he alone was flying. He alone knew how far he had come and how far he had to go. He was risking his life, and what he felt up in the air was the total lack of control, which had to send shivers down his spine. Flying without control was not flying: "That was the heart of the control problem; How to govern the movement of pressure around the center of gravity."[41]

In gliding, the two points came together when flying straight: "The elevator and wing-warping controls enabled the pilot to alter the position of the center of pressure."[42] In other words, one must control the air, and Wilbur seemed to be the only one who knew how far they had to go. Others assumed flight was like a train running down a track that was fundamentally stable. Wilbur believed that flight was unstable and had to controlled. He had come to believe that they had to start over and throw out all previous assumptions about flying. The mistake on the camber line (the curve of the wing) had led him to believe that Lilienthal's death, while unlucky, was also the result of a "problem with the information they had inherited from Lilienthal" himself.[43] The German simply did not understand the next step in controlled flight, and he had paid the ultimate price. Wilbur felt that men who flew without science were truly suicidal. Like the engineer, he had to understand the *physics* of controlled flight *before actually flying.*

Once home, the Wright brothers settled back into a routine. Katherine wrote her father, who was again on the road, "The boys walked in unexpectedly on Thursday morning. They haven't had much to say about flying. They can only talk about how disagreeable Mr. Huffaker was. Mr. Chanute was there for a week. Will is sick with a cold or he would have written to you before this."[44]

The sister was covering for the brother to keep her father happy. Wilbur didn't write, and he didn't talk about flying. There was nothing to say. He had left Orville long ago in the science of flying, and now he would leave even Chanute. But Chanute would prove invaluable still by funneling all known information to Wilbur, including secretive information from Samuel Langley: "Since beginning this letter I have received one from Prof. Langley in answer to one of mine some weeks ago. I enclose it herewith and beg that you will return it when you have absorbed his data for a surface very similar to yours. It is as he says confidential, i.e., the data are not to be published."[45]

Chanute was a sort of clearinghouse for Wilbur, who would return the Langley letter and say that his data differed, but one must imagine the sheer volume of information passed on by Chanute that made its way into Wilbur's final calculations. And yet Wilbur was down. A decade later, he recalled his feelings at the end of the 1901 experiments in Kitty Hawk: "Although we had broken the record for distance in gliding, and although Mr. Chanute who was present at the time, assured us that our results were better than had ever before been attained, yet when we looked at the time and money which we had expended, and considered the progress made and the distance yet to go, we considered our experiments a failure. At this time, I made the prediction that men would sometime fly, but that it would not be within our lifetime."[46]

Wilbur felt in his mind that he simply had to start over. He would have to finally break the tether of Chanute, Langley, Lilienthal, and others, and leap into the unknown to find his own answers.

WILBUR UNLEASHED—1901

W ilbur stepped off the train in Chicago at seven thirty in the morning on September 18, 1901. It had been eight years since he had been to the Windy City when he and Orville had gone to the Columbian Exposition at the World's Fair of 1893. He had been amazed at the beautiful white buildings and the well-dressed people who had attended the fair. In 1893 there was an Aeronautical Conference at the fair run by Octave Chanute, but there is no reason to believe the Wright brothers attended. Likewise, Wilbur and the people there didn't know that a madman named H. H. Holmes outside the fairgrounds would become famous a hundred and ten years later, when a bestselling book declared Holmes to be the first modern serial killer.

Chicago outside Union Station was grimy and gray. Coal from furnaces and dynamos coated the sidewalks and muddied the air. The steam engines belched black smoke, and horses dropped manure. Horses competed with electric cars and new gas-powered runabouts. People hurried by without tipping their derbies. Foul smells rose from the Chicago River as Wilbur walked across the Wacker Street Bridge and mixed with the Union Stockyards that reminded urbanites that on the south side, thousands of creatures were being slaughtered daily.

Few urban environments in America resembled Chicago. It was a rude city to Wilbur's Ohio sensibilities, and he wondered again if he should have come. "I have been talking with some members of the Western Society of Engineers," Chanute had written Wilbur upon his return.[1] "The conclusion is that the members would be very glad to have an address or a lecture from you on your gliding experiments. We have a meeting on the 18th of September and can set that for your talk. If you conclude to come I hope you will do me the favor of stopping at my house."

Wilbur was reluctant: "After your kindness in interesting yourself in obtaining an opportunity to address this society, for me, I hardly see how to refuse, although the time set is too short for the preparation of anything elaborate or highly finished."[2] Katherine had urged him to go, writing the bishop, "Through Mr. Chanute, Will has an invitation to make a speech before the Western Society of Civil Engineers, which has a meeting in Chicago in a couple months. His subject is to be gliding experiments. Will was about to refuse but I nagged him into going. He will get acquainted with some scientific men and it may do him a lot of good."[3]

Wilbur ate in a diner by himself. His clothes were tight. "We had a picnic getting Wilbur off to Chicago," Katherine wrote her father. "Orv offered all his clothes so off went [Wilbur] arrayed in Orv's shirt, collars, cuffs, cuff links and overcoat. We discovered that to some extent clothes do make the man."[4] Orville had stayed back, as it was Wilbur Chanute had asked to speak. Chanute had written him in a letter from Chicago, "The Secretary of the Society and the Publication Committee are greatly pleased that you consent to giving the Western Society of Engineers a talk on the 18th."[5]

Wilbur finished his breakfast, then walked north to Chanute's brownstone on the near north side. The class of homes improved, Wilbur noticed, as he neared the north-side enclaves of the well-to-do Chicagoans. Brownstones and graystones dropped granite stairs to the sidewalks, and it seemed fitting to Wilbur that Octave Chanute should be in the gentrified part of the city. Chanute had made lantern slides for Wilbur's speech on the two gliders and his experiments at Kitty Hawk. It was a primitive PowerPoint that would enhance Wilbur's speech, and there were also pictures of Lilienthal's gliders and Chanute's own double-decker planes. Wilbur could give an overview of the progress of aeronautics as he gave his speech.

He dined with Chanute that night in his elegant brownstone. "Mr. Chanute entertained him at his house and took him up to his study which Will declared was ten times dirtier and more cluttered than yours ever was," Katherine wrote to her father.[6] "It seems he has models of flying machines suspended from the ceiling so thick that you can't see the ceiling at all." They discussed his speech. Chanute told him to not worry about getting too technical. Wilbur could not help but be technical, but it gave him great relief to have a man like Chanute tell him he would be fine. The title of his speech was "Some Aeronautical Experiments."[7]

The next day, Wilbur was nervous as he waited to go on. His collar was too tight and his hands were clammy. He had tried to tamp down any enthusiasm for speaking to the assembly: "I must caution you not to make my address a permanent feature of your program as you will understand I make no pretense of being a public speaker."[8] Katherine told her father that she had asked Wilbur if his speech was to "be witty or scientific and he said it would be pathetic before he got through with it."[9]

Chanute was talking and explaining what had happened at Kitty Hawk. He spoke of two gentlemen, but of course he had only asked one gentleman to speak to the Western Society of Engineers. It was September 18th; four days before, President McKinley had been assassinated and Teddy Roosevelt became the youngest president in history. Wilbur felt the world had been off-kilter ever since, and now, waiting to speak to the august body of engineers, he wondered if the earth might just fly off its axis.

Octave Chanute stepped back, and Wilbur walked slowly to the podium, like a man moving underwater. The lights were dimmed for his lantern slides of the glides at Kitty Hawk. And then he was at the podium, facing the men and their wives. Wilbur Wright began to speak, and his audience did not move. Later, the speech would be quoted in *Engineering Magazine*, *Scientific Magazine*, *Scientific American*, *Flying*, and the *Annual Report of the Smithsonian Institution*. Chanute would order three hundred copies of the speech. "Some Aeronautical Experiments" would become a bible of aeronautics of the early twentieth century.

How did this happen when a relatively unknown bicycle mechanic had gone down to Kitty Hawk, North Carolina, for some glider experiments? The answer was that no one else was taking the methodical approach to flying that would solve the problem of *controlled* flight. Wilbur proceeded to explain that it was one thing to theorize how a bird flew but quite another to become that bird. He basically gave a speech on empiricism. He pointed out that a steamship would glide in the water once power was stopped to the propeller, but a plane would drop if power was cut. "However, there is another way of flying which requires no artificial motor and many workers believe that success will first come by this road. I refer to the soaring flight, by which the machine is permanently sustained in the air by the same means that are employed by soaring birds."[10]

He then showed a lantern slide of himself soaring in a glider. It is an amazing picture, with the sun shining down on the wings and the glider tilted at an angle much like a hawk. He related his own excitement in discovering these pictures in his darkroom behind the house: "In looking at this picture you will readily understand that the excitement of gliding experiments does not entirely cease with the breaking up of [*words missing*]. In the photographic darkroom at home we pass moments of as thrilling interest as any in the field when the image begins to appear on the plate."[11]

The experience of flying trumped the science of flying because one could not learn to tame the air if one did not attempt to fly. The high point of the speech came quickly. Wilbur held up a blank piece of paper in front of the crowd. "If I take this piece of paper, and after placing it parallel with the ground, quickly let it fall," Wilbur dramatically dropped the paper from his hand and pointed out the way it twisted and turned and flipped over. "It would not settle down as a staid sensible piece of paper ought to do, but it insists on contravening every recognized rule of decorum, turning over and darting hither and thither in the most erratic manner, much after the style of an untrained horse. Yet this is the style of steed that men must learn to manage before flying can become an everyday sport."[12]

This was central to his view of flight. Flying was inherently unstable, and therefore control was everything. It was not like a train that would continue down the track, but more like a ship in a stormy sea. Wilbur took the horse analogy further and pointed out that there were two ways to train a horse:

> One is to get on him and learn by actual practice how each motion and trick may best be met, the other is to sit on a fence and watch the beast a while, and then retire to the house and at leisure figure out the best way of overcoming his jumps and kicks. The latter system is the safest, but the former, on the whole turns out the larger proportion of good riders. It is very much the same in learning to ride a flying machine; if you are looking for perfect safety, you will do well to sit on a fence and watch the birds, but if you really wish to learn, you must mount a machine and become acquainted with its tricks by actual trial.[13]

There it was. The dividing line between he and his brother was there for all to see at that moment. It was Wilbur Wright's credo. The difference was the man who *actually dared* to fly. This left his brother and Octave Chanute behind, since neither man had ever ascended in a glider. Wilbur then praised Lilienthal and Chanute but pointed out that for all his gliding, Lilienthal had spent only five hours total in the air, and that was not enough. But he had flown, and that was the only way to tame the air. Chanute had made great advances with his biplane, and Wilbur told the audience their own glider at Kitty Hawk was based on advances pioneered by Chanute, a declaration that would later come to haunt him. What he didn't tell the audience was that he and Chanute had carried on a lively correspondence over the past year during which he worked out the science and theory of flying. He didn't tell them that over the next three months he would write to Chanute once a week, with many letters running nine pages.

Simply put, Wilbur Wright held a seminar, and he explained to the audience that flying was one thing but control was *everything*. "As long ago as 1893 a machine weighing 8000 lbs demonstrated its power both to lift itself from the ground and to maintain a speed of from thirty to forty miles an hour; but it came to grief in an accidental free flight, owing to the inability of the operators to balance and steer it properly."[14] He was referring to Sir Hiram Maxim's flying machine that was wrecked in 1894. It was a shot across the bow to Langley, who was proceeding on the same assumption that power equaled flight.

Wilbur aimed to control the air; he aimed to make a plane do what he wanted and take out the guesswork and the deadly experimentation that had killed Lilienthal. But first he doffed his hat to the German pioneer, saying he was on the right path: "Herr Otto Lilienthal seems to have been the first man who really comprehended that balancing was the first instead of the last of the great problems in connection with human flight. He began where others left off . . . he demonstrated the feasibility of actual practice in the air without which success is impossible. Herr Lilienthal was followed by Mr. Pilcher, a young English engineer and by Mr. Chanute, a distinguished member of the society I now address."[15]

Wilbur didn't tell the audience that he had come to suspect that Lilienthal's and Chanute's data was horribly flawed regarding lift, and that when he returned to Dayton he would have to establish a new baseline. He then dated his own interest in flight to Lilienthal's death in 1896: "The brief notice of his death which appeared in the telegraphic news at that time aroused a passive interest which had existed from my childhood and led me to take down from the shelves of our home library a book on Animal Mechanism."[16] The interesting part of this admission is there is no mention of his brother's interest. He then teased the audience with a general description of his wing-warping system. "Our system of twisting the surface to regulate the lateral balance was tried and found to be much more effective than shifting the operator's body."[17] The whole concept of remote control or a plane with actual controls to regulate flight was novel to the audience.

He then debunked Langley's theory of a powerful motor being the essence of getting a plane to fly: "Some years ago, Prof. Langley called attention to the great economy of thrust which might be obtained by using very high speeds and from this many were led to suppose that high speed was essential to success in a motor drive machine."[18] Wilbur's thesis followed, taking on the secretary of the Smithsonian, who was in the process of spending fifty thousand dollars of government money on an experimental plane. "However, there is another way of flying which requires no artificial motor and many workers believe that success will first come by this road."[19]

He was talking about gliding. He was saying that power had nothing to do with flying and if flight was understood, a man could fly with only the wind. There it is. Everyone who had tried to fly had been on the wrong track. Lilienthal, Chanute, Langley—none of them had tackled the science of controlled flight or had cracked the code that allowed birds to rise effortlessly. No one understood the science of flight, yet. But Wilbur had one on all the aeronauts of his time: *he knew the assumptions were wrong.* He knew what he didn't know. He didn't know what *would* work in terms of flying, but he knew what wouldn't work. In this he had an advantage over others who assumed the known data on flying was correct.

Wilbur then described the experiments at Kitty Hawk, complete with pictures of himself flying. The audience was astounded to see the man in front of them also on the screen in an airplane soaring through the air. Wilbur wound up the lecture by defining the central Rubik's Cube of flight that had yet to be cracked: "They [birds] spread their wings to the wind, and sail by the hour, with no perceptible exertion beyond that required to balance and steer themselves. What sustains them is not known, though it is certain that it is a rising current of air. But whether it be a rising current or something else, it is as well able to support a flying machine as a bird, if man once learns the art of utilizing it."[20]

The art of utilizing it. Wilbur knew that rethinking the science of aeronautics was required to discover the secret that allows birds to stay in the air, but there is an art to flying as well. There is something beyond human comprehension that must be considered, and it is this blending of art and science that will produce the plane that can fly in a sustained manner and be controlled. Wilbur knew that if the correct design could be discovered, a machine could ride the wind indefinitely. It was a vision beyond his contemporaries' at that time.

The people who watched Wilbur Wright that night in Chicago did not listen to a lecture by *the Wright brothers*; they listened to a lecture by a lone inventor named Wilbur Wright. The men and women of the Western Society of Engineers left filled with wonder. They did not talk about the Wright brothers. When they wrote about that night or thought about it or explained it to others, they talked about Wilbur Wright. He had gone down to Kitty Hawk and flown gliders. He was going to take the next step after Lilienthal and Chanute. He was the man who had dropped a piece of paper and explained that the capriciousness of air currents was his enemy and that he intended to tame them. They did not speak of his brother Orville Wright. Octave Chanute knew who was really going to get a heavier-than-air machine to fly under its own power. It was not Orville Wright. The majority of people who attended Wilbur Wright's speech that night in Chicago in 1901 didn't even know Wilbur had a brother.

After every speech there comes a relief. It is the giving away of information and then the satisfaction that comes from an audience that is held in rapt attention. Surely Wilbur, making his way back toward Union Station, saw himself as the man who would solve flight. It was there in the hall as a testament to how far he had come. It was his vision. It was his quest. And, riding back to the east, he must have been excited. He was at the jumping-off point and was ready to leave Octave Chanute and all known science behind. He had confirmed to himself that the known science of aeronautics was all wrong.

The artist must destroy what comes before to produce the new art. The engineer who solves what has not been solved must go in a radical direction. The genius cannot look aslant but must look forward and see nothing but the trail that must be blazed. The train clacked along toward the east, carrying the young man who now knew his charge. He would simply have to rewrite aeronautical science by starting over with the wings. Control the wings, and you control the sky. Like many pioneers, he realized that if he was going to solve the problem, he would have to do it entirely his way and ignore the work of others. Wilbur went home to find a new way to fly.

TUNNEL VISION—1901

The chief engineer of the United States Navy, Rear Admiral George Melville, did not believe flight was possible. He had looked around and assessed the various efforts and saw no clear path. In 1902, he wrote an article for the *North American Review*, stating, "A calm survey of certain natural phenomenon leads the engineer to pronounce all confident prophecies for future success as wholly unwarranted, if not absurd. Where, even to this hour, are we to look for the germ of the successful flying machine? Where is the preparation today?"[1]

The rear admiral would have had his answer had he visited the room above the Wright Cycle Company in Dayton, Ohio. Up there, two men had built "a small scale wind tunnel—a wooden box 6 feet long and 16 inches square, with one end open and a fan mounted at the other end, and this powered, since the shop had no electricity, by an extremely noisy gasoline engine. The box stood about waist high."[2]

The problem was lift and the Smeaton coefficient, which was a number determined by the equation for lift. This equation and coefficient, which had been used by Lilienthal and others, were wrong. Wilbur had based his own calculations on Lilienthal's data. He first performed a simple test by mounting Lilienthal's wing on his bicycle and pedaling like mad. It was a crude wind test of the wing, with the power of his legs creating the wind on the bicycle. He wanted to see if the 5° angle with a Lilienthal-cambered airfoil would remain stationary. He was testing the curve of the wing or the amount of lift the wing created. Basically, if the wing moved the mounted bicycle rim on his front handlebars, then it would show that there was too much lift or too much drag. If it didn't move, then it was the correct design. As he expected, the rim moved. This movement showed that Lilienthal's basic computations were incorrect on lift and, more specifically, that the Smeaton coefficient was wrong.

It was a mechanical age. Men worked out things with their hands, and mechanical problems were resolved in the physical space. The twenty-first century would be a digital age in which problems would be solved on computers. Wilbur sniffed a theoretical glitch in the mechanics of flying that was making his gliders, and all gliders, act like bucking broncos on which all the pilot could do was hang on and hope it didn't kill him.

After speaking in Chicago, Wilbur went to the room above the bicycle shop with his brother Orville. He had not told the engineers in Chicago that all the data that flying was founded on was wrong. He had told them about his methodology for solving the problem of flight. But now he had to tackle the physics of flight. So, there was Wilbur in the cold scent of oil and metal and wood and gasoline. He would build a mechanical device to solve a theoretical problem that would solve a mechanical one. If he had had a computer, he surely would have used it but, since those would not come into existence for many decades, essentially, he would have to build his own computer to simulate wind conditions for a fixed wing.

The wooden box with a fan mounted on the open end and powered by a loud engine was crude technology trying to solve very sophisticated problems, but it was all they had. The wind tunnel stood on four legs, and Wilbur began testing, using hacksaw blades cut up in various shapes to simulate the curvature of wings. He was trying to build a better mousetrap or a better wing, with Orville assisting. This went on for three months, with Wilbur shipping all the data to Chanute, who was amazed with the results. "You are evidently better equipped to test the endless variety of curved surfaces than anybody has ever been," Chanute replied.[3]

Even though Orville helped with the testing and construction, it was clearly Wilbur's wind tunnel and his computations:

> My brother Orville and I built a rectangle-shaped open-ended wind tunnel out of a wooden box. . . . Inside of it we placed an aerodynamic measuring device made from an old hacksaw blade and bicycle spoke wire. We directed the air current from an old fan in the back-shop room into the opening of the wooden box. . . . An old one-cylinder gasoline engine supplied the power to turn the fan. This was because there was no electricity in our shop.

In fact, even the lights were gas lights. It took us about a month of experimenting with the wind tunnel we had built to learn how to use it effectively.
... Occasionally I had to yell at my brother to keep him from moving even
just a little in the room because it would disturb the air flow and destroy
the accuracy of the test.[4]

Then the Wrights went after Langley. In a moment that presaged the
future, they re-created a sharp-edged wing that was preferred by the secretary
of the Smithsonian. They went over his data tables in *Experiments in Aerodynamics* and found the data flawed; in some cases, the data was grossly wrong.
Lilienthal's data was much more accurate. Langley and Lilienthal had differed
on many points. As the editor of *The Papers of Wilbur and Orville Wright*,
Marvin McFarland, explained, "Lilienthal believed and had demonstrated
experimentally that curved surfaces possessed considerable advantages over flat
planes. Langley, while admitting that curved surfaces offered slight theoretical
advantages, maintained that in practice, they were more apparent than real."[5]

If Langley had been listening or reading Wilbur's speech in Chicago,
he would have realized that Wilbur had given him some valuable advice on
powered planes: "A flying machine that would fly at a speed of 50 miles an
hour with engines of 1000 horsepower would not be upheld at all at a speed
of less than 25 miles an hour."[6] Wilbur was pointing this out because the
lift calculations were all wrong; therefore, brute power would only work in
limited situations. He then said to the world that the science of flight was the
problem, not the mechanics. "The flying problem was left over to the 20th
century because in this case the art must be highly developed before any flight
of any considerable duration at all can be obtained."[7]

In other words, the numbers must be right.

Wilbur worked many nights past midnight, with the gasoline engine
clattering away. The work being done above the bicycle shop would set the
bar for all aviators to follow. The tests illustrated that the cause of the poor lift
of the 1900 and 1901 gliders was due to an incorrect Smeaton value. Wilbur
continued to write to Chanute and forward his data. During that autumn,
Chanute went from mentor to pupil. His pupil had eclipsed him by so much
that Chanute had a tough time grasping the new data: "If your method and
machine are reliable you have done a great work and have advanced knowledge greatly. Your charts carry conviction to my mind and your descriptions

and comments are very clear. I must commend the system by which you went about to ascertain the best form of surface, instead of trying haphazard experiments."[8]

Then Wilbur took a strange detour. The bishop had ended up in a tussle with his church over the admittance of Masons. The liberals in the church wanted to admit the Masons, and Milton led the radicals against it. The liberals won, and the bishop's role in the church was greatly reduced. He was incensed, but he went back on the road, plotting his revenge. He saw an opportunity when he suspected Reverend Millard Keiter of embezzling $7,000. He asked Wilbur to examine the church books and find out what Keiter did with the money. Wilbur swung into action and quickly deduced that the books were a sham and that Keiter had used funds for his home, clothing, and insurance. Milton brought this evidence to the board of trustees, but they declined to prosecute, citing mismanagement over fraud. Wilbur kept going over the books and found even more fraud. Bishop Wright had Wilbur write it all up, and he launched his attack against Keiter, going public and accusing the reverend of criminal conduct.

The church turned against Reverend Wright, and Keiter sued him for libel. Wilbur stayed on it and issued a tract in defense of his father. Eventually, Milton would be exonerated from the libel charge and Keiter would leave the church. Here is the takeaway: Milton had turned to the son he thought most capable of handling a dangerous situation. His very livelihood and reputation were on the line. Orville was much more the man of business than Wilbur, but Milton instinctively had Wilbur, with his laser focus, dissect the church books and then mount his defense. In his father's eyes, Wilbur had the ability to do anything, while Orville was but a shadow beside a very brightly burning light.

When Wilbur stopped the experiments to handle his father's fight with the church and return to the business of manufacturing and selling bicycles, Chanute suggested he take some investor money from Andrew Carnegie: "I very much regret in the interest of science that you have reached a stopping point. . . . If however, some rich man should give you $10,000 a year to [*words missing here*] on, to connect his name with progress, would you do so? I happen to know Carnegie."[9]

Chanute wanted Wilbur to keep working on his aeronautical experiments, but the lone inventor was not ready to take on an investor, surely sniffing the tethers that would come with it: "Nothing would give me greater pleasure than to devote my entire time to scientific investigations and a salary of ten or twenty thousand a year would be of no insuperable objection, but I think it possible that Andrew too hardheaded a Scotchman to become interested in such a visionary pursuit as flying."[10]

Chanute offered his help then as a mathematician: "You will need to publish a table for each form of surface and aspect. I shall be quite at your service."[11] Chanute worked on the computations for the next six months and wanted to get them published. The new data went into the new glider that would be constructed after the bicycle season ended, but none of Chanute's hard work on tables ever saw publication. The world would have to wait until the summer of 1902 and the return to Kitty Hawk to see what Wilbur's wind tunnel had wrought.

THE SMITHSONIAN—1902

Chanute waited outside the large office. The august building smelled of old wood and the dust of time. Here men of science had plied their craft and set their names down in the annals of history. Octave tapped his foot and felt some grit down in his socks. The sand of Kitty Hawk was everywhere. It was in his luggage, in his glass case, on his papers, in his hair, in his shoes, on his toothbrush, in his razor, and even in his teeth. The food the Wright brothers had provided him at Kill Devil Hills was very good fare for being in a shed in the middle of nowhere, but the sand crept into the biscuits, the water, the bacon, and the eggs. That grit crushed between his teeth, and at night he felt like he was grinding his teeth.

Now his skin was dried out, windburned, and sunburned. His beard also had sand in it, and his eyes watered incessantly. He arthritis had kicked up from sleeping on the stiff cots, and now he had a cough. But it was an amazing time. He had seen the Wright brothers glide like no men before. Wilbur did most of the glides, but then Orville had done some, too, though Octave had only seen Wilbur. There had been an accident before he arrived: "My brother after too brief practice with the use of the front rudder," Wilbur had written him before he arrived, "tried to add the use of the wing-twisting arrangement also, with the result that, while he was correcting a slight rise in one wing, he completely forgot to attend to the front rudder, and the machine reared up and rose some twenty five feet and sidled off and struck the ground."[1]

Apparently, Orville was not hurt, but this set them back days. Octave's opinion of Orville Wright was of a man who did not talk much and seemed to wait to see what his brother thought. Why risk the machine with a man who was just learning to fly? Octave shifted in his chair. He looked at his pocket watch. Langley would make him wait, of course. Chanute had come from spending a week with four men in a large hangar, and he still felt the luxury of sitting in an upholstered chair.

Spratt had been there, and another Wright brother, Lorin; and, of course, Chanute had brought Augustus Herring with him to fly his own triplane. Chanute shivered at the Smithsonian. He still felt a chill, even though Wilbur had written him beforehand: "You should bring warm clothing and not less than the equivalent of two heavy double blankets for bedding, as we may have cool nights in October. We will arrange to have the necessities of life in the way of food but as our food was selected according to our tastes, it may be that it may lack what you prefer."[2]

Chanute had brought more blankets, and the six men had slept in the loft like sardines packed tightly together with their cots touching. The wind had shaken the hangar and came through the cracks in the wood. The ocean's roar seemed to be in that wind at times, and the cold scent of dead fish crept into the damp building. Chanute had awoken in the night, hearing the men snoring, and had thought it was odd that something as monumental as attempting to fly like the gods would be brought about by men sleeping in a shed on the edge of a sand dune. It was a long way from the rarified air of the Smithsonian, where he now sat, waiting for Langley. The early, bracing cold of September and then October had let Chanute know they were playing with Mother Nature, with northeasters and hurricanes possible any moment. Wilbur and Orville had taken in stride the wind that shook the shed to its foundations. That these men had spent time in a tent two years before seemed incredible to Chanute.

Chanute moved his legs and felt the pain in his hips. He would give anything to sink into a hot bath, but he wanted to see Langley first. He wanted to see him while the inspiration was still hot on him. In his mind, Wilbur Wright had solved the problem of flight. A breakthrough—the addition of a hinged rudder—had apparently occurred before Chanute had arrived. It was the problem of *well digging*, as the brothers called it.[3] It was the tendency of the plane in a turn to descend with the leading wing pointing down. Wilbur had then connected the hinged rudder to the cradle controlling the wing warping. There were now the three axes of control between the elevator or pitch for going up or down, the wing warping or roll for banking, and the rudder controlling yaw for turning. Chanute didn't know it, but this basic mechanical setup of control would set the bar for modern aviation for the next hundred years.

Bishop Milton Wright, Wilbur and Orville Wright's father. *Photo courtesy of the Library of Congress. Photograph by Harris & Ewing.*

Wilbur *(left)* and Orville Wright *(right). Photo courtesy of the Library of Congress. Wright brothers collection.*

Wright family home in Dayton, Ohio. *Photo courtesy of the Library of Congress. George Grantham Bain Collection.*

Orville *(second from the left)*, Wilbur *(third from the left)*, and Katherine Wright, with others. *Photo and caption courtesy of the Library of Congress. George Grantham Bain Collection.*

Captain William J. Tate, the Wrights' first host in Kitty Hawk, and his family on the porch of their home, the Kitty Hawk Post Office. *Photo courtesy of and caption adapted from the Library of Congress. Wright brothers collection.*

The Wright brothers' camp near Kitty Hawk (photo taken from the north). *Photo courtesy of and caption adapted from the Library of Congress. Wright brothers collection.*

Wilbur *(left, background)* and Orville *(right, foreground)* attempting to fly their glider. *Photo and caption courtesy of the Library of Congress. Wright brothers collection.*

Wilbur Wright in a prone position on one of his gliders just after landing. Its skid marks are visible behind it and, in the foreground, skid marks from a previous landing. *Photo courtesy of and caption adapted from the Library of Congress. Wright brothers collection.*

Wilbur gliding down the steep slope of Big Kill Devil Hill. *Photo courtesy of and caption adapted from the Library of Congress. Wright brothers collection.*

Crumpled glider wrecked by the wind on the Hill of the Wreck (named after a shipwreck). *Photo and caption courtesy of the Library of Congress. Wright brothers collection.*

Octave Chanute, 1832–1910. *Photo and caption courtesy of the Library of Congress. Photograph by Waldon Fawcett, Washington, DC.*

Glenn Curtiss at the pilot's wheel of his biplane. *Photo courtesy of and caption adapted from the Library of Congress. George Grantham Bain Collection.*

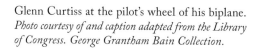

Samuel Pierpont Langley, secretary of the Smithsonian Institute. *Photo courtesy of the Library of Congress. Photograph by Harris & Ewing.*

Experimental tandem biplane embodying Langley principles on the Potomac River. *Photo courtesy of and caption adapted from the Library of Congress. Photograph by Harris & Ewing.*

Langley airship. *Photo and caption courtesy of the Library of Congress. George Grantham Bain Collection.*

Kitchen of the camp building at Kitty Hawk, North Carolina, with neatly arranged wall shelves holding dishes, canned foods, and other provisions. *Photo and caption courtesy of the Library of Congress. Wright brothers collection.*

Wilbur in his glider, turning rapidly to the left, with Dan Tate running alongside on Big Kill Devil Hill. *Photo courtesy of and caption adapted from the Library of Congress. Wright brothers collection.*

Left rear view of glider at a high altitude. *Photo courtesy of and caption adapted from the Library of Congress. Wright brothers collection.*

Rear view of Wilbur making a right turn in a glide from No. 2 Hill, with the right wing tipped close to the ground. *Photo courtesy of and caption adapted from the Library of Congress. Wright brothers collection.*

Wilbur gliding in level flight, with the single rear rudder clearly visible. *Photo courtesy of and caption adapted from the Library of Congress. Wright brothers collection.*

Orville making a right turn, showing wing warping, with a hill visible in front of him. *Photo courtesy of and caption adapted from the Library of Congress. Wright brothers collection.*

Rear view of the Wright brothers' four-cylinder motor as installed in their 1903 airplane. *Photo and caption courtesy of the Library of Congress. Wright brothers collection.*

The Wright brothers' 1903 flying machine at Kill Devil Hills, with camp buildings to the right. *Photo courtesy of the Library of Congress. Wright brothers collection.*

Kitty Hawk Life-Saving station crew that assisted in the 1903 flight. *Photo courtesy of the Library of Congress. Wright brothers collection.*

The 1903 flying machine on the launching track. *Photo courtesy of and caption adapted from the Library of Congress. Wright brothers collection.*

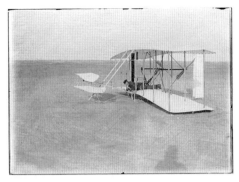

Wilbur in a prone position in the damaged machine, on the ground after an unsuccessful trial on December 14, 1903. *Photo courtesy of and caption adapted from the Library of Congress. Wright brothers collection.*

The first flight on December 17, 1903, at Kitty Hawk, North Carolina. *Photo courtesy of the Library of Congress. Wright brothers collection.*

Close-up view of the damaged 1903 machine, with its rudder frame broken in landing, on the ground at the end of its last flight. *Photo courtesy of and caption adapted from the Library of Congress. Wright brothers collection.*

Wright brothers' Type A plane in flight at Fort Myer, Virginia. *Photo courtesy of the Library of Congress. Photograph by Harris & Ewing.*

Chanute's own triplane had been a total disaster, and Herring had been rather unpleasant and jealous of the tremendous glides the Wright plane was making. Many of the glides were not over 200 hundred feet long, but the plane was making perfectly executed turns. Control of the air had been wrestled from the heavens, and Wilbur's glides resembled the soaring buzzards Chanute had observed over their camp. He had only been there for a week, but it was enough time for him to understand that Wilbur Wright was close to solving the problem of manned flight in a heavier-than-air machine. You could not watch that large glider cutting the sky, with Wilbur in full control, and not think that they were peering into a new age, a new world.

The door opened. "Mr. Langley will see you now."

Chanute popped up from his chair and walked across the marble floor. He couldn't help but feel that he was trailing sand behind him. Langley's office was so large that the Wright flyer might have fit inside it. Standing up behind the desk was Samuel Langley, a bearded sixty-eight to Chanute's seventy-two. He knew Langley was well funded and the Smithsonian was ramping up to produce the first airplane. Ever since the success of Langley's model aerodrome, he had been the undisputed leader as the man with the best chance to fly a plane under its own power.

The men shook hands, and then Chanute told him plainly what he had seen in Kitty Hawk. Langley kept his hands together under his chin and listened attentively. He gave Chanute no sign of his own progress, but that didn't surprise Octave. He was used to the paranoid secrecy of Secretary Langley and the Smithsonian. Langley listened with little visible reaction as Chanute finished.

He thanked Chanute for his time and saw him to the door. When he turned around, Langley felt a strange panic. It was like looking over your shoulder and seeing someone behind you who had seemingly come from nowhere. If what Chanute had said was true, then there was no time to lose. He would tell Manley, who was overseeing construction of Langley's own flyer, to continue with all deliberate speed. They must not be eclipsed by some bicycle mechanic. Secretary Langley sat back down behind his desk, pulled out some stationery, and picked up his pen. He immediately began writing a letter to Wilbur Wright, care of Kitty Hawk Post Office, Mr. William Tate.[4]

THE MOVABLE RUDDER—1902

O rville was staring up from his cot. Around him the men were snoring and the wind banged against the walls of the hangar. Below the loft where they were sleeping was the glider, freshly rebuilt after his accident. He had flown. He had flown on a tether and then he had flown in free flight. That was the disaster. Thirty feet up and the plane headed for the ground when he used the wing warping. He would later write, "I thought I must have worked the twisting apparatus the wrong way . . . the result was a heap of flying machine, cloth, and sticks in a heap, with me in the center."[1] Death. Yes, he saw it with the plane rushing for the ground, and then he was buried in canvas and wires and sand. Wilbur told him he forgot to use the elevator when he turned and the plane had slid down to the earth sideways. Three days of repairs.

And this was the improved plane. When Wilbur flew it, the plane was amazing. He flew off like a bird and seemed to control the sky. It was bigger, with a wing surface of 32 by 5 feet, and two tail fins or rudders. Everything was built according to the data tables from the wind tunnel. The camber, or the curve of the wing, was all vastly different. It was a new plane, but there was still the problem of well digging. When the plane turned, it pivoted on the wing and dug a hole in the ground. Orville looked at Spratt and his brother. They were peacefully sleeping, but he had drunk too much coffee; he just couldn't understand the tendency of the plane to head down and slip sideways when they turned. It was vexing. The rudders should have taken care of that, but there was something they were missing. Orville tossed and turned.

Here a legend was born. The Kelly biography paints the picture this way: "Then one night Orville drank more than his customary amount of coffee. Instead of going to sleep as usual the moment he got into bed, he lay awake for several hours. Those extra cups of coffee may have been important for the future of practical flight for, as he tossed about, he figured out the explanation of the phenomenon caused by the tail."[2]

The story goes that Orville awoke to an epiphanic moment. The rudder should be hinged. The story continues that his brother Lorin had come down to visit, and, while they were sitting around breakfast, Orville brought it up to Wilbur, expecting a fight: "Orville fully expected his suggestion to be brushed aside with an 'oh yes, I was already considering that.' . . . Instead Wilbur listened attentively and remained silent for a moment or two."[3] Then, without hesitation, he not only accepted the change but startled Orville by proposing that they connect it to the wing warping as well. So now when the pilot shifted his hips to turn the plane, the rudders moved in tandem. The three axes of control had just been achieved, and this would be the plane handed down to history.

In this story, Orville comes to the forefront as the man who made the breakthrough while Wilbur agreed and connected it to the other controls. Lorin is there to hand the baton to Orville as well, and the story seems to be traced back to Lorin with Orville's surprise at Wilbur's acquiescence. The problem with this is that none of it seems to be true. The true sequence of events will be made clear in a patent speech Wilbur will soon make. But what is true now is that they had arrived at Kitty Hawk on August 28 and made improvements to the shed while getting the new glider ready. They slept in beds up in the rafters now, and the kitchen had been well stocked and improved. They sunk a deeper well, filled in the cracks of the building, and built a bicycle that could run over sand and enabled them to go to Kitty Hawk to get supplies. So now it took them only one hour to get there and back, instead of three. The locals had accepted the brothers, and Kitty Hawker John T. Daniels summed up the locals' observation of their inventiveness this way: "They built their own camp, they took an old carbide can and made a stove of it, they took a bicycle and geared the thing so it could ride on sand."[4]

For the next week, they worked on the new glider, and on September 19 they flew it as a kite, then took it to Kill Devil Hills, where they flew fifty times in three days. Brother Lorin came to the camp. And they were expecting Chanute and Herring and Spratt. Here is where it would get interesting. For the first time, Orville began to glide. But there is some question as to how far he was gliding. In his diary, Orville said he made several short glides to learn the new method of working the front rudder. We know he did have a free glide that ended up in a crash. Was Wilbur yelling at him when he went down in a heap from thirty feet high? Did he let him fly again? The pictures of the 1902 glider flights are all of Wilbur, with only one of Orville. Would Wilbur have shut him down to keep him safe, and then covered it all with his father's admonishment that we are all one against the world?

Orville's account of the crash shows that he was in serious trouble:

> I was sailing along smoothly without any trouble at all from the fore and aft control when I noticed that one wing was getting a little too high and that the machine was slowly sliding off in the opposite direction. I thought that by moving the end control mechanism an inch or so I would bring the wing back again to its proper position ... By this time I found suddenly that I was making a descent backwards toward the low wing from a height of 25 or 30 feet.... The result was a heap of flying machine, cloth, and sticks in a heap, with me in the center without a bruise or scratch.[5]

This began three days of repairs, with Spratt and brother Lorin arriving in camp, and this sets up the whole hinged-rudder scene, complete with a wink to brother Lorin before Orville launched into his polemic. But immediately there are contradictions to this, beginning with Wilbur and the source of Orville's recollection. As Fred Howard wrote in *Wilbur and Orville: A Biography of the Wright Brothers*, "Wilbur's version appears in the deposition he made in a patent suit in 1912 and attributes the discovery of the cause of the well digging phenomenon to both brothers. The solution is not arrived in a single sleepless night but in the course of several days, during which they experimented to make sure that the fixed vertical tail was the cause of the difficulty."[6]

It gets even stickier when the source of Orville's story is none other than the authorized Kelly biography, which was written almost forty years on and which was heavily edited by Orville himself. The transcript of Wilbur's deposition then ends up in the Kelly biography as *quoted by Orville*. The patent deposition is all Wilbur, and he adopts the plural, spreading the credit to Orville as well. First Wilbur gives an explanation of well digging: "When the wings were warped to recover balance with the low wing having a greater angle of incidence than the upper wing, a still greater drag was produced upon the low wing with a result that its speed was further decreased. . . . These flights ended with a disaster to the machine in what is today called a tail spin."[7]

Then he explains the solution:

Our first change in the machine . . . was to remove one of the vertical vanes in the rear of the machine. . . . We found that this only slightly mitigated the evil influence of vanes. After a good deal of thought the idea occurred to us that by making the vane in the rear adjustable, so that it could be turned so as to entirely relieve the pressure on that side toward the low side of the machine, and to create a pressure on the side toward the high wing equal to or greater than the differences in the high and low wings . . . While this change to make the vane adjustable was being made the idea came to us of connecting the wires which operated the rudder to the cables which operated the wing warping, so that when the wings were warped the rudder was simultaneously adjusted.[8]

This did solve the problem of well digging and was an important break-through, so important, in fact, that Orville paraphrased it in Kelly's biography as his own discovery in a caffeine-induced high. Then Kelly paints a scene in which Wilbur listens and then "promptly saw that the explanation was probably correct and nodded approvingly."[9] Then in the Kelly biography there is paraphrasing of Wilbur's deposition and explanation for connecting it to the wing warping. All of this was given to Kelly almost forty years after the fact by Orville, whose brother Wilbur had died three decades before. There is the hand of the writer here as well. A good biography needs a hook, and the epiphany by Orville clearly takes him out of the role of mechanic and helper to his brother who is doing all the flying and heavy calculating required to produce a plane that will fly, and puts him squarely in the role of collaborator. Of equal.

The truth is that Wilbur has nothing to gain by lying in the deposition. Up until 1902, he was the man grappling with the problems of flight, a mission he started on his own. He had no biographer to satisfy, and he did not suffer from others suspecting that he might not be the man who was doing the problem solving and moving closer to the moment of powered flight. This could not be said for Orville, who moved in his brother's shadow at home and out in public. Wilbur only told the truth in his deposition in

1912 as he saw it. Sadly, it would be his last public statement on what happened at Kitty Hawk in 1902.

Wilbur wrote to Octave Chanute on his return:

> We left Kitty Hawk at daybreak on last Tuesday and reached home at 3 PM on Friday after a very exciting but tiresome trip. . . . Into the last ten days of practice we crowded more glides than in all the weeks preceding. In two days we made about two hundred and fifty. . . . This practice enabled us to very greatly increase our skill in the management of the machine. . . . We received a letter from Mr. Langley a few days before we finished our experiments at Kitty Hawk, a telegram and afterwards a letter inquiring whether there would be time for him to reach us and witness some of our trials before we left. We replied that it would scarcely be possible as we were intending to break camp in a few days. He made no mention of his experiments on the Potomac.[10]

The fact that the secretary of the Smithsonian was willing to trudge down to the Outer Banks of North Carolina to watch a couple of bicycle mechanics experimenting with their glider shows that from a very early stage Secretary Langley was aware of their progress. They had stayed at Kitty Hawk for two months and completed a thousand glides. Men like Spratt, Herring, and Chanute were astounded. The pictures of Wilbur gliding tell the tale, with his flyer making graceful turns against the barren sand. It was obvious that all he needed was something to power the plane. The brothers left their camp on October 28 in a chilly rain and walked the four miles to Kitty Hawk. Wilbur walked with his hands in his pockets, listening to the squish of his hard shoes. All he could think about now was building an engine to power the plane he had built.

UNITED STATES PATENT OFFICE—1903

People sent in all sorts of inventions requesting patents. It was as if the twentieth century had ushered in just about every kook who thought he could build the next car, washing machine, light, can opener, phone, fan, and of course the mother of them all: a flying machine. The examiner sat at his large wooden desk and opened the bulky envelope. It was another flying-machine application. For fifty years, the patent office had been bombarded with applications for flying contraptions. The examiner had personally seen applications for machines that blasted off, bounced off, went off ships or cliffs, and jumped around like a man on a pogo stick. There were machines that looked like cars with wings; machines that looked like boats with wings; men with wings; and machines that looked like butterflies, birds, bats, and praying mantises. He rejected them all.

The clock in the patent hall ticked loudly. As he pulled out the papers, the examiner listened to someone walk across the solid wood floor. There was some sort of design showing a double-decker wing with numbers and arrows and wires. He saw no engine. Just this elfin creation that, according to the applicant, could fly. The examiner frowned. He had seen this before.

He had returned it with a note instructing Mr. Wright that there had been six other patentees who had preceded his design. He told Mr. Wright that his design was "vague and indefinite."[1] This was standard language for 90 percent of the patent applicants he received. It would seem all of America was peopled with mad inventors seeking patents for their whimsical ideas hatched over their eggs and coffee and finished over their cigars and beers. This was another such whimsical design, and now Mr. Wright had sent back another application with more notes, more explanations, more diagrams, and a cardboard inner-tube box.

The examiner leaned back in his wooden rollaway chair and held up the tube. He showed it to the examiner next to him, who shook his head. He looked through the tube. "So, this is your airplane Mr. Wright," he murmured. He dropped the tube on his varnished desk and picked up the papers wearily. Mr. Wilbur Wright ran on and on about his "wing-warping system"[2] and explained that he would be glad to clarify how the cardboard inner tube demonstrated the concept. The examiner dropped the papers and shut his eyes.

Clearly this man was deranged. He had told Mr. Wright in so many words that nuisance applications would be dismissed unless the patent application could show that the machine described had *actually flown*. He had further told Mr. Wright that "the claims are furthermore all rejected as based upon a device that is inoperative or incapable of performing the intended function. The examiner is unable to understand how the machine is supposed to operate."[3] And so now Mr. Wright had persisted with a paper tube and expected him to grant a patent. What Mr. Wright did not know was that he had just received six other patent applications that looked much more promising than his.

Men like Samuel Pierpont Langley had been granted patents for machines that actually flew, even if they were models. Of course, he was the secretary of the Smithsonian and a man of science, and one knew he was not one of the many cranks who bombed their offices every day with harebrained ideas that would never see the light of day.

The examiner breathed heavily and picked up the cardboard inner tube. He flexed it as Mr. Wright had instructed him to do. Nothing happened. He rolled it across his desktop. Nothing happened. He even dropped it from his desk. Nothing happened. He scooped up the tube and put it on the corner of his desk on end. He picked up his pen. He began by thanking Mr. Wright for his application, again, but that the cardboard box would be of no assistance and that he once again would have to reject his patent application until he could demonstrate that his machine could *actually fly*.

The examiner paused and looked at the diagrams and the machine and then the tube. He looked at the letter that claimed great gliding success in some place called Kitty Hawk, North Carolina. Kitty Hawk? The examiner then wrote that if Mr. Wright wanted to carry this further, he would suggest a patent attorney be employed.

The examiner paused again and looked at the paper tube and the drawing of wires and arrows and numbers. He picked up the sketch of the flying machine and shook his head. He put his salutation on the paper and then suggested that Wilbur procure competent counsel.[4] The paper tube was enclosed herewith.

THE WESTERN SOCIETY
OF ENGINEERS—1903

The room was hazy, with cigar smoke rising into the lantern lights. Wilbur Wright stood in front of the crowd and spoke clearly. Gone was the timid man explaining his early experiments in the sands of the Outer Banks. He was not nervous anymore. He stood in front of the crowd of engineers in the Monadnock Building and told them the story of Kitty Hawk. He told them about the birds he had studied, and the art of soaring. He told them that people were far too concerned with the machinery of flying than with the science of actual flying: "The prime object in these experiments was to obtain practice in the management of a man carrying machine, but an object of scarcely less importance was to obtain data for the study of the scientific problems involved in flight."[1] What was needed was skill. The skill to be able to control a flying machine and understanding the air the way birds do, because only then could men soar like birds. A thousand glides, he said, were equivalent to about four hours of flying, and so there was "far too little to give anyone a complete mastery of the art of flying."[2]

The word *art* slipped by the audience, who listened to his descriptions like later people would watch men walking on the moon. This man had flown, it would seem. What he didn't tell the people was that for the last six months, a man named Charlie Taylor, an uneducated man without a high-school degree, had designed an aluminum block four-cylinder engine that could be mounted on an airplane wing. This was after Wilbur had written to manufacturers of engines about his needs and they all responded by saying that their engines would be too heavy.

So, like everything else, he would have to make it up. Wilbur then asked

Charlie Taylor, the mechanic who had been running his business and driving his sister crazy, if he could design a motor. Yes, he said. Had he ever designed one before? No, he said, but that didn't matter. Later he would be widely quoted as the homespun mechanic who did the impossible: "Those two sure knew their physics. I guess that's why they always knew what they were doing and hardly ever guessed at anything. . . . While the boys were handy with tools, they had never done much machine work and anyway they were busy on the air frame. . . . We didn't make any drawings. One of us would sketch out the part we were talking about on a piece of scratch paper and I'd spike the sketch over my bench."[3]

The engineers might have been interested in this pioneering work in the field of airplane engines. The use of an aluminum block sent on by the Aluminum Company of America, based in Pittsburgh, was to keep the weight below two hundred pounds and deliver 8 horsepower. The man with the bushy mustache used the same metal lathe and drill press in the back of the shop to bore out the cylinders and create the iron-cylinder rings. They would have been interested in the gravity-fed fuel system, the lack of a carburetor, and no spark plugs but a "make and break" contact system. The audience would have been interested to know if the engine ran at all and how it cracked the aluminum block, and how they had to send for another one, but this one worked just fine and delivered 12 horsepower instead of 8. The engine was started by priming the cylinders with gas, and the ignition switch was bought at a hardware store.

This was at a time when ingenuity was prized because it was necessary. There were no paths to follow. There was no corporate state to plug into. People had to make it up as they went, and building an engine no one else had ever built before went with building a plane no one else had ever built before. It was a way of looking at the world that is largely the purview of entrepreneurs now, but in 1903 it was the dominant thinking. Risk was not risk but a way of living. There were no road maps, and people like Wilbur Wright and Charlie Taylor had more in common with the pioneers than with the people sitting in the room.

But Wilbur kept that to himself, as he did the particulars of his control system with the breakthrough of connecting the hinged rudder to the wing warping and the vertical control of the elevator. Instead, he talked about soaring and Orville's accident:

> On this day my brother Orville did most of the gliding. . . . He started on a flight with one [wing] higher than the other. This caused the machine to veer to the left. He waited a moment to see if the machine would right itself but finding that it did not then decided to apply the control. At the very instant he did this the right wing rose up unexpectedly and led him to think that possibly he made a mistake. . . . The machine turned up more and more until it assumed a most dangerous attitude. . . . From the height of nearly thirty feet the machine sailed backward till it struck the ground. . . . How he escaped injury I do not know.[4]

The engineers and their wives sitting in the semidarkness with the lantern slides in front of them were enthralled. The pictures of Wilbur soaring across the wide, desolate dunes were not unlike Teddy Roosevelt's speeches in which he described his life in the Badlands in the 1880s. The man in front of them was a pioneer; this they knew. And he was out there tweaking death with his calm demeanor. Wilbur Wright was the man giving the speech, talking about flying as if it were an everyday occurrence: "While the high flights were more spectacular the low ones were fully as valuable for training purposes. Skill comes by the constant repetition of familiar feats rather than by a few over-bold attempts for which the performer is yet poorly prepared."[5]

Overbold attempts. He spoke of flying the way a man would of being careful in his bathroom. Then he spoke of the breakthrough with the movable rudder. This was a speech, and speeches rely on quips and anecdotes and colorful stories. What better story to tell than that of his brother laced up with coffee and coming down in the morning to tell of his epiphanic moment in the dead of night? But this did not come out in the darkened room with the flickering lanterns.

Wilbur continued,

> The lateral control still remained somewhat unsatisfactory. The tail was useful at times and at others was seriously in the way. It was finally con-cluded that the best way of overcoming the difficulty was by making the tail movable like a rudder. As originally built the fixed vertical tail or rudder was double but in changing to a movable rudder it was made single. . . . With this improvement our serious troubles ended.[6]

There was no mention of the breakfast conversation, nor of Wilbur's idea to attach the rudder to the hip cradle and conversely the wing-warping controls. This was omitted on purpose, as Wilbur had just been turned down for a patent on his plane, and that bit of information would allow someone to steal their plane intact. But if there was ever a place for the clever anecdote related thirty years later to Fred Kelly, this would have been the place. It would reveal nothing more than what had already been told, so the cause for omission was not proprietary information that needed to be kept secret. And Wilbur was not the type of man to ever take credit away from Orville. He was, in fact, the opposite, using the plural *we* or *my brother and I* at all times and especially in public. Big brother protecting little brother. In this sense, it is clear that Wilbur would only omit the story of Orville's coffee-fired epiphanic moment *if it did not happen*. He had no sense of competition with his brother regarding aviation, because he knew it was his vision they were fulfilling. So, undoubtedly, he would have thrown a bone to Orville if the movable rudder had been his idea. It is interesting to note that the only time Wilbur mentioned Orville to the audience was to describe the glider crash, a moment when things went terribly wrong.

Wilbur did omit the work his brother and he had been doing on propellers for the last six months. Here, too, they had to make it up as they went. As Orville would later write, "It is hard to find a point from which to make a start; for nothing about a propeller or the medium in which it acts, stands still for a moment. The thrust depends upon the speed and the angle at which the blade strikes the air, the angle at which the blade strikes the air depends on the speed at which the propeller is turning, the speed of the machine traveling forward, and the speed at which the air is slipping backward."[7]

Basically, all they had to go on was boats. Propellers were used to push boats through the water, and this gave Wilbur a starting point at least. Variables upon variables. It was decided that an "aeronautical propeller is essentially a wing rotating in the vertical plane."[8] Charlie Taylor cited many arguments between the Wright brothers on the propellers. Finally, they agreed on two propellers for the *Flyer*, one turning clockwise and one counterclockwise, so one would balance the other in thrust. Each had a diameter of 8.5 feet, and they were constructed of spruce laminations glued tougher and then shaped with a drawknife. The *Flyer* would slide along on skids, and the pilot would lie prone on the lower wing with the motor, radiator, and propellers behind him. Drive chains that were used for automobiles from the Indianapolis Chain and Stamping Company would power the propellers. This was the new *Flyer*, and Wilbur mentioned none of this during his speech. He already had the sense that Langley and others were racing to beat him as the first man to fly under power in the air.

What Wilbur did mention was probably the first account of wind shear, which is characterized by wind that moves at a much different speed over a short distance, either horizontally or vertically. The wind shear that has caused airliners to crash at airports is generally a strong down draft or vertical wind. Wilbur's experience with wind shear began with a strange tapping, with no apparent source, that had occurred during several flights. He explained:

> Some weeks later I was making a glide, the same peculiar tapping began again in the midst of a wind gust. It felt like little waves striking the bottom of a flat bottom boat. While I was wondering what it could be the machine suddenly but without any noticeable change in its inclination to the horizon dropped a distance of ten feet and in the twinkling of an eye I was flat on the ground. I am certain the gust went out with a downward trend which struck the surfaces on the upper side. The descent was at first more rapid than due to gravity, for my body apparently rose off the machine till only my hands and feet touched it.[9]

Neither Wilbur nor anyone in the audience understood what had happened, but it sounded very similar to a sudden downward draft or wind shear. If Wilbur had been higher, he might well have been killed.

In the following question and answer session, Wilbur was asked what he thought of Professor Langley's experiments. Wilbur ducked and responded by saying, "It is very bad policy to ask one flying machine man about the experiments of another, because every flying machine man thinks that his method is the correct one."[10] Wilbur then backed away from a question about engines and screws or propellers, the very two areas he had spent the last six months studying before creating an engine and a propeller. He said, "As none of our experiments have been with power machines, my judgement of the relative merits of screws and wings may be of little value."[11]

A lie, but a self-serving one in the current circumstances. Secretary Langley would be very interested in anything Wilbur Wright had to say. In less than two months, he would launch his vaunted fifty-thousand-dollar aerodrome on the Potomac. He had already tried to go to the Wright camp at Kitty Hawk and had failed after Chanute alerted him to their progress. Essentially, Wilbur Wright had left out of his speech the latest advances he had made in building an airplane that would fly under its own power. He had done this because he knew he was very close to solving human flight and did not want to tip his hand. His hard-found secrets were his, and not for someone to take and beat him to the punch. As any good writer knows, what the author leaves out is just as important as what he puts in. Wilbur had told the audience just enough to whet their appetite for more. He was learning the fine art of public relations. He left Chicago as the man closest to finding the secrets to human flight. Wilbur Wright had just told the world of his progress, and the people in Chicago again would have been hard-pressed to even know the name of his brother Orville. Wilbur rode the train home to Ohio and had no idea that Samuel Pierpont Langley was about to launch his aerodrome and set off a forty-year feud.

THE GREAT EMBARRASSMENT—1903

Charles Manley smoked his cigarette nervously and looked at the assembled reporters, other scientists, assorted government officials, and family members who had come to see man fly. He stared at the giant aerodrome on top of the houseboat. The fog was light off the river, and he brushed the droplets from the wings. The wings flexed. This bothered him. He had built a 52-horsepower engine to power the aerodrome, and it was heavy. It was more powerful than any engine so far that had been mounted to an airplane.

The aerodrome, according to his boss—the secretary of the Smithsonian, Samuel Langley—should fly like a bird. The model aerodrome had flown very well, and this was just a large version of that model, with floats for landing on water and a small cockpit mounted under the plane. The thing that bothered Langley was the flimsiness of the craft and the position of the cockpit. Even if he could land the plane, he would be underwater. The thought was that he could just swim out, but the water looked damn cold for swimming. Manley finished his cigarette and looked at the men who were waiting for his signal. It was October 7, 1903.

Another man who felt nervous was Charles D. Walcott; he was then the chairman of the executive committee of the National Advisory Committee of Aeronautics for the government, and he would eventually take over as secretary of the Smithsonian when Langley died. He had convinced the War Department to give Langley $50,000 to develop an airplane. The money was now gone, and five years had passed. He had been asked more than a few times where the airplane was. Secretary Langley had the dilettante's attitude. His model aerodrome had flown and, in his mind, this proved that man could fly in heavier-than-air ships. This would just put the seal on the bottle.

It was the same design, only larger and with a very powerful engine. The aerodrome should lift very easily into the sky, fly in great circles, and then land. Walcott could then tell the War Department its money was well spent. Secretary Langley was so confident, he didn't bother coming out onto the deck of the houseboat to observe. He would be notified by telegraph of the success.

Manley stripped down to his flying suit, dashed his cigarette, and climbed into the cockpit through the guide wires. He started the engine and allowed it to heat up. The engine was so large that it vibrated through the plane and shook Manley's body. He waited. This was the Smithsonian's big moment. Secretary Langley would prove that cutting-edge aeronautics were in the possession of the august institution and would not be in the possession of cranks flying out of garages, in backyards, or across the sands of Kitty Hawk. Manley gave the signal, and the great catapult shot him down the guiding ramps of the houseboat. He felt himself pressed back against the rickety chair in the bottom of the aerodrome, with the engine roaring furiously. Manley reached the end of the catapult track and found himself staring straight down at the water. The aerodrome fell like a sack of cement. The motor screamed in his ears the whole way down. There was no lift at all, just a horrible plunge straight down. It was as if they had built a fifty-thousand-dollar brick.

Manley felt the freezing water like an electric shock. He was beneath the plane under the surface of the icy Potomac. He struggled to get free of the sinking plane and had a moment of panic when he couldn't get free of the cables from the wings. The motor was an anchor heading for the bottom of the river. Manley finally managed to get to the surface, spitting out river water, where he waved to the reporters, family members, witnesses, and government officials who were staring at him from above as if they had just seen a sea creature. Manley could not escape the feeling that they were staring at him as if he were at fault. The term *pilot error* had not been coined yet, but it was coming.

The man who stared at Manley the hardest was Walcott. This would not do. The War Department was furious. They had spent fifty thousand on a brick with wings. Secretary Langley immediately went into damage control and assured the press that it was a technical glitch with the launching mechanism. The catapult had failed, and that was why the plane took a header into the river. Manley was fished out, and then he smoked a cigarette. He was wrapped in a blanket and later interrogated by Langley. He agreed quickly. He had felt something at the end of the catapult, and that had tripped up the plane. He told Langley that if they would fix that, she would fly like a soaring eagle.

The *New York Times* ran a headline the next day: "FLYING MACHINE FIASCO Prof Langley's Airship Proves A Complete Failure." The *St. Louis Republic* followed with, "FLYING MACHINE BUILT BY LANGLEY AN UTTER FAILURE." The *San Francisco Call* wasn't much better: "LANGLEY'S FLYING MACHINE FAILS COMPLETELY." An editorial in the *New York Times* went after Langley personally: "The ridiculous fiasco which attended the attempt at aerial navigation in the Langley flying machine was not unexpected, unless possibly by the distinguished Secretary of the Smithsonian Institution who devised it, and his assistants."[1]

Brutal. It was all blamed on the launching catapult. Surely it was not the plane itself. On December 8, the aerodrome was ready again. The houseboat was put into anchor at the confluence of the Potomac and Anacostia Rivers. The Potomac had ice on it, and a freezing wind punished the assembled reporters. The press had been alerted again, and the shores were lined with reporters, along with boats chartered by newspapers. Secretary Langley was there this time and had brought a party of friends and Smithsonian employees. People drank champagne and smoked cigars. It had the feeling of a holiday. Christmas was coming. Langley was confident. This time, he would show the world what science can do in the hands of a farsighted and competent man like himself. Walcott was not there but was waiting for news. The press has been brutal to him, too, so Walcott's reputation was on the line as well.

The weather was not cooperating. There was ice in the river, and the sky had darkened. Wind gusts kept moving the houseboat out of position. Manley went down to meet with Secretary Langley and others to make sure they would still launch. They had to. The money was gone. Patience was gone. Besides, it would be a brilliant success, and they all would have some brandy by the fire when it was over. And they sure didn't want to be eclipsed by the bicycle mechanics at Kitty Hawk, North Carolina. Manley stripped down again. This time, he wore a union suit, a cork-lined jacket, socks, and light shoes. He did not want to drown in the Potomac.

He once again climbed into the aerodrome and ran the engine up. He checked the controls and waited for the engine to warm. At 4: 45 p.m., he gave the signal, and once again he shot down the tracks of the catapult. Manley reached the edge, and this time the plane rose quickly, then turned on its back and headed straight down into the icy Potomac. Once again, the engine whined furiously until the great gulp when the plane flipped over, and then silence. Manley felt the freezing water like a thousand knives. His breath went out, his body feeling the shock like a bucket of ice water on a hot day. Manley began to struggle furiously to get free, but he was even farther under water this time.

The plane had hit the icebound water like a downward-plunging missile. Manley found himself in total darkness underwater and, worse, his jacket had caught on a sharp edge of the plane. He struggled out of his jacket and swam for the surface, where he hit a ceiling of ice. He was blocked under an ice paddy, and he was freezing to death. Manley swam frantically, punching the ice with his fists, until he finally found open water.

He emerged again, this time screaming and swearing. The people on the ship once again stared at him as if he were some sort of beached whale that had washed up on the shore. Manley waved his arms, which felt like they were weighed down by lead, and shouted to get him *the fuck out of the water.* This was at a time when profanity was seen as very bad form. He didn't care. He was freezing while the people stared down.

Manley was fished out of the water again. He was so frozen that his clothes had to be cut off of him. Workers wrapped him in a blanket, and by the time he reached the houseboat, he had drunk some whiskey. When Secretary Langley came over to him, Manley began to curse and didn't stop. The old man Langley had nearly killed him. Manley was shivering uncontrollably and cussing in a way few had heard before. Listening to the blasphemies of his engineer, Samuel Langley knew that his quest for flight had ended, and the great embarrassment was at hand for himself and the Smithsonian.

Walcott got word that the War Department was done funding anything to do with flight, or the Smithsonian for that matter. Langley tried again to pass it off on the launching mechanism, but nobody was buying it. The verdict on Langley came from "army engineers who finally studied the design and realized that the aerodrome was fatally flawed, lacking both sufficient power and sufficient lift. Going from a model to a full-sized aircraft involved computing weight to thrust ratios that aerodynamicists had yet to formalize; with no background in mathematics and scant in engineering, Langley had ignored computations of scale and had never realized it requires eight times the lift to keep a craft double the weight in the air."[2]

Secretary Langley pledged to fight on, but the money faucet was shut off. A congressman from Arkansas, Joseph Taylor Robinson, twisted the knife further: "The only thing Langley ever made fly was government money."[3] Fifty thousand dollars was out the window. Secretary Langley abandoned aviation and died three years later, a defeated man who had dragged the reputation of the Smithsonian down with his aerodrome. The aerodrome had been fished out and lashed to the boat like a harpooned whale and towed back to port. The Langley flyer's wings trailed in the water, and the propeller turned from the current. It was as if the flyer wanted to go again.

After Langley's death, when Charles Walcott became secretary of the Smithsonian, his goal quickly became to restore not only Langley's reputation but also the Smithsonian's, and—more importantly—his own. He had egg all over his bearded visage from Langley's folly. This would not do. Something had to be done. The damaged Langley aerodrome was crated and stored in a Smithsonian warehouse with other artifacts. The pilot Manley, of all people, knew Langley's plane was not airworthy, and, had someone told him that it would one day fly, he wouldn't have believed it. He knew a brick when he saw one, and that fifty-thousand-dollar brick had almost cost him his life. Charles Manley didn't understand that there were people who would do anything to turn a brick into a plane. He didn't even know Glenn Curtiss's name.

GREAT THINGS—SEPTEMBER 23, 1903

The year 1903 promised great things. Teddy Roosevelt was president and the swaggering cowboy set a new tempo for the country. The *Chicago Tribune* declared that times were better than ever and would improve more once "science and new methods and new educations have done their perfect work."[1] Music had found ragtime, and everyone was working. The country was on the verge of greatness and had undertaken the building of the Panama Canal. So, the *Philadelphia Inquirer* asked, "why so far after so much attention had been paid to aerial navigation, have there been so few results?"[2]

The man with the answer to that question was staring at the burned ruins of the freight depot at Elizabeth City, North Carolina. Orville and Wilbur stood in their high collars, dark suits, and shined shoes and stared from the station platform with the locomotive hissing steam behind them. This, then, could be the end of the dream of flight. In the charred ruins there might be hundreds, if not thousands, of hours of work. Everything that came through the station and was headed for Kitty Hawk passed through the depot. To make matters worse, they thought they saw the carbide can they used for heating. They walked over with the sinking feeling of men descending to the bottom of a pool. The carbide can turned out to be a lard container. They spoke with a freight agent and found that their lumber and the crated goods had already passed through and were at Kitty Hawk. The *Flyer* was en route.

So, the great catastrophe had not happened. "We were glad to find, on reaching camp, that our groceries and tools had not burned in the depot fire at Elizabeth City," Orville would later write his sister.[3] It was September 23, 1903, and they caught the Ocracoke on a midnight journey to Roanoke Island, arriving at one in the morning on September 25. In Manteo, they hired a steamboat to take them the rest of the way to Kill Devil Hills. Their old hangar/cabin had been lifted from its foundation the previous winter by a 90 mph wind and was "several feet nearer the ocean than when we left last year, and about a foot lower in places."[4]

The gale had hit in February, and it reminded the brothers that they were in hurricane season. There would be no early warning for them. No evacuation orders. They would simply have to ride out whatever Mother Nature threw at them. They immediately put the building back in shape and began work on a new building to house the new flyer. Then they took out the old glider and had what Wilbur called "the finest day we ever had in practice.... We made about 75 glides, nearly all of them about 20 seconds' duration. The longest was 30 2/3 seconds which beats our former records," he wrote Octave Chanute.[5]

Dan Tate joined them, and they erected a building of sixteen by forty-four feet for assembling and storing the new flyer. They were still working on the new building when a storm struck with 75 mph winds. Wilbur later wrote his sister Katherine, "The wind suddenly whirled around to the north and increased to something like 40 miles an hour and was accompanied by a regular cloudburst.... The second day opened with the gale still continuing. ... The climax came about 4 o'clock when the wind reached 75 miles an hour. Suddenly a corner of our tar-paper roof gave way under the pressure and we saw that if the trouble were not stopped the whole roof would go."[6]

Orville then ascended a ladder with hammer and nails and began making repairs in the storm. The storm blew his coat over his head. "As the hammer and nails were in his pocket and up over his head he was unable to get his hands on them or pull his coattails down," Wilbur related later, "so he was compelled to descend again. The next time he put the nails in his mouth and took the hammer in his hand and I followed him up the ladder hanging on to his coattails."[7]

The storm continued for four days, and on the morning of the third day "their doorstep was six inches under water and the water was sloshing against the undersides of the floorboards in their living room."[8] Then the Wrights went out and flew their glider. The wind had suddenly stopped, along with the rain. They were in the eye of the hurricane, but the brothers had no idea. Orville was gliding when a gust threw the plane to the ground, and the wing just missed Wilbur's head. Five ships were wrecked on the Outer Banks that day.

When the storm passed, the men from the Life-Saving station dropped by and were presented with framed pictures of themselves taken the year before. The brothers made many flights with the 1902 flyer on the Big Hill. On October 8, Captain Midgette's sailboat arrived with the crated 1903 *Flyer*. It was pulled on a sand road along Kitty Hawk Bay and delivered to their camp at Kill Devil Hills. They began work on construction of the plane. The fourth week in October, Wilbur received a clipping from their neighbor in Dayton, George Freight. "I see that Langley has had his fling and failed," Wilbur wrote in a letter to Octave Chanute.[9] "It seems to be our turn now and I wonder what our luck will be. We will still hope to see you before we break camp."

The work on the new flyer continued through October, with temperatures beginning to dip. On October 25, Wilbur wrote in his diary, "Rain and wind continued through entire night, forming ponds all about the camp. Temperature lower. Air so damp and cold that we made a stove out of a carbide can and built a small fire, avoiding smoke as much as possible by sitting on the floor. Enclosed small space with carpets to keep out wind."[10]

George Spratt arrived and worked on the motor with Dan Tate on October 27. The motor weighed 152 pounds and generated 12 horsepower. The aluminum block was advanced for engine construction of the time while the fuel system was primitive at best: "A one-gallon fuel tank was to be suspended from the wing strut, and the gasoline fed by gravity down a tube to the engine. . . . There was no carburetor. . . . Fuel was fed into a shallow chamber in the manifold. . . . The engine was started by priming each cylinder with a few drops of gas."[11]

The temperature continued to dip, and the three men froze in their bunk beds; they "passed a very miserable night on account of cold."[12] More carpets were hung for insulation, and a wood-burning stove was rigged up with one of the carbide cans. Then disaster struck, according to biographer Fred Howard:

> By November 5th the machine was more or less in a finished state and Wilbur and Orville ran up the motor for the first time. Suddenly they were faced with a crisis. . . . The magneto did not produce a satisfactory spark at first and the propeller shafts vibrated ominously at every missed explosion. . . . All at once the motor racketed away, filling the shed with exhaust, it backfired. The cross arms that connected the propeller shafts to the airframe were jerked loose and one of the shafts were [*sic*] badly twisted.[13]

The twisted shaft would have to be repaired, and the other shaft reinforced. Charlie Taylor, who was back in Dayton, had to do the repairs, so Spratt left with the shafts to go with Captain Jesse Ward of the Life-Saving station, who was leaving that afternoon for Manteo. The day after Spratt departed, Octave Chanute arrived. It was a miserable, cold, wet day, and the hung carpets did little to improve the heating situation in the new hangar. The wind was so uneven that they couldn't even show Chanute the progress they had made with the 1902 glider.

There was nothing to do but huddle around the stove. "Storm all day with rain. We hardly got out of the building at all, but spent our time in conversation with Mr. Chanute, who told us of some of the plans he hoped to carry out this year," Orville wrote Katherine.[14] Chanute showed the brothers photos of Langley's first crashed plane. Wilbur stared at the plane in the Potomac as a sad testament to the years that Langley had spent trying to get to that moment. Chanute had passed through Washington on his way and snapped the photos prior to his arrival at Kitty Hawk. Chanute then told them he was looking to buy a plane built by engineer and inventor Clement Ader in France. The steam-powered plane looked like a bat and did not look like a machine that could leave the earth.

Octave Chanute wanted Wilbur and Orville to repair and fly Ader's plane. The machine was from 1890 and posed a serious risk for anyone who chose to fly it. Chanute, like many men when confronted with real genius, did not recognize how far Wilbur had come. He had been corresponding with Wilbur for three years, and long ago the pupil had surpassed the teacher, but Chanute had recently given a talk at the Aero Club de France, where he referred to the Wrights as his "devoted collaborators." The impression he left with people was that the Wrights were completing "his" work.

Now he wanted them to repair and fly an old plane, completely not understanding how close Wilbur was to heavier-than-air flight powered by an engine. Wilbur would later fume to his sister, "He thinks we could do it! He doesn't seem to think our machines are so much superior as the manner in which we handle them. We are of the reverse opinion."[15]

Chanute would never be able to get his hands on the plane he talked about, since it was given to a Paris museum and heralded as the first machine to ever fly until official test results proved it wasn't. Still, this little incident shows the blind spot that would fester between Wilbur and Octave Chanute and would later lead to a split between the two men. For now, all they could do was wait for the repaired propeller shafts to arrive from Dayton.

Octave Chanute left several days later, glad to get to some place where he didn't have to wear five blankets and keep a fire burning to stay warm. He would not see the first twelve seconds of manned flight. The fact that Chanute left showed his assumption that Wilbur was not close to solving the problem of manned flight. Had he really thought Wilbur Wright might fly, he would have never left Kill Devil Hills. The truth was that Chanute still viewed Wilbur Wright as his protégé, not the man who would crack manned flight.

Besides, visitors slowed down progress. It was good that Chanute left, because now Wilbur could turn to the final preparations for the first attempt at powered flight. They didn't even know if their launching system would work at this point. "Mr. Chanute left with Mr. Dough of the Kill Devil Station in the sailboat for Manteo at eight o'clock," Orville recorded in his diary.[16]

> On our return to camp we began work in planning down the starting track. A breeze of ten meters soon sprang up from the North. We decided to test our method of starting from the track with the old machine, so we took two rails to Big Hill. Five starts out of six were successful. . . . The flights, however, were very irregular and made in some danger. Probably as a result of the fire we keep in the building, the cloth and trussing seemed very loose allowing the surfaces to swing considerably in twisting the wings. . . . After four or five flights we took the machine back to camp. Spent most of the afternoon chopping wood and reading.[17]

So now the launching system of two rails with bicycle hubs for wheels had proved reliable. They only needed the propeller shaft to launch their plane. Skim ice had already appeared in puddles around the cabin, and water in their basin had frozen overnight. It was November in North Carolina, and the weather was only getting worse. It was November, and time was running out.

Spratt had decided not to return after handing off the damaged shafts in Norfolk to be sent on to Charlie Taylor. Snow began to fall on Kill Devil Hills, and the temperature dropped even further. Now the water in their basins froze every night. It snowed again before Thanksgiving Day. The temperature dropped to below 20°, and the wind howled and pressed through the boards of their shed. The smoke poured from the stovepipe in the corner of the frame structure. Soot literally dropped off the rafters.

"We are now alone again, the first time for about a month," Orville wrote Katherine.[18] "The past week and half has just been a loaf, since we have nothing to do on the machine until the shafts come. The weather has been fairly cold at times but with a half cord of wood on hand we have not suffered any."[19] They hung the machine from the rafters to see if it could support the weight of a man. They made last-minute adjustments and checked the controls, but there wasn't anything to do until the shafts arrived. Some days it was just too cold to do anything. "We found it very cold trying to work, so soon gave it up. Spent time in fixing up about the beds so as to keep them warm. . . . About midnight wind shift to the north bringing a rain which continued throughout the morning. . . . On arising found ponds around camp frozen."[20]

On November 23, Orville wrote to Charlie Taylor that the new, heavier propeller shafts arrived: "After a loaf of 15 days we are down to work again. The shafts arrived day before yesterday noon."[21] If someone looked across the dunes of this blustery gray day on November 27, they would have seen two forlorn gray buildings against a great plain of sand, with smoke wisping out of the corner of the smaller one. They would not know that inside were two men trying to determine when would be the best day for them to be the first humans to undertake controlled powered flight.

The Wrights had done everything they could think of while waiting for the propeller shafts. They had put together the launching track and fit the 1902 glider onto it and tested the running and speed of the bicycle hubs. They had conducted thrust tests on the propellers using fifty-pound buckets of sand and grocer scales. They tested the flyer's hip cradle and put on extra padding. They would have done more gliding with the old glider, but the weather was not cooperating and the carbide stove had dried out the satin canvas, so it was no longer safe. They ran the motor the day before Thanksgiving and did another load test with the plane suspended and 440 pounds on the wings. She was ready.

So, it was the Wednesday before Thanksgiving when they rolled the *Flyer* out of the shed and looked up at the sky. It began to rain. They took a quick picture, then rolled the plane back in to wait for the weather again. They passed time by making a crude flight-data recorder. On Saturday they started the motor again, with the flight data recorder attached, and immediately they saw that something was wrong with the propeller. "We spent morning in testing speed of engine," Orville wrote in his diary. "After six or seven runs from two to three minutes, we discovered something wrong, which turned out to be a cracked propeller shaft. Went to Kill Devil Station and made arrangements for going to Manteo Monday Morning."[22]

One of the shafts had cracked, and there was no choice but for Orville to go back to Dayton and get it replaced as fast as possible. They decided to go with solid shafts of high-grade steel. "One of the shafts twisted off in the middle and Orville has gone home to make new ones, leaving me to keep house alone,"[23] Wilbur wrote George Spratt on December 2. Orville had left for the Kill Devil Life-Saving station and departed on November 30. The man who had begun the quest to fly was now alone with his plane in the middle of nowhere.

Wilbur chopped wood to pass the time. He practiced German. "I am sorry to find you back at your old habit of introspection, leading to a fit of the blues. Quit it! It does no good," he had written to Spratt.[24] This went all the way back to a time when he, too, had gone down into the dark place. Now he was alone with nothing to do but wait. One wonders if he was telling Spratt or himself to not be introspective. He also recognized that this was their "Langley moment."[25] He didn't know Langley had tried again and failed. But their plane would not go into the Potomac; worse, it might never leave the sandy loam of Kill Devil Hills. There would be no newspapers deriding his effort; there would simply be the indifference of silence.

Spratt suggested in a letter that he might go work for the Smithsonian, to which Wilbur replied, "I doubt whether your friendship with us would be a recommendation in the eyes of the Secretary. . . . The fact you are acquainted with some of our ideas need not stand in the way so far as I can see, for it is now too late for Langley to begin over again."[26] It is interesting to note that even in this early stage Wilbur recognized that Langley might well take their ideas but that he had had his shot and was essentially done with aviation. Wilbur knew that a man has only one big chance to test his theories, and if he failed mightily, as Langley did, then it might be over for him as well. They were at a similar juncture where failure would mean basic assumptions had proven false.

Orville did a quick turnaround and was back on the train headed toward Kitty Hawk with the propeller shafts. He had picked up an old newspaper and read of Professor Langley's second and final attempt to fly. The plane had plunged into the Potomac, but the newspaper did not say if it had been recovered. It went on to say that the total spent on Langley's aerodrome was $50,000.[27] Orville marveled at the sum and, while he was on the train, totaled up every single dollar they had spent on their flyers, including transportation. It was less than a thousand dollars; such was the difference between private enterprise and government effort.

Langley had spent $50,000 more on human flight and an incalculable amount in human capital. He would die a fallen man two years later. The playing field had been cleared for the man waiting patiently for his brother back at Kitty Hawk, North Carolina. There would be no reporters, no champagne, no cigars, no government officials, just a few men and a boy, and a camera.

On December 14, they signaled the life-saving crews. John T. Daniels, Robert Westcott, Thomas Beacham, W. S. Dough, and "Uncle Benny" O'Neal helped to get the 750-pound glider to the launching site. They used the launching track to move the glider, laying track in front and then picking it up from the rear and putting it back in front again. The bicycle hubs on the bottom of the *Flyer* had ball bearings that allowed it to roll along like a train from the future.

They reached the Big Hill and laid the track out, then Wilbur started the motor. He warmed it up and then walked over and faced his brother. The wind made their eyes water, burned their cheeks, and numbed their fingers. The ocean moved in the distance. The *Flyer* rocked in the wind. They said a quick prayer, then Wilbur fished a coin out of his pocket.[28]

The destiny of humankind taking flight was now up in the air with a piece of copper revolving in a 25 mph ocean wind. Orville watched the flipping copper disc.

The coin landed back on Wilbur's palm. He moved his hand.

It was a moment in time. He won the toss.

Wilbur lay down on the *Flyer* with the engine running and the propellers blasting sand behind him. The plane was vibrating horribly and straining against the rope that was keeping it from taking to the sky. The men from the Life-Saving station had to push the *Flyer* back to release the pressure. The thrust of the propellers was not allowing the *Flyer* to take off. They had brought the *Flyer* to the Big Hill by laying track the whole way and finally,

Wilbur was facing down the track that ran down the Big Hill. They would use the assistance of gravity to launch their plane.

Orville held the right side of the wing tip. When the rope released, the *Flyer* took off down the hill. Wilbur stared straight into the wind that made his eyes tear and bit his cheeks with cold. He was a human cannonball at the long end of a motor churning the wind furiously with two giant wooden propellers. The *Flyer* was moving agonizingly slowly, and it seemed to have no lift; the biggest sensation Wilbur felt was the vibration of the engine in his belly. The end of the track was approaching. If he did not lift off, the plane would auger into the sand. At the end of the track, Wilbur pulled hard on the elevator; the plane lifted, and he felt the free motion of being above the earth. Then the sand rushed up to meet him as the plane nosed down and landed in the sand after flying a hundred feet. Wilbur forgot to shut off the motor, and the plane pivoted around in the sand and splintered a strut, a brace, and a spar. Wilbur had flown all of 3.5 seconds and had gone fifteen feet up into the air. The silence was deafening when the motor ceased.

Orville would later write to his sister that he barely had time to grab hold of the plane. He described the first test to her: "We tossed up a coin and to make the first trial, and Will won after getting adjustments of the engine ready I took the right end of machine. Will got on. When all was ready, Will attempted to release fastening to rail, but the pressure due to weight of the machine and the thrust of screws was so great he could not get it loose. We had to get a couple of men to help push back the machine until the rope was loose."[29]

The plane then started down the track. "While I was signaling the man at the other end to leave go but before myself was ready, Will started machine. I grabbed the upright the best I could and off we went. By the time we had reached the last quarter of the third rail the speed was so great I could stay with it no longer. I snapped watch and the machine passed the end of the track. . . . The machine turned up in front and rose to a height about 15 feet from the ground at a point about 60 feet from the track."[30]

For Wilbur, though the flight was short, it was all he needed. He wrote to his father that night:

> We gave the machine first trial today with only partial success. . . . The real trouble was an error in judgement in turning up suddenly after leaving the track, and as the machine had barely enough speed for support already."[31]

In other words, pilot error.

> It was a nice landing for the operator. The machinery all worked in entirely satisfactory manner and seems reliable. The power is ample but for a trifling error due to lack of experience with this machine and this starting the machine would undoubtedly have flown beautifully. There is now no question of final success.[32]

Wilbur had flown first, but two things happened. One, the flight was very short, lasting only 3.5 seconds in duration and traveling a distance of only 105 feet. The second and biggest reason this flight was not regarded as the first moment of powered flight is that there was no photographic record. This, going all the way back to Lilienthal, was crucial for proving to the world that flight had occurred. Even with the photographic record, the world was skeptical, but without it there was literally no proof.

The plane had been damaged, but not severely, from Wilbur forgetting to shut down the engine: "The machine swung around and scarped the front skids so deep in sand that one was broken and twisted around until the main strut and brace were also broken, besides the rear spar to lower surface of front rudder."[33]

It would take a couple of days for repairs, and then it was Orville's turn. It was eleven days before Christmas, and the weather had turned very cold, with a strong 30 mph wind off the ocean. The winter weather was quickly moving in, and if the *Flyer* was not put into the air soon, then it would have to wait until spring or summer.

THE PHOTOGRAPH—DECEMBER 17, 1903

The repairs took two days. They laid the track just outside the two buildings this time so that they didn't have to take the *Flyer* so far. Taking off from a flat plain would also prove that the plane took off under its own power, with no help from an incline. On December 16, they were ready to try again. "Wind of 6 to 7 meters blowing from west and northwest in morning," Orville wrote in his diary.[1] "We completed repairs by noon and got the machine out on the tracks in front of the building ready for a trial from the level. The wind was gradually dying and by the time we were ready was blowing only about 4 to 5 meters per sec. After waiting several hours to see whether it would breeze up again we took the machine in."

On December 17, the wind was blowing at 20 miles per hour, and they hung a white sheet on the side of the shed as a signal for the men at the Life-Saving station. They waited for the men to arrive so they could transport the *Flyer.* They were two men and a flying machine next to two sheds in the middle of nowhere. Wilbur saw a man crossing the sand toward them. The stranger crossed the sands along the desolate coast of Kitty Hawk. He had seen a contraption in the distance and wondered what it was. He approached the two men who were dressed in ties, high collars, and dark suits. *What is it,* he wanted to know. *It is a flying machine,* they answered. *Did they intend to fly it?* he persisted. *Yes, as soon as they have a suitable wind,* Wilbur answered. The stranger stared at the contraption with the track laid out in the sand. "Well it might fly," he conceded, "if it had a suitable wind."[2] He then continued across the sand and disappeared. No one in history would ever identify the man.

John T. Daniels, Will Dough, and Adam Ethridge came from the Life-Saving station, along with a dairy farmer named W. C. Brinkley and an eighteen-year-old boy named Johnny Moore, who had heard about the flying machine, and Bob Westcott watched from the station with a spyglass. He wanted to be sure he did not miss the flight if the brothers succeeded. The men laid the track down 100 feet west of the camp and faced the freezing wind. They positioned the *Flyer* on the track as Orville and Wilbur huddled together, brim to brim, their suit coats too thin for the 30° wind.

Hard to know what was said. Wilbur was giving the instructions. It was his plane, and he was telling his brother to not pull up on the elevator too quickly, as he had done. He was telling him to be sure to keep the wings level and concentrate on keeping the plane in the air. He had positioned his Gundlach Korona V 5 × 7 glass-plate camera with the pneumatic shutter 30 feet from the end of the rail and had given John Daniels instructions to press the bulb when the *Flyer* passed. This would be their only chance to prove that they had flown.

"After running the engine and propellers a few minutes to get them in working order I got on the machine at 10:35 for the first trial," Orville later wrote in his diary.[3] The whole plane was shaking from the drive chains turning the propellers, with the motor creating a deafening, clattering racket and the propellers churning the air like giant fans. The December wind was stiff and cold at 27 mph. Orville stared down the track with his hard shoes bottom up, his tie on, and his eyes blurring from the gusting, freezing wind off the ocean. "On slipping the rope the machine increased to probably 7 to 8 miles an hour."[4]

Wilbur walked along with the wing, keeping his left hand on the edge. His footsteps in the sand were less than twenty. He walked with the *Flyer* and, like a parent letting his child go, the *Flyer* lifted from his hand. Orville would later write, "The machine lifted from the track just as it entered the fourth rail. Mr. Daniels took a picture just as it left the track. I found control of the front rudder quite difficult on account of it being balanced to near the center."[5] Orville would later characterize the flight as "extremely erratic."[6] "The *Flyer* rose, dipped down, rose again, bounced and dipped again like a bucking bronco when one wing struck the sand."[7] The distance flown had been 120 feet—less than half the length of a football field. When asked if he was scared, years later, Orville replied, "Scared? There wasn't time. . . . It was only a flight of twelve seconds and it was an uncertain, creeping sort of a flight at best, but it was a real flight at last."[8]

As the plane reached the end of the monorail, Wilbur was walking briskly, and maybe he had just begun to jog when the plane lifted and Daniels squeezed the camera bulb. The camera shutter opened, and in came the image upside down. The emulsion was exposed, and even though it was cold, the silver crystals burned with the light. Etched into the chemical plate for all time was the image of two men: one with his arm akimbo against the plain of sand and another lying down in a contraption that had two wings and was slightly tilted. Then the shutter slammed shut, with its frozen history once again in darkness.

The picture would remain a secret until the Wright brothers returned home. Then, in the darkroom in the back of their Dayton home, the image would emerge under a safety light in a bath of developer. The image would change history for all time, and, ten years later, the glass plate would survive two days underwater in a flood in Dayton. Other pictures would be lost in the flood. It was a stubborn image of a moment in time, and it would define Orville, Wilbur, and the history of powered flight.

In the darkroom back in Dayton in late December, the photo that would change the course of history began to develop. The photographic paper slowly emulsified under the translucent developer, and first there were shadows, then a man with his arm slightly up and another man lying down in the middle of a plane, with the soles of his shoes visible. The plane is ten feet above the sand, with propellers slightly blurred and wings slightly titled. It is the first twelve seconds of flight, and the year is 1903. Historians have grappled with this photo ever since, and many would describe it in the barest terms. As stated in *The Papers of Wilbur and Orville Wright*:

> The starting rail, laid in a south to north direction on the level ground some 25 to 30 yards west of the camp buildings and 1000 feet north of Big Kill Devil Hills was constructed of four fifteen-foot two by fours, topped with a thin metal strip. The truck which supported the skids of the plane during take-off is visible in the sand at the end of the starting rail.... Orville Wright is at the controls of the machine, lying prone on the lower wing with hips in the cradle which operated the wing-warping mechanism. Wilbur Wright, running alongside to balance the machine, has just released his hold on the forward upright of the right wing.[9]

We do see Orville lying down with the soles of his patent-leather shoes facing the camera. The exposure was slow enough that the propellers' revolution is visible. The short length of the takeoff into a wind of "20 to 27 miles an hour"[10] is apparent from Wilbur's footprints in the sand. The plane is slightly tilted, with "the horizontal rudder tilted up to its extreme position."[11] There is the stool for keeping the wing off the ground and the C-clamp to keep the plane level before launch. The coil box and trailing wires for starting the motor are in front of a shovel, a bucket of nails and tacks, and a hammer.

But the footprints in the sand show Wilbur walking, then jogging along with the plane he had conceptualized. The footprints go straight, then veer right and then stop, and it is here that history is recorded as the plane lifts off. It is Wilbur, though, who is caught in time. He is running with one hand by his waist, with his suit coat open, and he is watching the plane lift off the ground, barely—but his plane *is flying*. He is watching something that began after a three-year depression. He should have been on the plane, but Orville was there, and if John Daniels had not snapped the picture, and if the photo had not been exposed, then the world would not have seen Orville flying. In fact, Wilbur would fly next and longer. Had that photo been the first one, then Wilbur would have been etched into history as the first man to fly. This made the Gundlach Korona V one of the most important things on the dunes of Kill Devil Hills, besides the *Flyer* itself.

Without the historic photo, December 17, 1903, would not have mattered. It would have been the telegram sent to their father from Kitty Hawk: "Success four flights Thursday morning all against twenty-one-mile wind started from level with engine power alone average speed through air thirty-one miles longest 57 seconds inform Press home Christmas."[12]

The importance of a photograph cannot be understated. It is the flag raising on Iwo Jima that was snapped by the photographer and later stood for more than all the men who had died there. In this image, the photo shows Wilbur staring as the plane passes him in flight, and all that would follow and who would claim they flew first would have to contend with that photo of two men on a desolate sand dune and a white-winged plane with propellers spinning furiously to lift itself into the air and leave the earth. It is the record of man finally freeing himself from the terrestrial plane. It is the record of Wilbur's dream born out of the dark agony of an existential crisis. It is the white pennon flapping out of the darkness.

This more than any other photographic moment in history would usher America and the world from the nineteenth century into the modern age of aviation, electricity, electronics, computers, television, space travel, and the atomic bomb. It is no mistake that a piece of the *Flyer* would go with Buzz Aldrin to the moon.[13] It was the bridge between the old world of people who lived and died in a contained world of farms or city blocks and the new world of modern globalism. The photo, the moment frozen, was a recording of that first step out of the darkness of superstition and suspicion into the bright light of science. Man could now look down from a high perch and see the world below. This sea change was evident in the stranger asking what that machine was in the sand. It was a flying machine. It was a spaceship. It was a time machine. The stranger had to know that, as he walked across a sand dune in the year 1903 and saw two men dressed in their Sunday best, bright and clean, with a white flying machine—he must have intuited that this new century would be very different from the last. The flying machine had flown.

After receiving Orville's telegram from Kitty Hawk confirming the successful flights, Katherine Wright fired off a telegram to Octave Chanute at once. His star pupil had just cracked the Gordian knot. "Boys report four successful flights today from level against twenty-one-mile wind. Average speed through air thirty-one miles. Longest flight fifty-seven seconds."[14] How did Chanute take this news? Did he understand that the world had just changed? Did Joe Dosher, the lone telegraph operator in Kitty Hawk, understand the importance of the keys he was pressing? We rarely understand a momentous event until later. Still, man had flown, and the men from the Life Saving stations had cheered. A man could throw a ball farther than Orville had flown, but still. . . .

Wilbur wrote to Octave Chanute two weeks later and summed up the flight:

> The conditions were very unfavorable as we had a cold gusty wind blowing, almost a gale. Nevertheless, as we had set our minds to be home by Christmas we determined to go ahead. Four flights were made, the first lasting about 12 seconds and the last 59 seconds. The "Junction Railroad" worked perfectly and a good start was obtained every time. The machine would run along the track about 40 ft propelled by the screws alone. . . . It would then rise and fly directly against the wind at a speed of about ten miles an hour. . . . One of the most gratifying features of the trial was the fact our calculations were shown to have worked out with absolute exactness. . . . Orville and I alternated in the flights according to our usual custom.[15]

Wilbur did fly after Orville. He "went off like a bird"[16] for 175 feet, then Orville flew again for 200 feet, and then they made a final test in which Wilbur flew a half a mile for almost a minute. The final flight was really where sustained controlled flight occurred. We can only imagine his excitement at creating a machine that actually could be controlled in the air. In his letter to Chanute, he continued: "The controlling mechanisms operated more powerfully than in our old machine so that we always turned the rudders more than necessary.... The machine possesses greater capacity of being controlled than any of our former machines."[17] This letter is interesting because Wilbur does not specify who flew first; he says only that they alternated.

"At just 12 o'clock Will started on the fourth and last trip," Orville wrote in his diary later.[18] "The machine started off with ups and downs as it had before but by the time he had gone over three or four hundred feet he had it under much better control and was traveling on a fairly even course. It proceeded in this manner till it reached a hummock out about 800 feet from the starting ways ... the distance was 852 feet in 59 seconds."

The first three flights were literally up and down and over in seconds. The final flight with Wilbur was the first moment of *controlled flying*. If a photo had been taken of that fourth trial, it would have had the moniker, "the First 59 Seconds of Controlled Flight" instead of "the First Twelve Seconds of Flight." But there was no photo of this flight, and when Wilbur writes to Chanute and describes the control of the plane, he is talking about the 59-second flight.

But here is what Wilbur doesn't know. The exposed plate inside their camera will be revealed in the darkroom in Dayton, and that will change the narrative entirely. The four flights will be immediately reduced to *one* by the photograph. The photo will alter history and will put Orville in the *Flyer* in the historic moment of flight, not the man who was the guiding force for breaking the mystery of flight. The plane had flown, and Wilbur was willing to spread the credit around, not knowing a photo would put his brother front and center as the man who had been first in human flight. Even the telegraph announcing to the world that man had flown would not be signed by Wilbur, although both were there. It is Orville who is listed as the sender.

It is a cruel joke on Wilbur and would allow historians from Kelly on to say that Orville Wright was just as instrumental in the creating of the first modern airplane. *He had flown first.* If the photo had been overexposed or if John Daniels had missed the moment, then Wilbur could have given his version, which could have easily pointed to the 59-second flight as the first controlled flight. In this case, history was determined by the emulsion-based glass plate of a Gundlach Korona V, and that not only superseded any account Wilbur could put forward but also would be a powerful arrow in the quiver that the Wright brothers were equal in every way, and that Orville had made history.

Wilbur's untimely death would be the nail in the coffin of the truth of December 17, 1903, that Orville's short flight in reality was similar to Wilbur's three days before. Control was not there yet in the 12 seconds of flight that John Daniels had captured, and control is the essence of being the first to fly. In his diary, Orville would later affirm this lack of control: "The machine lifted from the track just as it was entering the fourth rail ... I found the control of the front rudder quite difficult on account of its being balanced too near the center.... A sudden dart when out about 100 feet from the end of the track ended the flight."[19]

In fact, Orville nosed back into the sand a second after the photo was taken, when one wing struck the ground. It was not a landing but a controlled crash: "The lever for throwing off the engine was broken and the skid under the rudder cracked."[20] Again, it wasn't until Wilbur took over and worked out the problems again (in the way he had with the gliders) and flew the new *Flyer* for almost a minute that the first controlled flight occurred. *That* was truly the first 59 seconds of powered flight during which man had tamed the air.

This accounts for the tone of Wilbur's letter to Chanute in which the 12-second flight is given no real precedence over the other flights. In a 1913 *Flying* article after Wilbur's death, Orville would characterize the December 17, 1903, 12-second flight as, "the first in history of the world in which a machine carrying a man had raised itself by its own power into the air of full flight, had sailed forward without reduction of speed and had finally landed at a point as high as that from which it started."[21]

Others would not see it that way.

After Wilbur's final flight, the flying for that day in 1903 ended abruptly. Orville would later write:

> After removing the front rudder, we carried the machine back to camp. We set the machine down a few feet west of the building, and while standing

about discussing the last flight, a sudden gust of wind struck the machine and started to turn it over. All rushed to stop it. Will who was near one end ran to the front but too late to do any good. Mr. Daniels and myself seized spars at the rear but to no purpose. The machine gradually turned over on us. Mr. Daniels having no experience in handling the machine of this kind hung on to it from the inside and as a result was knocked down and turned over with it as it went.[22]

Daniels was caught inside and turned over with the *Flyer*. Amazingly, he was not hurt. But the plane that had flown first was now a wreck. "The engine legs were all broken off the chain guides badly bent, a number of uprights, and nearly all the rear ends of the ribs were broken."[23]

The amazing events of December 17, 1903, were over. The wrecked *Flyer* was put back into the hangar, and the Wrights began a long, cold walk to Kitty Hawk to report to the world what had happened. The 1903 *Flyer*, now twisted, bent, broken, and sand-covered, would never take to the air again and would be shipped back to Dayton, Ohio, to be crated and stored in a shed behind their home. There it would sit for ten years, moldering and rotting, until it was submerged in the great flood of 1913. Then, in 1928, it would cross the Atlantic Ocean and leave America.

PART 3

LANDINGS

"Nobody who has not experienced it for himself can realize it. It is a realization of a dream so many persons have had of floating in the air. More than anything else the sensation is one of perfect peace."

—Wilbur Wright 1905

1940

Near the Village of Corsham, England

They moved the *Flyer* one hundred miles out of London and put it in an underground storage facility near the village of Corsham. The *Luftwaffe* was bombing every night now. The pilots high above in the night sky, using radar to hone in on London, were letting their bombs go. They used their rudders and their ailerons and throttled up their engines and their elevator flaps and didn't have any idea that below them and deep underground was the reason they were able to fly through the night and drop 500-pound bombs on a city. They used the very controls that were encased in the crates marked *1903 WRIGHT FLYER*.

The shockwaves passed and maybe dust puffed off the wings. It had been thirty-seven years since Orville had lifted off for the first twelve seconds of flight and then had come back to Earth. Thirty-seven years since Wilbur flew for almost a minute and then landed back on the sand. As the bombs fell on London, it was too risky to try to bring the plane across the ocean again. Besides, Orville Wright didn't want the *Flyer* to come back to America. Yet.

FLIERS OR LIARS—1906

C aptain Baldwin's dirigible had taken off on its own. He was all set to perform for the crowd when the balloon suddenly became unmoored and went sailing off into the windy, dusk-laden evening. Wilbur had come with his brother to the Dayton fair to watch Baldwin fly, and now the two men watched the giant balloon take flight, with its ropes dragging through the dust, toward the cornfields. Wilbur and Orville leapt to their feet and ran after the dirigible. They grabbed onto the trailing ropes, along with Glenn Curtiss, who had come to perform maintenance on his motor for Baldwin.

The brothers manhandled the dirigible back to its moorings. Wilbur later wrote Chanute on September 4, "Captain Baldwin is at the fair this week, but the wind has been too strong to attempt a flight. . . . Mr. Curtiss who is building the motor for Prof. Bell's experiments this fall, called to see us."[1]

The dirigible taking off is a perfect metaphor for what would happen to Wilbur and Orville in the years after 1903. Wilbur's fine sense of control slipped away over the years, and here we have a moment in time during which the three men who would seek to destroy each other in future years are all trying to pull an errant dirigible down from the wind that wanted to take it away. But once man had ascended to the skies, there was no turning back. It would be a fateful night for all involved.

Hours later, Glenn Curtiss walked through the summer night with Captain Baldwin at the Dayton County Fair. He was kicking dust up with his hard shoes, and he watched the dirt float and settle back down. He might have been just a supplier of motors for hot-air balloons, had it not been for the Aero Club of America. In 1905, the Automobile Club spawned an off-shoot called the Aero Club of America, with luminaries Colonel John Jacob

Astor, William K. Vanderbilt, and Alexander Graham Bell. The inventor of the telephone and many other innovations had long been interested in flight. Thomas A. Watson, his aide in the invention of the telephone, remembered: "From my earliest association with Bell he discussed with me the possibility of making a machine that would fly like a bird. He took every opportunity that presented itself to study birds, living or dead. . . . I fancy, if Bell had been in easy financial circumstances, he might have dropped his telegraph experiments and gone into flying machines."[2]

The cross-pollination occurs here. At the very time Chanute was conversing with Wilbur Wright, he was also trading letters with Alexander Graham Bell, who would later thank Chanute for sending him a copy of *Experiments and Observations in Soaring Flight*, a pamphlet by Wilbur describing the early gliding experiments at Kitty Hawk. By the end of 1905, Bell had built a kite capable of lifting a man and powered by an engine he ordered from Glenn Curtiss.

The Aero Club planned an aeronautical show in 1906 in New York. Bell was there, as was Octave Chanute. The Smithsonian supplied Langley's model Aerodrome, and the Wright brothers sent the crankshaft and flywheel of their 1903 *Flyer*. Samuel Langley had died that year, and Wilbur had written a letter earlier to Chanute that would come to haunt him: "The knowledge that the head of the most prominent scientific institution of America believed in the possibility of human flight was one of the influences that led us to undertake the preliminary investigation that preceded our work. He recommended to us the books which enabled us to form some ideas at the onset. It was a helping hand at a critical time and we shall always be grateful."[3]

Glenn Curtiss was there with his engine exhibit for the auto show. Bell, a stout, gray man with a white mustache and dressed in tweed, went on in a booming voice, proclaiming that one day man would cross the Atlantic in a plane. Bell gave a speech proclaiming "the Age of the Flying Machine is not in the future. It is with us now."[4] He broke the news at the exhibition that the Wright brothers had flown twenty-five miles in Dayton, Ohio. He then went home and later ordered a Curtiss engine. Bell and Curtiss probably met at the show, but neither man understood how their lives would intersect again.

Alexander Graham Bell wanted to pursue flying using the model of Chanute's early biplane, the Chanute I, a goal toward which he would employ the talents of many young men whom he deemed to be on the cutting edge of aeronautics. As Cecil Roseberry explained in *Glenn Curtiss: Pioneer of Flight*, "A program to gather around himself a team of bright, dedicated young men to help him over the final hurdle of putting a mechanical kite in the air . . . now he had three promising candidates for the team but he lacked the key person of all—an engine specialist. He considered Glenn Curtiss the greatest motor expert in the country."[5] The Aerial Experiment Association (AEA) was quickly formed, with Curtiss as the man who would put engines on the aircraft. Stationery with letterhead was printed with "Alexander Graham Bell" at the top and "G. H. Curtiss, Director of Experiments," just beneath. This new title would give Curtiss one more chance to approach the Wright brothers and offer a free engine. He had tried twice before.

Although he still regarded all fliers as cranks, Curtiss wanted to expand his market. Maybe Bell gave him an idea that the airplane market would be viable. If the Wright brothers did fly, then they probably needed a better motor. He sent off a letter to Dayton in May 1906. It was the first time he would reach out to the Wright brothers, and their fates would be forever intertwined.

He wrote, "Dear Sirs, We have read of your success with the Aeroplane and thinking we might be of service to you in getting out a light and powerful motor with which to carry on your work we have taken the liberty of writing to you on the subject . . ."[6] He told the Wright brothers of his sale to known fliers of airships and Captain Baldwin and then made his case: "Of course, we understand that your work is of a somewhat different character, but we mention these to prove that our motor has great power and reliability. . . . We recently shipped to Dr. Bell's Nova Scotia Laboratory a motor designed for Aeroplane work, and we hope that this experience will be of service to you."[7]

Glenn then informed the Wright brothers that he would be in the area the next week and they might meet. Wilbur was not impressed and sent back a reply informing Curtiss that they use their own engines, thank you very much. Glenn never received the letter and headed for Dayton to meet the biggest aviation crank of the age.

Wilbur had no intention of using anyone else's engine in his plane: "We have never considered light motors the important point in solving the flying problem," he wrote to Chanute.[8] Glenn wired the Wrights from Columbus, "IF CONVENIENT LIKE TO TALK WITH YOU SIX O'CLOCK BELL PHONE."[9] Glenn called, and the conversation didn't go well with

Wilbur, who was showing no interest in Curtiss engines. Still, Curtiss said he might drop in but then decided against it. When he returned home to Hammondsport, he found a letter from Wilbur that he had missed. He immediately wrote back: "On my return I find your letter. Trust I did not cause you any inconvenience in getting you to the phone. . . . Was delayed a day in Columbus and thought of going over to see you. Am glad, however, to have made your acquaintance and hope to meet you at some future time."[10]

Wilbur Wright remained suspicious. He had good reason. Ever since 1903, the world had not yet recognized his achievement at Kitty Hawk. After they had sent the first telegram home proclaiming success to Bishop Wright, the world had only yawned. The first scientific publication to report that man could fly was a magazine on bee culture, *Gleanings in Bee Culture*. That would not be until March 1, 1904. Amos Root would wiggle into history as the first newspaperman to break the story of flight. His timing was perfect, since Wilbur was about to attempt to fly a full circle around the field at Huffman Prairie.

Root described for his readers what he saw as the plane flew low to the ground and then turned back toward him:

> When it turned that circle, and came near the starting point, I was right in front of it and I said then and I believe still, it was . . . the greatest sight of my life. Imagine a locomotive that has left its track and is climbing up in the air right toward you—a locomotive without any wheels . . . but with white wings instead . . . a locomotive made of aluminum. Well now imagine that locomotive with wings that spread 20 feet each way, coming right toward you with a tremendous flap of its propellers.[11]

Root then described the landing of the plane for his readers: "When the engine is shut off, the apparatus glides to the ground very quietly and alights on something much like a pair of light sled runners, sliding over the grassy surface perhaps a rod or more." He then predicted what the invention of the airplane will mean to the world: "We shall not need to fuss with good roads nor railway tracks or bridges . . . at such enormous expense. With these machines we bid adieu to all these things."[12]

Root published his article in January 1905, in *Gleanings in Bee Culture*, and many papers scoffed at the story. The editor of *Scientific American* wrote, "If such sensational and tremendously important experiments are being conducted in a not very remote part of the country on a subject in which almost everybody feels the same profound interest, is it possible to believe that the enterprising American reporter, who, it is well known, comes down the chimney when the door is locked in his face."[13]

In other words, Amos Root was not to believed. It was not surprising. The *Dayton Journal*'s editor refused to publish the story offered by Milton at Wilbur's direction. The telegraph operator in Kitty Hawk who had transmitted the cable letting their father know that they had flown had leaked it to the *Virginia Pilot*, which printed a fantastic story of a long-extended flight that was picked up by several newspapers and then dropped: "FLYING MACHINE SOARS 3 MILES IN TEETH OF HIGH WIND OVER SAND HILLS AND WAVES AT KITTY HAWK ON CAROLINA COAST."[14]

H. P. Moore of the *Virginia Pilot*, who had taken the story from the telegraph operators and put it on the front page, had then sent it to twenty-one other newspapers. As Fred Kelly wrote in *The Wright Brothers*, "Of the twenty-one newspapers to whom it was offered, only five ordered the story. They were the *New York American*, the *Washington Post*, the *Chicago Record-Herald*, the *Philadelphia Record*, and the *Cincinnati Enquirer*."[15] Three of the newspapers delayed the story, and some didn't print it at all. They simply didn't believe anyone had flown at Kitty Hawk. The morning after the first flight, there was not a single item in the *Dayton Journal*, even after brother Lorin had seen editor Frank Tunisson, who didn't bother looking up, murmuring the now-immortal words, "Fifty-seven seconds, hey? If it had been fifty-seven minutes then it might have been a news item."[16]

Orville and Wilbur ended up writing a press release to correct the fabrications printed in the newspapers:

> It had been our intention not to make any detailed public statement concerning the private trials of our power "Flyer" on the 17th of December last; but since the contents of a private telegram, announcing to our folks at home the success of our trials was dishonestly communicated to the newspapermen at the Norfolk office, and led to the imposition upon the public by persons who never saw the Flyer or its flights, of a fictitious story incorrect in almost every detail . . . we feel impelled to make some correction. The real facts are as follows.[17]

The press release to the Associated Press on January 6 then became a dry rendition of the four flights at Kitty Hawk. The AP had previously sent out a 350-word summary of the flight at Kitty Hawk on December 18, complete with the fantastic claims made in the *Virginia Pilot* that "the machine flew for more than three miles."[18] Many of the Associated Press newspapers did not pick up the brief dispatch. The Wrights' press release did not fare much better. Finally, on January 17, the New York *Herald* in its magazine section published an article titled "The Machine That Flies." It was full of half-truths and fabrications, including "a diagram, showing the two six blade propellers, one behind the machine and one beneath it to give it elevation!"[19]

This was during the Wright brothers' momentous step of closing the bicycle shop and going full-time in an effort to market their invention. Wilbur had thought on this after Christmas of 1903, after enjoying the warmth of family and a porterhouse steak and a "fancy dessert" on his first night home:

> We found ourselves standing at a fork in the road. On the one hand we could continue playing with the problem of flying so long as youth and leisure would permit but carefully avoiding those features that would require continuous effort and the expenditure of considerable sums of money. On the other hand, we believed that if we would take the risk of devoting our entire time and financial resources, we could conquer the difficulties in the path to success before increasing years impaired our physical ability. We finally decided to make the attempt but as our financial future was at stake we were compelled to regard it as a strict business proposition.[20]

This was a fork in the road, and an extremely risky one. Wilbur knew what they had, but no one else did and their patent had yet to be approved. He now had to make a living from their invention in a field of study within which no one had ever considered a money-making occupation. Selling planes or flying planes had never been considered for monetary gain. So not only did he have to invent the airplane but then he had to monetize it. This would lead eventually to charges of greed being Wilbur's motivation—and by none other than Octave Chanute. But Wilbur had no fortune to fall back on, and protecting his invention was protecting his livelihood.

Thus began the era of the great secret at a time when they needed to prove to the world that they had flown, so they could sell their invention.

They didn't have a patent yet, and they did not want anyone stealing their secrets. This paranoia would end up in their application for the widest possible patent, which would set the stage for infringement on any airplane constructed: "The value of such a monopoly would be enormous. With no serious rivals in sight, there was no reason for undue haste. . . . They would continue working toward the production of a practical flyer while guarding the secrets of their technology."[21]

Octave Chanute thought this a grave mistake, showing his view of Wilbur's invention as one of using existing technology in a different way. As Tom Crouch wrote in *The Bishop's Boys*, "He saw the Wrights as extraordinarily gifted mechanics who had put old ideas into new bottles. Their genius he thought was to be found in the ability to make other men's ideas work. . . . Simply put they saw things others missed, made correct decisions where others erred, and persevered when others lost faith."[22] Chanute simply didn't believe Wilbur had invented the technology, nor did he believe that "the idea of flexing the wing . . . was patentable."[23]

This view would tear apart their friendship in the years to come. Wilbur and Orville concentrated on building another flyer in 1904 to fly in nearby Huffman Prairie. As described in an article in *Harper's Magazine*, "A cow pasture, fairly level, handy to an interurban railway, at Simms Station, eight miles from Dayton. . . . This field often called the Huffman Prairie, was part of a farm belonging to a Dayton bank president."[24] The press came out to the prairie several times to watch but were unimpressed when the plane didn't leave the ground. An interurban train car passing by gave passengers a glimpse of manned flight in its earliest stages. Wilbur later wrote of the ragged start in the cow field, "We took the machine out Monday but just as we [were] ready the wind died out. . . . On Wednesday we took it out but were driven in by rain. Again, on Thursday we took it out and again the rain compelled us to take it in, but in the afternoon we again took it out."[25] Then, when they started the flyer, mechanical problems left onlookers unimpressed. "The engine was not working right but there was no time to see what the trouble was then. The machine rose six or eight feet but the power was insufficient and it came down."

The Wrights began flying soon, though, and people on the interurban train cars watched in disbelief as a machine circled over Mr. Huffman's pasture. Wilbur's description of flying was now becoming more ethereal. "When you know, after the first few minutes, that the whole mechanism is working perfectly ... the sensation is so keenly delightful as to be almost beyond description. Nobody who has not experienced it for himself can realize it. It is a realization of a dream so many persons have had of floating in the air. More than anything else the sensation is one of perfect peace."[26]

Flying gave him the escape he must have always thought it would. In the air he was fulfilled and earthly cares fell away. He and Orville invited Milton and Katherine out along with friends to watch them fly. The new *Flyer III* that they built had improvements in the wing design, the tail, and control, and a 25-horsepower engine and allowed Wilbur to circle Huffman Prairie twenty-nine times in one flight. Bishop Wright would write, "I saw Wilbur fly twenty four miles in thirty eight minutes and four seconds in one flight."[27]

People often called the local papers to report what they had seen, but still the press did not take notice. Even Fred Kelly, writing for the *Dayton Journal* at the time in a branch office at Xenia, did not believe anything had happened there. In his biography years later, he wrote about himself, "Did he investigate the story? No, he didn't need to investigate it to feel sure it must be nonsense. If true, surely it would be in the Dayton papers."[28] Wilbur in the 1904 *Flyer* was able to make complete circles around the field, but the problem was that nobody saw him do it. The only photos of the flights were taken by the Wrights, and these did not impress anybody. The reason was that people simply didn't believe the Wrights were flying. James M. Cox, the publisher of the *Dayton Daily News*, summed up public sentiment at the time when years later he admitted, "Frankly, none of us believed it."[29]

Finally, several Dayton newspapers took note, but it was hard to prove anything to a skeptical public. A druggist, W. C. Fouts, was quoted, "When I went out to Huffman Prairie I expected to see somebody's neck broken. What I did see was a machine weighing 900 pounds soar away like an eagle. ... I told a friend about it that night and he acted as if I had gone daft or joined the liars club."[30] The Wrights took the unusual position that no one would catch up with them, and so they believed that they were quite safe in taking their time to prove their achievement to the world. This secrecy was based on their business decision: "the entire package, protected by an airtight patent could be afforded to a potential buyer—presumably a national government."[31]

This led to a basic problem of disbelief. The words "alleged experiments" crept into many articles covering the Wrights at this time. The Paris edition of the *Herald Tribune* headlined an article in 1906, "FLYERS OR LIARS?"[32] An editorial in the New York *Herald* summed it up this way: "The Wrights have flown or have not flown. They possess a machine or they do not possess one. They are in fact either fliers or liars. It is difficult to fly. It is easy to say, 'we have flown.'"[33]

But there were two men who appeared in the Huffman Prairie who did believe the Wrights had flown. As John Kelly described in *The Wright Brothers*, "The Wrights saw two men wandering nearby fields during most of one day and thought they must be hunters. . . . The next day the two strangers were seen and finally they came across the field." One man carried a camera and asked if visitors were allowed. "Yes, only we'd rather you didn't take any pictures," one of the Wright brothers courteously replied.[34]

The man set the camera down, and then they proceeded to examine the machine. The Wrights assumed they were newspapermen, and one man said he had written for some publication, but Charlie Taylor overheard the men talking and later said after they left, "that fellow's no writer. At least he's no ordinary writer. When he looked at the different parts of the machine he called them all by the right names."[35] Later, Orville and Wilbur would identify the man as the former chief engineer for Professor Langley of the Smithsonian Institution.

Then, in 1905, the Wrights compounded the problem of people not believing they had flown by refusing to fly for anyone unless the two brothers had a firm offer in hand for their flying machine. They had made 105 starts in Huffman Prairie and still had no approved patent, and Wilbur was afraid someone would steal their ideas. So, they hid their plane, their knowledge, and their achievements, and they waited for the world to catch up to them. From then on, the business of flying would overtake them, especially Wilbur, who would make it his mission to protect their patents. Others would step into the vacuum of advancing aviation, eventually using what Wilbur had learned and then taking it a step further. Like a man sticking his fingers in the dyke, Wilbur would spend the rest of his life in perpetual litigation, protecting what he had discovered in the sands of the Outer Banks.

This brings us back to the night at the fair in 1906, when the Wright brothers assisted in retrieving Baldwin's escaped hot-air balloon and finally met Glenn Curtiss. The very secret that Wilbur had so meticulously guarded was now going to be exposed. There was little chance a man like Glenn Curtiss could have stumbled on Wilbur's system of aeronautical control if he hadn't gone to the Dayton Fair. Curtiss felt that the Wrights had proved amenable and much friendlier than he had previously thought. Prior to meeting with them, the word Curtiss got was that the Wright brothers didn't do business with people they didn't know. But now they had offered to have him drop by their shop.

Curtiss was impressed with the simplicity of the Dayton workshop. It was efficient, organized, and clean. Wilbur pulled out the photographs of their machine in flight at Kitty Hawk and at Hoffman Prairie. Curtiss was very proud of his lightweight, powerful motors, just as Wilbur was of his flyer. The conversation was far ranging, and Curtiss asked him question after question about control, rudders, wing warping, propulsion, and flying. Glenn believed knowledge was like the air and just as free. He asked so many questions that George Baldwin later chastised him for his obnoxious manners on the way back to the fairgrounds. Glenn Curtiss didn't care. He left the Wrights that night with his head full of ideas.

He followed up with a letter again.

> Gentlemen—
>
> This is my first opportunity to write you since getting back from Dayton. . . . It may interest you to know that we cut out some of the inner surface of the blades on the big propeller, so as to reduce the resistance and allow it to speed up and it showed a remarkable improvement.[36]

Curtiss then listed several other improvements, finishing up by saying, "we are getting well started on the 8-cylinder motor for Jones. It certainly looks good on the drawings. Will let you know how it pans out as to power."[37]

This moment of cross-pollination would prove portentous for all parties involved. Over the next two years, Glenn Curtiss would build airplanes with ailerons that many would say were based on the wing-warping concept of the Wright brothers. Ailerons used hinges, Curtiss would later point out, and you cannot copyright an idea. He had walked back to the fairgrounds with dust on his shoes and his head exploding with ideas. Years later, some historians would say this was the night Glenn Curtiss stole Wilbur Wright's invention. As Roseberry wrote in *Glenn Curtiss: A Pioneer of Flight*, "The Wrights and their partisans repeatedly cited it as evidence that Curtiss attempted to pick their brains at their first meeting."[38]

Under the aegis of the AEA, Curtiss fired one more shot across the bow and approached Wilbur directly in 1907:

> Dear Mr. Wright—
>
> Although I have been endeavoring to keep track of your movements by the newspapers, I am not sure which of the Brothers is in Dayton. Therefore, address you as above. I just wish to keep in touch and let you know that we have made considerable progress in engine construction. [Curtiss then describes his latest engine.] The 50 H.P. engine will weigh about 200 pounds and the 100 about 350 pounds. We would be glad to furnish you with one of these gratis, providing you are in the market for engines, as we have great confidence in them. This proposition you will appreciate is not at all regular and is made to you confidentially. . . . I should like very much to have you come to Hammondsport at any time you will feel it convenient, not only that we may talk engines, but we would feel honored to make you our guests as long as you care to stay.[39]

Wilbur smelled a rat and turned Curtiss down on both counts. He wrote back, "Your very interesting letter of December 30th has been received. We thank you for your offer to us of your powerful motors for use on our flyer. We believe, however, that our own motor of 25 to 30 will meet all the requirements. . . . We remember your visit to Dayton with pleasure. The experience we had together in helping Captain Baldwin back to the fairgrounds was not one soon to be forgotten."[40]

Like a bride wary of an aggressive suitor, Wilbur instinctively knew there was a condition in Curtiss's offer: *Tell me all that you know*. It was Glenn Curtiss's last attempt to do business with the Wrights. From then on, he would take what he could.

DEATH IN THE SKY—
SEPTEMBER 17, 1908

lexander Graham Bell looked around, then walked quickly into the shed and saw the smashed up Wright flyer. He pulled out a tape measure and began taking measurements. The rain pattered on the shed roof. He noted the wing span, the curvature of the wing itself, and the mountings of the smashed motor. He examined the controls of the flyer, the wing, the movable rudder, and the warping edges of the wings that were controlled by cables. He walked around in his suit and kneeled down and saw blood on the white, muslin canvas. He didn't know if it was Orville Wright's or Captain Selfridge's. He stood up, and then walked quickly away, passing a soldier outside the door. Aviation just had its first fatality.

It began with the army committing to buying a Wright plane. All the Wrights had to do was fly the plane with an army officer, and the contract would be signed. Wilbur was in France demonstrating to the world that they had built a plane that could actually fly, so it was up to Orville to do the test. It was damp, and the sky was low at Fort Meyer, Virginia. The smell of the earth rose under the plane as Orville walked around inspecting the wings, the wheels, the rudder, the engine, and the propeller. The press was there with a good-sized crowd. Some people asked for Orville's autograph.

He turned back to the plane. The propeller was wooden and built in layers. Wilbur always inspected the propellers very closely. All seemed to be in working order, but Orville was not very familiar with the new controls of the 1908 plane; he sat in the seat going over possible scenarios, moving the rudder and the ailerons, and checking the cables.

He stood and watched Captain Selfridge crossing the wet field. A light fog was dissipating. Orville felt a disgust well up over him. "I understand that he does a good deal of knocking behind my back," he wrote Wilbur.[1] Selfridge was part of the Aviation Experiment Association that included Glenn Curtiss and Alexander Graham Bell. Curtiss had already infringed on their patent and sold a plane using their wing-warping technology. "I learn from Scientific American that your June Bug has surfaces at the tips of the wings, adjustable to different angles on the right and left sides for maintaining lateral balance," Wilbur wrote him in a formal letter.[2] "Claim 14 or four patent No. 821,393 specifically covers the combination which we are informed you are using."

After retaining a lawyer and resubmitting their patent, Wilbur had struck pay dirt. The patent had been granted on May 22, 1906, for "new and useful improvements in Flying Machines."[3] For three years since Kill Devil Hills, Wilbur and Orville had essentially refrained from flying in public, under the fear that someone would steal their secret, and it had paid off with a far-reaching patent. Now anyone who wanted to fly had three choices. As Mark Eppler summed it up in *The Wright Way*: "Sign a license agreement, pay royalties, or stay grounded. For all intents and purposes, Wilbur and Orville Wright now controlled the skies."[4]

And now Orville was supposed to take Capt. Tom Selfridge flying with him because the army required one of their own to make a flight before the Wrights could get a contract. It was like taking a spin with Benedict Arnold or a spy. "I will be glad to have Selfridge out of the way," he wrote to Wilbur after arriving in Fort Meyer. "I don't trust him an inch. He is intensely interested in the subject and plans to meet me at dinners where he can pump me."[5]

Bell and Selfridge were associated with Curtiss, and that was enough for the Wrights to detest the men.[6] Wilbur had flatly told Glenn Curtiss that he must pay to use the technology discovered at Kitty Hawk: "We believe it will be very difficult to develop a successful machine without the use of some of the features covered in our patent [granted in 1906]."[7]

There it was. In their view, and the court's, anyone building an airplane owed the Wrights royalties, and Curtiss built the *June Bug*, which clearly used their technology. The Wrights had a stranglehold on the budding aeronautical industry and would stifle progress to the point that when World War I broke out, the United States would be behind other countries in producing advanced biplanes. Curtiss obfuscated in his reply and said that the AEA was merely experimenting, and any conflict of patents should be handled by the secretary of the organization—none other than the man with whom Orville had to fly, Tom Selfridge. Curtiss was basically stalling the Wrights while he moved ahead to design his next plane. Selfridge had even sent a letter inquiring about the patent, but Wilbur saw subterfuge. "Selfridge," he had written to Orville, "is infringing our patent on wing twisting."[8] Best to get this flight over with quickly.

Selfridge nodded to Orville, took off his uniform jacket and hat, and handed them to a friend. He sat down next Orville, who nodded to the men to push the propellers. The engine coughed to life, and the plane vibrated like a caged animal. Just after 5 p.m., the counterweight for the catapult was dropped, hurling the Wright flyer into the air. The plane lifted quickly, and Orville struggled with the unfamiliar controls, then made three circles around the parade ground. Selfridge seemed to be enjoying himself, and Orville started thinking about landing when he heard a slight tapping behind him.

They were moving toward the wall of Arlington Cemetery. Orville turned around and looked behind him but saw nothing wrong. Two thumps shook the plane, and the flyer turned violently to the left. Orville cut the power to the engine and fought with the controls. Then came a crack, and the plane nosed down.

W. S. Clime, a photographer on the ground, wrote later:

> There was a crack like a pistol shot coming from above. I saw a piece of a propeller blade twirling off on to the Southward. For a brief period, [the plane] kept on its course, then swerved to the left and with a swoop backwards, but in an almost perpendicular manner it fell for half the distance to the ground. Then suddenly righting itself regained for an instant its normal position only to pitch forward and strike on the parallel planes in front for altering elevation.[9]

Orville would later write to Wilbur and explain the last seconds of the flight:

> The machine suddenly turned to the right and I immediately shut off the power. I then discovered that the machine would not respond to the steering and lateral balancing levers which produced a most peculiar feeling of helplessness. Yet I continued to push the levers, when the machine suddenly turned to the left till it faced directly up the field. I reversed the levers

to stop the turning and to bring the wings on a level. Quick as a flash, the machine turned down in front and started straight for the ground. . . . Lieutenant Selfridge up to this time had not uttered a word, though he took a hasty glance behind when the propeller broke . . . but when the machine turned headfirst to the ground he exclaimed *Oh Oh* in an almost inaudible voice.[10]

The plane smashed into the ground nose first and buried Selfridge and Orville in the wings, wires, earth, and engine. Selfridge was under the engine and choking on his blood. A deep gash in his forehead pulsed blood. Orville was unconscious and bleeding from the head as well. The crowd rushed to the wreck, and the two men were put on stretchers. Orville had a concussion, a broken femur, four cracked ribs, and a dislocated hip. Selfridge had two skull fractures and internal injuries. He died on the operating table at 9 p.m. The wreckage was put in a shed, and it was found that one of the propellers had cracked lengthwise, which knocked the other propeller out of balance and cut a stay wire. The Wright flyer then went out of control.

The army interpreted it as a freak accident. Alexander Graham Bell of the AEA intimated that it was Orville's lack of experience with the new controls that contributed to the crash and that if it had one propeller instead of two, the crash wouldn't have happened. In Orville's mind, what caused him to lose control was the fact that he had to fly with a man whom he considered a spy and a thief. In Wilbur's mind, it was his brother's carelessness that caused the crash that killed Selfridge. He wrote to Milton and called the crash "a great pity," then went on to say, "I think the trouble was caused by the feverish conditions under which Orville had to work. His time was consumed by people who wished to congratulate him and encourage him."[11]

He then wrote this to his sister, Katherine:

I cannot help but thinking repeatedly, if I had been there, it would not have happened. . . . It was not right to leave Orville there to undertake the task alone. I do not mean that Orville was incompetent to the work itself, but I realized that he would be surrounded by thousands of people. . . . A man cannot take sufficient care when he is subject to continual interruptions and his time is consumed by talking to visitors. I cannot help suspecting that Orville told Charlie to put on the big screws instead of doing it himself and that if he had done it himself he would have noticed the thing that made the trouble, whatever it may have been. . . . People think I am foolish because I do not like the men to do the least important work on the machine. . . . Hired men pay no attention to anything but the particular thing they are told to do.[12]

It was not the first time he had accused Orville of carelessness. When the *Flyer* had been shipped to France earlier in the year, Wilbur found it damaged beyond belief: "I . . . have been puzzled to know how you could have wasted two full days packing," he wrote Orville caustically.[13] "I am sure that with a scoop shovel I could have put things in within two or three minutes and made fully as good a job of it. I never saw [such] evidence of idiocy in my life." Wilbur kept up his attack on his brother's competency for days until Katherine stepped in: "Orv looks perfectly terrible . . . so pale and tired. I wouldn't fuss at him all the time. You have troubles too but I can't see any sense in so much complaining at him."[14]

In a letter to Chanute, Wilbur came to terms with the root cause of the crash: "One blade of the right propeller developed a longitudinal crack which permitted that blade to flatten out and lose its pushing power. . . . This brought the uninjured blade in contact with the upper stay wire to the tail and tore it loose, the end of the wire wrapping around the end of the blade and breaking it off."[15]

Selfridge's funeral was not attended by any of the Wrights, nor did Glenn Curtiss attend. Alexander Graham Bell of the AEA was named as a pallbearer. After the funeral, Bell and others walked by the shed containing the mangled flyer. Bell hesitated, looked around, then walked into the shed and took some measurements. The sergeant guarding the wreckage confirmed the measurement by Bell later. When Orville and Wilbur learned this, they accused Bell, the AEA, and by connection Curtiss, of using the funeral as a cover to steal more of their secrets. Orville was still in the hospital, flat on his back, and Wilbur was certain that even in death Selfridge had managed to conspire to infringe even further on their patents. Glenn Curtiss was singularly loathed by Wilbur for being behind Orville's distracted flight, the taking of measurements of their flyer, and the infringement on their patent. A case could be made by the Wrights that Curtiss was a factor in Selfridge's death. It wouldn't be the last time a death would be blamed on the upstart aviator, Glenn Curtiss.

25

RETURN TO EDEN—1908

The boys ran over the sand dune. They had walked the four miles from Kitty Hawk to see where the flying fellas had flown their airplane. Someone said that there were airplanes in the old shacks at the foot of the dunes. The wind was blowing, and it was still cold for April. The roof was gone and one wall had collapsed in. They had passed a wing sticking out of the sand, and they figured the plane was somewhere inside. Maybe they could go for a ride.

They had just reached the building when they saw a man walking briskly toward them and they ran off. The man did not look like anyone from the island. He wore a suit with a white shirt and a derby. He had on shiny leather shoes. He had just appeared like a god from another planet. He walked with a purpose, his eyes straight ahead, barely noticing the boys tearing across the dunes. He was already cataloging the damage.

The sand had invaded and claimed the floor and had come crashing through one wall. In a few more years, it would bury the shed and the building where he had lived and broken the code of flight. Wilbur Wright stared at the remnants of Octave Chanute's glider that had crashed from the rafters to the floor. The roof was open, and one wall was down. Even now the sand was blowing into the building. The new building they had built for the 1903 *Flyer* was simply gone. A nor'easter had carried it off, William Tate had told him upon his arrival.

Wilbur turned slowly. Here is where he had found the secret. Here is where he had been allowed to take to the air. Here he had been supremely happy in his pursuit of a singular dream to fly like the winged creatures of the earth. He had done it, and yet he had lost something that had been there in the Outer Banks of North Carolina. This remote outpost, this shelf on the edge of the continent, had given him the moment "to lie motionless between a pair of seventeen-foot wings on a sea-scented updraft," and now he wanted it back.[1]

Wilbur turned, stared out the window, and heard the wind whistling through the boards. Sand. Yes, the sands of time would cover it all. He turned and stared out to the dunes, where he saw a skeleton poking out of the sand. He walked outside and struggled over to the small dune. It was the wing of the 1902 flyer. They had flown it one last time and just left it there, and time had buried it until this one bit of wing was the only marker of all that effort. Wilbur touched the rotted fabric, the pine struts that he had cut and bent. This was one of his babies. Of course he would never have children and lately he couldn't escape the feeling that his time was limited. His health had not been good, with the stress of the patent wars and the impending suits with Glenn Curtiss.

Wilbur turned back to the building they had built in 1900. It was small against the giant dunes. A few cans were on the ground. A few boards of better times. The wind. It never stopped. It was always blowing. That's why he came here. This place, this magical outpost in the middle of nowhere, had wind for lift and sand for a soft landing. It had the isolation he craved. The great silence to think into. Like any artist, he needed solitude to create, and he had found it when he had arrived at Kitty Hawk.

He turned again and stared where it had happened. Yes, the first flight had happened in a 25 mph wind five years before. December. It was cold. There was ice on the dunes. Christmas was just eight days away, and it was now or never. If they didn't fly on that day, then who knows what would have happened. He had won the toss, and then it was Orville's turn. Wilbur felt his eyes water. It was 1903.

26

THE INJUNCTION—1910

The sheriff knocked on the door of the Herring-Curtiss Corporation. The door swung back, and the sheriff asked the man to identify himself. He then handed Glenn Curtiss an injunction that would basically freeze his company. It was January 3, 1910. Curtiss had just come out with his newest plane, the *June Bug*, in 1909. It was superior to anything the Wrights had come up with: "a biplane with parallel wings instead of AEA bows, a twenty-nine-foot span and 4.5-foot chord and a double front elevator with a horizontal panel halfway up. Control was generated by a movable steering wheel rather than a lever."[1]

But the thing that broke the mold was "movable surfaces at either extremity of the main planes, each movable surface half within the main cell and half without."[2] In modern language, Curtiss had just created a plane with ailerons. Every modern jetliner today has ailerons—the lower flaps on the wings that move up and down. No more wing warping. Ailerons were more efficient, faster, and mechanically more sound. They were the future. Glenn added a lightweight, newly designed motor that "develops more power per square inch of piston area than has ever been secured in a gas engine."[3] Then he sold it for $5,000 to the Aeronautical Society of America after they passed on a Wright flyer.

This was the last straw for Wilbur, who saw it as a violation of the promise Curtiss had made not to infringe on their patent. Curtiss had believed Augustus Herring when Herring told him that he held patents that predated the Wrights'. That patent ownership was the basis of the incorporation of the Herring-Curtiss Corporation, and Curtiss proceeded thinking that legally he was on firm ground. Herring had a contract with the army to deliver a plane while Glenn entered race after race with his planes and won. Promoters had found that people would come to see these races of daredevils with experimental planes, so they offered substantial prizes. The Wrights, meanwhile, met with their lawyers in New York. Curtiss and Wilbur had tried to settle it, but the truth was that Curtiss did not want to pay the Wrights for what he felt belonged to all men who flew. The airplane could not be held hostage to the whims of someone just because he happened to discover something first. So, in the end, he declined to pay, and that brought a final letter from Wilbur:

> The negotiation was initiated at your request and now seems to be similarly closed by you. As I stated in one of our conferences, an agreement, in order to be effective must possess sufficient elements of advantage to each party to make both satisfied. If you do not consider that such advantages exist so far as you are concerned, it is well for both parties to revert to the established mode of settlement. We are compelled to push through a test case anyway against someone, and there is nothing in our former affidavits in this case which will do us harm or embarrass us when the case comes up for regular trial. Although I entered upon the negotiations without enthusiasm, I have endeavored in good faith to reach a mutually satisfactory basis of settlement and disarranged my plan to give you time to consider the matter carefully. . . . I must consider the negotiation at an end unless you do something at once.[4]

He did do something. Curtiss entered a race at Rheims, France, with a new plane, the *Rheims Racer*, with an 8-cylinder 50-horsepower motor and ailerons on the wings. It was light, maneuverable, and fast. The day of the race, Curtiss learned that the Wrights had filed a patent-infringement suit against the Herring-Curtiss Corporation and the Aeronautical Society in New York and himself in Buffalo. Curtiss quipped, "I should like to ask the Wrights if they really believe my machine is an infringement of their patents. It is quite absurd to say."[5] Curtiss raced his plane and won, thereby becoming the fastest man on Earth and in the air. Quentin Roosevelt, President Theodore Roosevelt's youngest son, congratulated Curtiss and told him his victory was "bully." "The Star-Spangled Banner" played at the field in France. The Wright brothers, on the same day, had Curtiss's wife served papers in Hammondsport.[6] In their view, Curtiss had won at Rheims with technology stolen from them.

Curtiss returned from France as an American hero being sued by two other American icons. The papers made little note of it until Wilbur Wright and Glenn Curtiss ended up in hangars side by side on Governors Island, preceding flights to Grant's Tomb in New York and back. Wilbur saw this as a chance to demonstrate to the world who the real inventors of flight and the real aviators were. Curtiss made a point of strolling into the hangar with the Wright plane and chatting with Wilbur.

Newspapers reported that they discussed Curtiss's win at Rheims and that "no ill feeling exists because of the suit which the Wright brothers have brought against the Herring-Curtiss Corporation for alleged infringement of patents. Wright asked Curtiss if he found the information given him by the Wrights before he sailed of any value to him. Mr. Curtiss replied that he had and they exchanged further pleasantries."[7]

But Grover Loening, an engineering student who ended up working for the Wrights and who was allowed into the hangars, overheard things not intended for the press. In his eyes, it was all a lie: "Wilbur was furious at this controversy and openly despised Curtiss and was convinced he was not only faking but doing so with a cheap scheme to hurt the Wrights and here on this very occasion was the first public appearance of that vicious hatred and rivalry between the Wright and Curtiss camps."[8]

Loening saw Curtiss as merely a promotor and cited a moment when he asked Curtiss about the tail assembly of his plane, where Curtiss answered offhandedly, "Oh I don't know but if it isn't right the boys will fix it."[9] Loening saw this as further evidence that Curtiss was a not a real aviator but a walking publicity stunt. Wilbur, on the other hand, would have explained in detail about the tail, and then some. Loening went further and recalled that "one of the interesting things about Wilbur . . . was the hours of practice he would put in on the controls of the plane, sitting in the seat, hangar doors all closed, no one around, quietly sitting there imagining air disturbances and maneuvers and correcting the rudder and warping wings and elevator to suit."[10]

Wilbur understood the danger of flying, and so he practiced. Curtiss was an intuitive flier who was always onto the next thing, faster, better, bigger. Loening recalled what it was like to fly the early planes and gave more understanding as to why Wilbur would practice in a closed hangar:

The modern aviator has no conception of what those early planes were like. The stability was nil—flying them felt like sitting on the top of an inverted pendulum ready to fall off on either side at any moment. The speed range was nothing at all. High speed, landing speed, climbing speed were all within one or two miles an hour, because the planes got off into the air with no reserve whatever, and only because of the effect of the ground banking up of which was not then understood. . . . Turns had to be carefully negotiated because the excess power was so low that the plane would often sink dangerously near the tree tops.[11]

A fog rolled in, and Curtiss took off the next day for Grant's Tomb, but no one saw him make his flight. Loening, among others, said he was lying about having made the flight to Grant's Tomb and back. "Curtis never got off the ground," he later wrote. "The required run into the wind would have brought him right by where I stood. . . . Also Curtiss never could, in my opinion in that morning fog, again have located the landing area on the island."[12] The press didn't pick up on it, but Curtiss had wheeled his plane back to the hangar and left for his hotel.

Wilbur saw an opportunity and took off. He flew around Long Island to test the winds, then flew to the Statue of Liberty and circled the beacon of liberty, then banked over the giant ocean liner *Lusitania* as thousands cheered and foghorns echoed off the skyscrapers. Wilbur then made another flight up the Hudson River and then shot back to Governors Island. There are many famous photographs of his flight, and they are the earliest pictures of a plane over a major American city. People in New York stared up in wonder at the plane that had a canoe tied underneath. The canoe was there in case Wilbur was forced to land on water. For the first time, the publicity-hungry Curtiss was pushed off the papers and Wilbur was declared the king of aviation.

Then the Herring-Curtiss Corporation descended into chaos when, in an October board meeting, Herring was ordered to produce the patents that he had previously told Curtiss he had in his possession. During a recess, Herring snuck off with his lawyer and hightailed it to New York. The company was broke, and their only chance was to sell some airplanes in order to remain solvent. Then came the sheriff, who knocked on the doors of the Herring-Curtiss Corporation. A district-court judge had granted an injunction "enjoining the Herring-Curtiss Corporation and Glenn Curtiss and Augustus Herring personally from selling or flying airplanes for profit."[13]

It was a death knell for Curtiss. Generally, defendants in patent suits can continue to do business. Here, however, US District Judge John R. Hazel was "preempting the decision, effectively putting Curtiss out of business in advance, denying him the opportunity to sell his airplanes and thereby perpetuate the income stream necessary to defend himself in court."[14] The decision put all airplane manufacturers on notice of potential litigation, but it put Glenn Curtiss out of business.

Curtiss sat in his office and shook his head. He really didn't understand Wilbur Wright. How could he claim for himself that which came from the air? When Curtiss built his first motorcycle, he didn't claim that technology for himself. He would never think of it. Something that came to him in the dust and grime of his own shop was not his. It belonged to everyone. Wilbur wanted to claim what really belonged to God, the divine inspiration of the heavens. If man was to fly, he could not be paying a toll every time he ascended to the skies. That simply wasn't fair; and now the Wrights were trying to put him out of business. Glenn sat in his quiet office and shook his head again. He had to find some way around the Wright patent if he was ever to make a living again.

WARPED BY THE DESIRE
FOR GREAT WEALTH—1911

27

I t burned deep down in his stomach. He had been wronged. The world had wronged him again, much like it had wronged him as a young man, when absolute evil took away his life. Wilbur went to bed thinking about it, and it was the first thing that occupied his thoughts in the morning. It was the itch that couldn't be scratched. The legal process was like that. It moved at a glacial pace. And even though he and his brother had been granted the patent, he still believed that Glenn Curtiss and others were stealing from him.

Wilbur had visions of himself in court, dressing down Glenn Curtiss, many times. In his fantasy, he would shame Curtiss in front of the world. That would give him satisfaction. He nodded as he sat in the darkened hangar in his airplane. He moved the elevator and then the wing warping and rudder control. He envisioned one problem after another. He thought of down drafts, bumpy air, rain, the engine dying, dips, ascending, descending, turning, taking off, and landing. He went through it all in a silent pantomime. But this time he wasn't thinking of flying; he was thinking of Glenn Curtiss, and he felt the pain down in his stomach. He felt the headache, the gritting of his teeth. It happened whenever he thought about the way people were stealing from him.

That is what Curtiss was doing. He was stealing his money by stealing his patent. He was taking what he had invented and using it to make money and not paying a licensing fee or royalties. He had just told Curtiss that they would settle in court, but everywhere he looked now he saw infringement. It was not only that Curtiss was stealing from him; really, anyone who flew a plane was stealing from him. The judge said it. Anyone who flew an airplane was using his technology, his three axes of control that encompassed an elevator, wing warping, and a hinged rudder that moved in tandem with the

208

wings. Everyone owed him licensing fees and royalties, and yet hardly anyone was paying him.

Take Curtiss, who had asked his price in a letter. Wilbur gave him a fair licensing fee of $1,000 per plane sold and $100 on every event where he flew a plane. That was fair, but Curtiss wouldn't even do that; and, even though he had an injunction against his company, Curtiss kept forming other companies with other people to get around Wilbur. They just had to launch another suit when he tried to say that separately controlled ailerons were not derivative of Wright technology. It was all a lie, and Curtiss knew it.

Wilbur sat in the darkness. He hated the feeling of being a victim. Just three years before, in Le Mans, close to Paris, in 1908, Wilbur had proved to the world that he had invented the first machine capable of flight. The French were the first to recognize his accomplishment—even before his own country. This was after the plane had been nearly destroyed by customs officials and he had to take two months to rebuild the machine, during which he was scalded by radiator steam. Then he flew at Le Mans, and the world stood at attention. The crowds kept coming to Le Mans by train and automobile and from increasingly farther distances. "Every day there is a crowd of people not only from the neighborhood," Wilbur reported to Orville, who was still recovering from injuries sustained in his crash at Fort Meyer, "but also from almost every country in Europe."[1] He would fly for over 200,000 people in the end.[2] He flew with women, men, princes, and millionaires. They all wanted to have their picture taken with him. He had become an international celebrity, and for once the world stood at moral attention in recognition of his accomplishment.

At the Aéro-Club de France's banquet, he received the gold medal and a prize of 5,000 francs. It was a celebration of Wilbur, not Orville. This was the man who had flown; and, to the world, this man had invented the airplane. As Major Baden Fletcher Smyth Baden-Powell wrote after flying with Wilbur, "Mr. Wright, with both hands grasping the levers, watches every move, but his movements are so slight as to be almost imperceptible. . . . All the time the engine is buzzing so loudly and the propellers humming so that after the trip one is almost deaf."[3]

The Wright brothers were mentioned in the press, but the French looked upon Wilbur as the man who had flown. Louis Barthou, the minster of public works, said in a speech at the Aéro-Club banquet, "Mr. Wright is a man who has never been discouraged even in the face of hesitation and suspicion."[4] It had the feel of the Western Society of Engineers in Chicago, where people listened to the man who had gone down to Kitty Hawk and were barely aware of his brother. Then Wilbur rose and addressed the crowd. After thanking the French for his warm reception, he gave his own vision of man's quest to fly: "I sometimes think that the desire to fly after the fashion of birds is an ideal handed down to us by our ancestors who, in their grueling travels across the trackless lands in prehistoric times, looked enviously on the birds soaring freely through space, at full speed, above all obstacles, on the infinite highway of the air.... Once again, I thank you with all my heart and in thanking you I should like it understood that I am thanking all of France."[5]

And then he was toasted, written about, celebrated, and feted from one ceremony to another. Kings came to see him fly, as did princes and other royalty. Then his sister came over with Orville, and he took her for a seven-minute ride on a cold February day. When asked if she felt like a bird, she replied, "I don't know exactly how a bird feels. Birds sing... but like the birds I sang best when the flight was over."[6]

France changed everything for Wilbur. David McCullough wrote in *The Wright Brothers*, "At Le Mans and Pau he had flown far more than anyone ever had and set every record for distance, speed, altitude, time in the air, and made the first flights ever with a passenger and all this after so many years of the near secrecy.... The whole world now knew."[7] And he had made $200,000 between contracts and prizes. The four months he spent in Europe had portended only good things on the horizon. In this moment, people saw the inventor of the airplane, and Wilbur Wright doffed his hat to their praise.

But this was now years ago, and since then he had become increasingly bitter at the turn of events. In France alone factories were opening rapidly to produce airplanes. As Lawrence Goldstone cited in *Birdmen*, "On April 25 the *New York Times* reported that no less than fifteen factories were now in operation" in the United States and France.[8] Wilbur hated feeling like people were reaching into his pocket and stealing the diamond he had found down at Kitty Hawk. He alone had risked everything. He alone had flown down in Kill Devil Hills and fought the elements and froze and baked and walked through the pouring rain while pulling a glider with his brother. He alone had emerged out of a three-year depression and pursued flying like a man possessed. He alone had written almost five hundred letters to Octave Chanute to work out all of the mind-numbing data that had to be changed.

He had built the wind tunnel when he realized that the data was wrong and he would have to start over. He had designed a motor lighter than anyone else could have manufactured, and he alone had flown when no one else could. No one had suffered like he had. He had put his business on hold and had tracked down the men of science who could help him, from the Smithsonian to Octave Chanute, and now they wanted to take it all from him.

He had tamed the air and learned control when no one else could. *It was his.* The judge confirmed this, but Curtiss didn't respect that. A man like Curtiss just wanted to steal from him and, what's more, he would never stop stealing. Asserting and maintaining ownership of his own ideas was like trying to contain water in his hands—it just kept slipping through his fingers.

Wilbur sat in the darkness of the hangar. Where was the great payoff? When could he relax and enjoy the fruits of his discovery? He was consumed with business. He now thought back on Kitty Hawk, which had the quality of a dream. Everything was right there. The world was clear while he methodically experimented and worked out the mechanics of flying through the air. There he could control events just as he had learned to control an airplane in the sky. But now nothing was in his control.

He had returned to Kitty Hawk on April 10, 1908. Five years had passed since 1903, and Wilbur had breathed in the scent of the ocean and felt the stress slithering off his limbs. "Went down to camp . . . found things pretty well wrecked," he later wrote in his diary.[9] "The side walls of the old building still stand but the roof and north end are gone. . . . I strike various relics of the 1901, 1902, 1903 machines. A few months ago some boys stopped at the camp and ripped the cloth on the 1902 surfaces and ripped up our cots. The floors of both buildings are a foot under the sand. Two of the carbide cans are still on hand."

Returning to his Eden, Wilbur must have marveled at how far he had come and how the world had changed since then. The lawsuits and endless rounds of meetings and patent fights had replaced the clear days of a single dream to fly. Wilbur now sat in the plane, in the darkness of the hangar. The suits would drag on and on. Curtiss would never settle. Every time Wilbur thought he had him, he melted away. It didn't matter that that crook Herring had run out on Curtiss and his company was in receivership. It didn't matter that he was broke and had a federal injunction on his company. The man continued to fly, continued to find backers, and continued to humiliate him with his flouting of his patent. The worst was that Curtiss won the races and made improvements on planes using *their technology*, and the press ate it up and put him on the front pages of the paper. Wilbur believed Curtiss was doing nothing less than stealing the Wrights' moment in history. The injunction should have destroyed Curtiss, but it had not. He simply wouldn't die. [10]

His teacher and mentor had turned on him as well. Chanute had said Wilbur was greedy and questioned his legal suits: "I think the Wrights have made a blunder in bringing suit at this time. Not only will this antagonize very many persons but it may disclose some prior patents which will invalidate their more important claims."[11] They said Wilbur was impeding the progress of aviation in America. The people who didn't want to pay said that. He wasn't impeding anything. He just wanted what was his due. He had invented the airplane. He had cracked the sky, and people were profiting from his work, his toil, and his intellectual drive that had solved the hard questions. No one even knew the correct lift coefficients before he fixed them. They were all wrong! Wrong! And if he had not built his wind tunnel and worked out the new coefficients, then men would still be flying off cliffs and hills and crashing to the earth without any idea why they flew or why they crashed. He had broken the code, but no one wanted to pay for his efforts.

Then Octave Chanute accused him of pursuing wealth in the protection of his patent. Chanute said wing warping was an ancient art that had been invented in France and that Wilbur had merely perfected it. In a letter to an editor of the *World*, Wilbur wrote, "We have repeatedly acknowledged our indebtedness to the Chanute double decker for our ideas regarding the best way of obtaining the strongest and lightest sustaining surfaces. But it is an absolute mistake that he suggested the warping tip idea. We were using the warping tip long before we made Mr. Chanute's acquaintance."[12]

Wilbur felt he had developed the system of control that every plane used, and he wanted his due. It was the principle, not greed. Chanute didn't believe Wilbur had invented something original. Wilbur suspected that Chanute could never really accept that he was able to discover what his mentor could not. "The *New York World* has published several articles in the past few months in which you represented as saying that our claim to have been the first to maintain lateral balance by adjusting the wing tips to different angles of incidence cannot be maintained, as this idea was well known in the art when we began our experiments," he wrote Chanute in 1910.[13] "I do not know if this is newspaper talk or whether it really represents your present views."

Chanute then fired back a letter that would drive a permanent wedge between pupil and mentor, friend and teacher. It was the coup de grace as far as Wilbur was concerned. Chanute wrote:

When I gave you a copy of the [Louis Pierre] Mouillard patent in 1901 I think I called your attention to his method of twisting the rear of the wings. If the courts will decide that the purpose and results were entirely different and that you were the first to conceive the twisting of the wings, so much the better for you, but my judgement is you will be restricted to the particular method by which you do it . . . This is still my opinion and I am afraid, my friend, your usually sound judgement has been warped by the desire for great wealth.[14]

This arrow went straight to the heart. Chanute then took umbrage to the impression Wilbur had given to several newspapers that the old scientist had sought him out:

In your speech at the Boston dinner, January 12th, you began by saying that I "turned up" at your shop in Dayton in 1901 and that you then invited me to your camp. This conveyed the impression that I thrust myself upon you at that time and it omitted to state that you were the first to write me, in 1900 asking for information which was gladly furnished, that many letters passed between us and that both in 1900 and 1901 you had written to invite me to visit you, before I "turned up" in 1901. This coming subsequently to some somewhat disparaging remarks concerning the helpfulness I may have been to you.[15]

Wilbur, clearly stung, responded immediately.

Neither in 1901, nor in the five years following, did you in any way intimate to us that our general system of lateral control had long been part of the art. . . . As to the inordinate desire for wealth, you are the only person acquainted with us who has ever made such an accusation. . . . You apparently concede to us no right to compensation for the solution of a problem ages old except such as granted to persons who had no part in producing the invention. . . . When I went to France I found everywhere an impression that we had taken up aeronautical studies at your special instigation; that we obtained our first experience on one of your machines; that we

were pupils of yours and put into material form a knowledge furnished by
you, that you provided the funds, in short, that you furnished the science
and money while we contributed a little mechanical skill.

He then fired his final salvo at his teacher:

We also have had grievances extending back as far as 1902 and on occasion
several years ago we complained to you that an impression was being spread
broadcast by newspapers that we were mere pupils and dependents of yours.
You indignantly denied that you were responsible for it. . . . One of the
World articles said that you felt hurt because we had been silent regarding
our indebtedness to you. I confess that I have found it most difficult to for-
mulate a precise statement of what you contributed to our success.[16]

Wilbur knew the friendship would not survive. The eclipsed mentor had
protested the lack of recognition in the development of flight, and the pupil
wanted to fly alone now and declare his independence. Neither man could be
blamed for his position, but the casualty was clearly their friendship. Herring
had come out of the woodwork and demanded compensation for his part in
the development of the 1903 *Flyer*; what that was could never be determined.
But to Wilbur, the world had become unjust and had proven that their father,
Milton, had been right all along. Only the family could be trusted; all else
was suspect, all else was evil. Evil had knocked out his teeth and broken his
jaw and sent him into the heart of darkness and on a quest to leave the earth.

Wilbur felt the pain in his stomach and stared straight ahead. He had
devoted the last twelve years of his life to the quest to fly, and it was unfair
that he should be so tormented. The world was not just. He had been treated
unfairly once again, just like his father, who had found that even the church was
corrupt. His father was right. Anyone outside the family was a potential enemy.

Wilbur gripped the control stick and went over possible scenarios in his
head. It was all about turbulence. There was no way to anticipate turbulence,
no matter how much you planned for it. It was always different. It came out of
nowhere and could throw a plane to the ground or cause a tail spin or a stall,
or even knock a pilot out of the plane. Wilbur stared into the darkness of the
closed hangar as he went over scenarios and moved the stick and the elevator.
No matter how much you planned, the fact of the matter was that an errant
wind could still kill you.

FINAL FLIGHT—1912

Wilbur was flying again. He was out over the dunes of Kitty Hawk and looking down at the two sheds he and Orville had built. He could smell the ocean, and felt the rising heat. Now he was riding the thermals, rising up like the hawks he had observed. He turned off the engine and could see the ocean and the Albemarle Sound he had crossed with Israel Perry in 1900 and nearly drowned. He was banking now and soaring with the gulls and the eagles in an updraft. He was happy again. He was back at Kitty Hawk, and when he landed he would have some biscuits and coffee and discuss the flight with Orville and make adjustments. Maybe they would sleep in the tent for old time's sake. But now, now he was going higher than he had ever been before, in fact, he was leaving the earth. He felt like he could fly forever.

The premature death of Wilbur Wright would have far-reaching implications. He had been steadily getting run down by the incessant legal demands. As Tom Crouch wrote in *The Bishop's Boys*, "He was constantly on the move from mid-December 1911 through the early spring of 1912, shuttling back and forth between New York and Dayton in an attempt to deal with the Grahame-White, Lamson, Winkley and Herring-Curtiss suits."[1] Orville would later recall that his brother "would come white" after court appearances and long hours with his lawyers. It was his quest, his plane, and Wilbur would do whatever it took to protect what he had discovered in the sands of Kitty Hawk.

It was May 4, 1912, when Wilbur had shellfish in a hotel in Boston and didn't feel well. He had written an angry letter to his attorney regarding the Curtiss patent suit. It had dragged on way too long and had been all-consuming for the last few years. And now his attorney wanted to wait unit the fall to begin hearings. Wilbur wrote, "Unnecessary delays have already destroyed fully three-fourths of the value of our patent. The opportunities of the last few years will never return again."[2] It was his last letter, and it is fitting that it was about the case that would not be resolved in his lifetime. He had written to a French friend, M. Hievesy, earlier in the year and revealed his understanding of the time wasted by the litigation: "We wished to be free from business cares so that we could give all our time to advancing the science and art of aviation, but we have been compelled to spend our time on business matters instead during the last five years."[3]

Four days after he returned from Boston, he was noticeably weaker. Dr. Conklin examined him and wrote, "there seems to be some sort of typhoidal fever prevailing."[4] Typhoid fever had nearly killed Orville twenty years before, and now it was coming for Wilbur. The doctors thought it might be malaria and did not see Wilbur in any immediate danger. Wilbur, as always, knew better and dictated his last will and testament. Orville caught a train back from Washington to be by his side on May 20, when he took a turn for the worse. His father, now eighty-four years old, began recording his forty-five-year-old son's condition in his diary.

On May 15, Bishop Wright wrote, "Wilbur has not a high fever as some days, Roosevelt spoke in Dayton tonight, and Orville went to hear him, but was crowded and heard a suffragette instead. . . ." Then he wrote on May 16, "Fever is unchanged. Orville left for Washington City." May 18: "Wilbur is no better, he has an attack mentally for the worse. He is put under opiates. He is unconscious mostly." May 19: "Wilbur asks to take opiates, but is mostly quiet and unconscious." May 20: "Dr. Spitler came afternoon and at night with Dr. B. Conklin. Wilbur's case very serious, he notices little." May 23: "The *Journal* represents Wilbur as changed for the worse . . . he seems about the same."

May 24: "Wilbur seems better in every respect . . . the doctors have a long examination before noon." May 26: "Wilbur was worse in the night, Orville slept little." May 27: "His fever was higher and he has difficulty with the bladder and his digestion inadequate. . . . I slept with my clothes on. We thought him near death. He lived through till morning." May 28: "Wilbur is sinking the doctors have no hope of his recovery."

Then, finally, May 29: "Wilbur seemed no worse, though he had a bad chill. The fever was down but rose high. He remained the same till 3:15 in the morning when, eating his allowance 15 minutes before his death, he expired without a struggle. His life was one of toil."

Wilbur died on May 30 at 3:15 in the morning. He would not escape the clutches of typhoid fever the way his brother had. It might have been the fact that he was older or tired, or it might have just been fate. Milton wrote in his diary, "A short life, full of consequence. An unfailing intellect, imperturbable temper, great self-reliance, and as great modesty, seeing the right clearly, pursuing it steadily, he lived and died."[5]

A thousand telegrams poured in. Newspapers cleared their front pages with bold headlines, "INVENTOR OF THE AIRPLANE, FATHER OF FLIGHT, DEATH OF CONQUEROR OF THE AIR, THE MAN WHO MADE FLYING POSSIBLE."[6] Many of the papers declared boldly that Wilbur Wright was the true inventor of the airplane. A funeral was to be held at First Presbyterian Church. The family considered a private funeral, but the world demanded a public mourning. Twenty-five thousand people filed past his coffin. At 3:30 p.m., on June 1st, Wilbur Wright was lowered into his grave as all activity in the city ground to a halt: the switchboards shut down, the trolleys didn't move, and automobiles pulled to the curb. The inventor of human flight was being laid to rest.

Orville and Katherine pulled together; they were even more determined to fight on for their brother. They were bitter in their grief and, in a very Miltonian way, they held the world responsible for Wilbur's death, but one man in particular. Tom Crouch surmised in *The Bishop's Boys,* "They did not regard Wilbur's death as pure providence—other factors had been at work. He had been worn out by the patent fight, his energy drained and his resistance lowered. The men who had forced them into court time after time bore a share of the responsibility."[7]

To Orville Wright, Glenn Curtiss was responsible for the death of his brother. Curtiss had hoped that with the death of Wilbur Wright, things might get better; but by January 31, 1914, things got much worse. Curtiss could now hear the faucet on the factory floor. It dripped in the rhythm of the clock that ticked in his office.[8] He sat with the green shade of the desk lamp cutting just under his eyes. The cuffs of his shirt had grease painted around the edges, and his vest had dark oil stains that shone in the sunlight. He couldn't resist working on an airplane even if he was in a suit. But all that was over now.

He had just hung up with his lawyer, and the US Circuit Court of Appeals had just handed the Wrights their final victory and awarded them a pioneer patent.[9] The Hammondsport factory he had built with his own hands was dormant. His company was in bankruptcy, and now the Wrights had a pioneer patent[10] that said everyone had to pay them to use technology associated with flying.

Orville was ecstatic over the New York Court of Appeals' decision and wrote later: "Claim 3 which was for warping wings or ailerons without a rudder was sustained as I hoped. This will give us an absolute monopoly as there are no machines at the present time that do not infringe this claim. . . . Of course we will make a claim for damages done by Curtiss. . . . This covers every machine that is being flown today . . . all of them have ailerons."[11]

It was the motherlode for Orville. A pioneer's patent could not be contested, and it said that all technology associated with the patent had to be derivative of the original invention. The courts had ruled that not only were the Curtiss systems of control derivative of the Wrights' but that all aerial-control systems associated with flying came from the Wright system. Basically, if you wanted to fly, you had to get a license through Orville Wright and pay up.

Back in November 1910, Glenn had tried to work it out with Wilbur. Everyone knew he was the decision maker and the power broker. They had met before a race in Belmont, and Curtiss had asked for terms. Wilbur came back with a fee of $1,000 for every plane sold and $100 for each day Curtiss few in an exhibition. It was outrageous, and Curtiss wrote Wilbur again asking for terms. The same terms came back, and Curtiss responded, "It had been my intention to make you a counter offer but in thinking the matter over, it has occurred to me to accept a license, even at no cost to us, might not improve our condition."[12] Wilbur had written back on November 30, obviously irritated: "The negotiation was initiated at your request and now seems similarly closed by you. . . . It is well for both parties to refer to the established mode of settlement."[13] In other words, let the suit go through the courts.

Curtiss was broke in 1910, and then his company had been served again by Orville Wright with a secondary suit when he tried to get around the patent by making the ailerons a separate control. Orville's suit would win with the precedent of the pioneer patent that essentially grounded him, along with all other pilots who did not pay the Wrights a licensing fee. Curtiss had to somehow break the essence of the Wright pioneer patent, or he was doomed. He had to prove that someone else had invented the control system of the modern airplane first.

Curtiss put his feet up on the desk and stared at the photos of his various planes on the wall. If he could show that someone had flown before the Wrights—really, anyone would do—then the patent would not be valid. To hold a pioneer patent, you had to be first. His eyes settled on a picture of Samuel Pierpont Langley's plane. In the photo, the plane was on the house-boat just before it went into the Potomac. The damn thing looked like a giant bug on top of a boat. But he had flown a model aerodrome before. Curtiss stared at the picture for a long moment. The basics might have been fine, and Curtiss wondered if it had been in the execution or the launching mechanism, as Langley claimed.

Langley had died in 1906, and Charles D. Walcott had taken over as secretary of the Smithsonian. Langley had given them all a black eye when his plane nosed into the Potomac, and Curtiss knew the Smithsonian wanted to redeem its fallen hero of aviation. Walcott had gotten the army to invest $50,000, and he had heard only blame and recrimination since they fished Langley's plane out of the water. No funding was coming the way of the Smithsonian anytime soon. But if he could show that Langley's plane *could have* flown, then that would circumvent the Wright patent. If he could just get his hands on Langley's flyer. He knew Walcott either still had it or knew where it was. But he couldn't be obvious. He needed a third party to approach the Smithsonian.

Curtis picked up the phone and gave the operator a number. He picked up a pencil and flipped it into the garbage can across his office. This was why he was a good pilot—he had very good reflexes.

THE GREAT FLOOD—1914

The wooden crates in the shed behind the bike shop in Dayton looked like nothing. They were not marked, and they had been there for eleven years. The shed held bicycle parts, bicycles, wheels, tires, and tools. The large wooden crates were an imposition, really. They were bulky and took up a lot of the space. The floor of the shed offered no real protection against the elements. Occasionally, rain leaked down onto the crates from the roof. The men who had put the crates in the shed had long forgotten them. Wilbur had died in 1912, and Orville was busy. The crates with sand in the bottom from Kitty Hawk in 1903 remained silently moldering.

Floodwaters had rampaged through Dayton six times before, but on March 23, 1914, the worst flood was yet to come. The rain began and didn't stop. Dayton was a floodplain between the Miami, Mad, and Stillwater Rivers. And there was Wolf Creek, which added its own water to the torrent of floodwater racing through Dayton. The streets of Dayton became their own rivers, and then the Laramie Reservoir earthen dam collapsed and the levee at Stratford Avenue was breached. A wall of water was headed for the Wright home and bike shop.

Orville and Katherine had left their home on Hawthorne Avenue that morning and found it impossible to return. Their father was trapped.[1] They spent the night at a friend's house but were unable to contact their father. Phones were down, and fires had broken out all over the city from broken gas mains. A lurid glow was in the sky as the water rose steadily higher.[2] Hawthorne Street and other low-lying areas of Dayton were under eight feet of water. Orville was worried about his father, but he had other worries as well. As Tom Crouch pointed out in *The Bishop's Boys*, "The priceless photographic negatives of the flying machine experiments of 1900–1905 were in the old shed at the rear of the house. Letters, diaries, and other records of inventions of the airplane were stored in the second floor at the bicycle shop on Third Street where the water was said to be over twelve feet."[3] And then there were the crates in the shed behind the bike shop. These gave him the most concern of all, for in those crates was the 1903 *Wright Flyer*—the plane that had made human flight possible.

Bishop Wright was rescued, along with his neighbor Mrs. Wagner, by a man with a canoe. Orville and Katherine returned to devastation the next morning. The lives of 371 people had been lost, and property damage was estimated at $100 million.[4] A reporter later described the damage of the direct hit that Dayton had taken:

> The streets are seas of yellow ooze. Garden fences and hedges are twisted or torn away. Reeking heaps of indescribable refuse lie moldering where there were smooth lawns and bright flower beds. The houses that stand are all smeared with dirt that shows the height of the flood. But inside the houses, that is the dreadful thing. The rooms that the water filled are like damp caves. Mud lies thick on the floors, the walls are streaked with slime, and the paper hangs down in dismal festoons. . . . But the worst is the reek of death about the place.[5]

Orville went directly to the bicycle shop, which had been underwater. The glass-plate negatives had survived; a few of them had been damaged, but all were salvageable. The most important one, the photo taken by John Daniels showing the 1903 *Flyer* lifting off from the sand at Kitty Hawk on December 17, had been underwater but survived with slight damage. But what of the *Flyer* itself? Orville left the bicycle shop and saw the low shed. A thick mud encased the building and he had to scoop it away to get the door open.

The mud had entered the structure and covered the crates. Orville got down on his knees and scooped the muck off and pulled out the first crate. He opened it and stared down at the fabric-covered wings. Amazingly, the mud had acted as an insulator and kept the water out of the crates. The fabric was damp and the wood was wet, but it was undamaged. The only plane the Wright brothers had saved had been in danger of being swept away forever, but the 1903 *Flyer* had survived to fly one more time, in the Wright brothers' biggest battle yet to come.

Orville and his secretary, Mabel Beck, tirelessly dried out the old *Flyer* in his laboratory and stretched the canvas over the frame. To Mabel, the canvas smelled of time and sand.[6] In 1925, the *Flyer* would be unpacked again for a very different reason. Mabel at that time would write, "the original cloth was in bad shape, very frail and worn. . . . Mr. Wright decided to recover the machine with new cloth. . . . Mr. Wright and I laid out and cut all the cloth, and I did the sewing."[7] She worked alongside Orville, for hours and hours. The smell of the ocean had come into the room, and sand collected on the floor. At the end of the day, Mabel brushed away the grit of history. She had never seen the ocean and wondered about the place Orville talked about many times—Kitty Hawk. The name sounded like a magic bird to her.[8]

TO FLY AGAIN—1914

Eight days after the Wrights were declared victorious in the US Circuit Court, Charles D. Walcott sat behind his desk in the Smithsonian and stared at the telegram on his desk with the attached note from the Smithsonian administrator, Richard Rathbun. The telegram was from the famous American stunt pilot Lincoln J. Beachey, who was closely allied with Glenn Curtiss, though Walcott had no way of knowing this. Beachey had flown at the Curtiss school, had been a performer on the Curtiss exhibition team, and was a Curtiss stockholder.

He had wired the Smithsonian "requesting to borrow the surviving parts of the 1903 aerodrome so that he could rebuild and fly the craft."[1] It was a strange request for the Langley flyer of 1903 that had gone down like a rock into the Potomac River. The flyer had been fished out of the river and hung from the side of the houseboat. From there it had been put into permanent storage; everyone wanted to forget the disaster that had cost both the Smithsonian and Langley their reputations.

Walcott had vouched for Langley and cajoled the government into giving him the fifty thousand dollars. When the flyer went down twice, that was it. He took over as secretary of the Smithsonian in 1906, and immediately he tried to resurrect Langley's tarnished, if not destroyed, reputation. He had the Langley Memorial Tablet put into the wall of the Smithsonian castle. He then established the Samuel P. Langley Medal for Aerodromics, and later he created the Langley Laboratory for aeronautical research. He even proclaimed the day in 1896 when the first steam-powered aerodrome models had flown as Langley Day, an official holiday for the Smithsonian.[2]

None of it worked. There were no funds coming for research anytime soon. Langley was a black eye. Just eight days prior, the Wrights had been declared pioneer patent holders for airplane-control systems, thereby making Orville and Wilbur Wright the patriarchs of modern aviation. It was over, really, until . . . this.

Walcott picked up the telegram and then looked at Rathbun's recommendation: "I do not think you want to grant Mr. Beachey's request."[3] There was another note, from Alexander Graham Bell, cautioning against trying to do anything with the flyer since it was too valuable an artifact. "An artifact of what?" Walcott almost muttered. Failure. Disgrace. Reputations ruined. It was an artifact alright, down in the dungeon of the Smithsonian, never to be seen again.

Walcott leaned back in his chair and smoothed his beard. That valuable artifact was a cross he and the Smithsonian had to bear ever since the great dunk in the Potomac. It was really a fascinating idea. Fly the Langley aerodrome and prove to the world that Langley had the technology to fly first, and that he should have taken the honors given to Wilbur and Orville Wright. Samuel Pierpont Langley's name could then be side by side with the Wright brothers, and the Smithsonian would be redeemed as the august center of science it once was.

Walcott looked at the telegram again. Still, Beachey was sort of a loose cannon. Bell had suggested that an exact replica of the Langley flyer should be constructed for display. That would be something, but really it had to fly, or what was the point? He would turn Beachey down but leave the door slightly open.

The door was kicked wide open when Secretary Walcott bumped into Glenn Curtiss at a Langley Day celebration. Curtiss had brought down one of his float planes and had mentioned "that he would like to put the Langley airplane itself in the air."[4] Walcott had been pressured before by the Smithsonian regents and Bell not to release the flyer to Beachey, but this time he acted alone and consented to give the plane to Glenn Curtiss.

The secretary of the Smithsonian instructed A. F. Zahm, a Curtiss witness in the patent trial who now happened to run the Langley Laboratory, to turn over "the fuselage, engine, propellers, various bits of tubing and a few wing ribs of the old flyer to Curtiss."[5] Walcott then gave Curtiss $2,000 for improvements and testing. Zahm, who had been humiliated by Orville Wright during the trials, put out a covering statement: "The main object of these renewed trials was first to show whether the original Langley machine was capable of sustained free flight with a pilot, and secondly, to determine more fully the advantages of the tandem wing type aeroplane."[6]

The real reason was to show that Langley's plane could have flown in 1903. Everyone involved had a vested interest. "Curtiss, the Smithsonian, and Zahm all stood to benefit if the craft proved airworthy. Curtiss could return to court and argue the pioneer status granted the Wrights patent was unwarranted and he could start selling planes again. Walcott would demonstrate to the world his old friend Langley had not failed after all and restore the Smithsonian's reputation as an institution worth further funding for projects. And Zahm would gain revenge on Orville for supposed slights offered to him at the patent suit in 1910."[7]

If Curtiss could get Langley's old machine to fly, then everything would work out just fine. The problem was that Walcott was not all that sure it would fly the way it had been originally designed. At the time of the two crashes, the rumor was that Langley really didn't understand lift and that some engineers said the wings could not have provided nearly enough lift for a man and a heavy engine. Walcott had heard that all Langley had done, really, was make a bigger aerodrome model and hope for the best. He was certain Curtiss would get the plane to fly one way or another. After that, he didn't really want to know anything else.

Curtiss and Zahm proclaimed that they would simply restore the Langley plane back to its original design. Nothing was further from the truth. As Tom Crouch observes in *The Bishop's Boys*, "The wings constructed in the Curtiss plant differed from the originals in chord, camber, and aspect ratio. The trussing system that linked the wings to the fuselage also bore little resemblance to the 1903 original. The kingposts had been relocated and the wires were trussed to different spars at different points. This was particularly important, for most knowledgeable authorities believed that the failure of the wing structure, not a catapult defect, had been responsible for the disaster of 1903."[8]

Then Curtiss fitted the plane with his own control system. He did away with the catapult system, put the plane on floats, and tied off the original rudder. The tail was altered to serve as both rudder and elevator, something Langley had never thought of. Now all they had to do was fly the plane and prove to the world that the Wright brothers were not the first to build an airplane capable of powered flight. The Wright brothers were the second men to build a plane capable of sustained flight after Samuel Pierpont Langley, secretary of the Smithsonian.

HAMMONDSPORT, NEW YORK—1914

Glenn Curtiss looked over the parts of the 1903 Langley flyer that had arrived that morning in wood crates stenciled *SMITHSONIAN*. It made Curtiss feel very important to be associated with the making of history. He had his workmen spread out the parts on the factory floor of the Herring-Curtiss factory. Zahm and Walcott had told Curtiss to restore the aerodrome to its 1903 condition. Curtiss could see right away that this wouldn't do if the plane was to fly. No, he would approach this plane the way he approached all planes—with one simple question: How could he make it better?

He pulled the musty parts and stared at the body of the plane. Time and the crash had done its work. Curtiss felt it should have stayed in the Potomac, but here it was. He instructed his men as he replaced the wings with new Curtiss wings that had the correct chord, camber, and aspect ratios that reflected the data Wilbur had found with his wind tunnel. He then linked the wings to the fuselage with wires trussed to different points. This was critical. Many had claimed that Langley's machine spiraled into the Potomac because not only did the wings not have enough lift, but they folded up when the catapult flung the flyer into the air. Curtiss gutted the old control system and put in a yoke-and-wheel control system based on his own planes that led directly back to the 1903 *Wright Flyer*, with the three-axes-of-control center. A large cruciform tail was added and altered to serve as rudder and elevator. Then Curtiss put the Langley flyer on floats, forever leaving the catapult system in the ash heap of aviation history.[1]

He and his men stepped back from the aerodrome and surveyed their work. It was maybe 30 percent 1903 technology and 70 percent 1914. It was time to see if it would fly. On May 28, 1914, Curtiss sat in the aerodrome on

Lake Keuka, with the water slopping over the floats. It was early morning, which was better for avoiding the press. He pushed up the throttle all the way and felt the plane start skimming across the water. Curtiss eased back the elevator, and the Langley aerodrome left the earth for the first time under its own power and flew 150 feet. The plane splashed back down. Curtiss shook his head. It just didn't have the power. He tried a few more times, but each time the plane barely lifted off. He had the plane taken back to his plant, where he finished the job by replacing the 1903 engine with a modern Curtiss engine with twice the horsepower. He also made some changes to the structure of the plane to improve its aerodynamics. Only the fuselage was original when Curtiss finished. Curtiss went back to the lake for several more flights that were longer in duration. None of the flights were sustainable, but it was enough that the Langley flyer flew.

It was at this time that Orville Wright's older brother Lorin Wright stepped off the train in Hammondsport. Orville had asked him to help protect their invention, and Lorin was willing to do his part to protect his brother's honor and reputation. He was doing this for Orville, but he was doing it for Wilbur too. If Wilbur had been there, he would have taken care of Glenn Curtiss once and for all. But Wilbur was gone and so it was left to Lorin to protect the family name.[2]

It was a beautiful morning as he took a cab to the Curtiss hangars on Lake Keuka's shore. He felt like a secret agent. He was carrying a small camera and knew what had to be done. After an Englishman named Griffith Brewer met the brothers in 1908 and had flown with Wilbur at Le Mans, he had the distinction of being the first Englishman to fly. Brewer had spent three months with Orville in Dayton and had learned about the Smithsonian and Glenn Curtiss, they realized what had happened. Griffith had taken a tour of the Curtiss factory after Orville told him that the Smithsonian had snubbed the Wrights in 1910 by refusing the offer of their plane for exhibition and had given people the impression that they were heavily dependent on the research of Langley for their 1903 *Wright Flyer*.[3]

Then Orville told him the story of Curtiss and the Langley aerodrome and asked him if he would request a tour of the Hammondsport facility to see what he could find out. Griffith took the tour and found out that the 1903 aerodrome had been heavily altered so that it could fly. He took photographs and forwarded them to Orville. That's when Orville asked his brother Lorin to find evidence of the alterations to the Langley plane and the results of the trials.

The taxi let Lorin off on a rain-soaked tarmac. He looked around, then walked straight toward an open hangar and immediately saw the aerodrome. He took some pictures. In his writing about the events there is a natural drama to his narrative. "I arrived at Hammondsport about one o'clock Friday afternoon June 4th. Went immediately to Curtiss training camp on the lake shore near the village," Lorin wrote in a memorandum.[4] "I found three Curtiss boat machines containing the controls and one which had the wings removed. I also saw the so-called Langley machine which they were preparing to give a trial. Mechanic told me it would be tried Friday evening if the wind died down."[5]

The next morning, June 5, he watched with binoculars from a field as the Langley aerodrome was tested on the lake: "The distance from the launching place I think was about 600 feet. . . . About ten o'clock Mr. Walter Johnson mounted the machine and started the motor. The machine gradually speed[ed up] and after running as near as I could judge 1000 ft the rear wings broke."[6] The wings had folded up during the trial as Curtiss pilot Walter Johnson attempted to take off. He had gone only 330 yards when the plane fell apart. Lorin went back to the hangar when Johnson came in with the soggy aerodrome. Orville's brother began to snap more pictures.

Johnson, still wet from the lake, demanded his film. Johnson was a small, pugnacious man who looked like he might take a swing. Lorin later wrote, "I took four pictures of the machine when some of the workman noted the fact and notified Mr. Johnson. He demanded that I should give up the films. At first, I refused and started to leave the grounds. Mr. Johnson and several others left the machine and came running up to me demanding the films, saying that they could not allow any pictures of the wrecked machine to be made."[7]

It was here that violence started to creep in. In Lorin's camera was proof that the altered Langley plane still couldn't fly, and the futures of Langley, Walcott, and Curtiss were riding on the contents of the Wright brother's camera: "At this juncture a man who I am informed was Mr. Henry Weyman came up and apparently took charge of the situation. He insisted that I should not leave the grounds until I had delivered up my pack of films. I asked him why. He replied because of legal complications they wanted no pictures of the machine in its present condition to get out."[8]

At that point, Lorin Wright was surrounded by men who were not letting him leave. It was incredible to think that the brother of Wilbur and Orville Wright, who was holding proof of a fraud being perpetrated against the history of flight, a company, the holders of a patent, and in a sense the American people, was being held against his will. Lorin liked the idea of a being a secret agent, but he was really just a family man. "I finally yielded the film pack and he insisted on supplying me with another to replace it. I insisted that he should not but he sent a boy on a wheel uptown and in a few minutes the boy returned with a pack."[9] The contest of wills became intertwined here, and the situation became even more dangerous. Mr. Weyman insisted that Lorin take the replacement film. "I refused and Mr. Weyman laid the pack on my knee. (I had gone over and sat down on the edge of the runway.) I laid the pack down on the runway and left it there."[10]

Clearly Weyman wanted no one to be able to say that he stole Lorin Wright's film. He had merely replaced it. This ominous standoff ended, and Lorin reported back to Orville that the aerodrome was in the process of being heavily altered so it would fly. Orville thanked him and pondered on what to do. The Smithsonian was intent on rewriting history with a clear message to the world. In this alternate narrative being written by the Smithsonian, the Wrights may have been the first to fly, but Langley had been capable of doing it before them. If such a fabrication went public, it would destroy their pioneer status as patent holders and, worse, distort the history of flight for all time. He must do something that would make Walcott and the Smithsonian sorry they had ever cooked up this scheme to defraud both him and Wilbur. It had to be something that would put the issue front and center and would make the world take notice.

When Curtiss returned to his factory, he called Secretary Walcott and A. F. Zahm and let them know that the tests were a great success. They were overjoyed and lost no time in publishing the results of the tests in the 1914 Smithsonian *Annual Report*. Zahm led off by claiming that "with its original structure and power, the 1903 Aerodrome is capable of flying with a pilot and several hundred pounds of useful load. It is the first airplane in history of which this can be truthfully said."[11] Zahm followed up by reporting that the Langley flyer had flown "without modification." He concluded by saying, "the Langley aerodrome without floats, restored to its original condition and provided with stronger bearings, should be able to carry a man and sufficient supplies for a voyage lasting the whole day."[12]

A year after, a 1915 report finished the job by stating, "the tests thus far made have shown that former Secretary Langley had succeeded in building the first airplane capable of sustained free flight with a man."[13] In other words, Wilbur Wright and his brother Orville would no longer be the first men to build a plane capable of heavier-than-air flight with an engine. Samuel Langley had beaten them to the punch. If the 1903 Langley flyer was a bullet, then the Wright brothers' legacy was the target. Their pioneer patent would certainly be in danger.

Curtis then shipped the Langley aerodrome back from Hammondsport, and Walcott quietly had it returned to its original 1903 condition and had it exhibited in the Arts and Industries Building with a label, "The First Man-Carrying Aeroplane in the History of the World Capable of Sustained Free Flight."[14] The cover-up was complete. Walcott had his trophy that would rescue not only his reputation but also the Smithsonian's and Langley's. He never thought Orville Wright might object, and who cared if they did? The Wright family could not really do anything. They could still say the Wright brothers were the first men to fly; they just couldn't say that they had invented the first airplane. Langley and the Smithsonian had done that.

The fix was in, and Walcott could now claim that Langley had been vindicated and by proxy his and the Smithsonian's reputations were restored. No longer would there be derision when Langley's aerodrome was spoken of. Now Langley had been the man who had solved the problem of flight, and the proof was on display at the Smithsonian. And for Glenn Curtiss, it was a dagger to the heart of the sanctimonious Wright brothers and their claim to a pioneer patent.

Walcott was only too glad he had turned down the Wright offer to display the 1903 *Flyer* years before in 1910. Now there was the Langley flyer saying that here was the plane that had solved the problem of manned flight. He would eventually put the 1903 *Wright Flyer* in the Smithsonian; he was sure Orville Wright would donate it, since he had already offered the *Flyer* to the Smithsonian once before.

When in 1915 the Massachusetts Institute of Technology asked to exhibit the 1903 *Flyer*, Orville and Jim Jacobs, who worked for the Wright Company, began to put the old flyer back together. They used new material only when absolutely necessary and fixed the damage the wind gust had caused when John Daniels was thrown off his feet. The year after Walcott put Langley's plane on display in the Smithsonian, claiming it was the first airplane capable of flight, "the world's first airplane was displayed at MIT on June 11–13, 1916."[15]

Walcott immediately requested to have the Wright machine displayed at the Smithsonian as well, but Orville did not even consider the request. The Smithsonian was sticking by the Hammondsport trials and claiming that Langley had built the world's first flyable airplane. Orville finally had a chance for revenge. The 1903 *Flyer* was exhibited at the Pan-American Aeronautical Exhibition in the Grand Central Palace in New York in 1917 and then twice in Dayton during the years 1918–1925.[16]

In 1925, Orville played his card against Walcott and the Smithsonian. If they continued to support the claim that Langley's plane had been airworthy in 1903, then they would not get the 1903 *Flyer* that was the first plane to fly, and not only would the Smithsonian lose Wilbur Wright's vision of a manned flight, but the United States as a country would lose the *Flyer*. He would send it to the Science Museum in London.[17] Secretary Walcott was sure Orville was bluffing. Surely, he would not ship away a national treasure that belonged to America.

MIDDLE OF THE
ATLANTIC OCEAN—1928

The crates down in the hold of the ship were lashed and stenciled and marked *WRIGHT FLYER*. It would take a full week to cross the Atlantic. In 1903, the *Flyer* had lifted off from the sands of Kitty Hawk. Now, twenty-five years later, it was headed for London and no one knew when it was coming back, if ever.

When in 1925 Orville had decided to ship the *Flyer* to the Science Museum in London, the crates were once again unpacked. Mabel Beck assisted in the rebuilding of the flyer once again. "Actual work was not started on the machine until December 1926,"[1] Mabel would write later. "The original cloth was in bad shape, very frail and worn from having been handled too much in setting up the machine in various exhibitions. Mr. Wright therefore decided to recover the machine with new cloth. . . . Jim Jacobs [again] was hired to do the woodwork and assembly and Mr. Wright and I laid out and cut the cloth, and I did the sewing. Jacobs later did the crating. Only the three of us had anything to do with the final work on this machine."[2]

The 1903 *Flyer* was ready to go to Britain in March 1927. It remained in Orville's laboratory for the next nine months, under the guard of Mabel Beck, who went there every day to check on it. Then, in June, Orville called her at home early one morning and told her to meet him at the laboratory. Mabel went there, and in walked Charles Lindbergh, just weeks back from his famous flight.[3] The young man stared at the 1903 *Flyer* with Orville beside him and Mabel just behind.

Orville then went to Canada for vacation that summer, and Mabel stayed with the plane. In January 1928, it was crated up and Mabel made the arrangements to have the 1903 airplane shipped to London. America demanded to know why Orville would send the 1903 *Flyer*, the plane that conquered the skies, to the Science Museum of London. He had responded with a letter.

> I believe that my course in sending our Kitty Hawk machine to a foreign museum is the only way of correcting the history of the flying machine, which by false and misleading statements has been perverted by the Smithsonian Institution. In its campaign to discredit others in the flying art, the Smithsonian has issued scores of these false and misleading statements. They can be proved to be false and misleading from documents. But the people of today do not take the trouble to examine the evidence.
>
> With this machine in any American museum the national pride would be satisfied; nothing further would be done and the Smithsonian would continue its propaganda. In a foreign museum the machine will be a constant reminder of the reasons for its being there, and after the people and the petty jealousies of this day are gone, the historians of the future may examine the evidence impartially and make history accord with it. Your regret that this machine must leave the country can hardly be so great as my own.[4]

Then the 1903 *Flyer* left for the Old World. Mabel had thought about that journey across the Atlantic ocean. It was her job to make sure the treasure of the Wright brothers arrived safely. She imagined America was far behind in the stormy gray seas that tossed the ship and stressed the ropes holding the crates. A journey to Britain took seven days. The steady thrum of the steam engines and the ship's propeller cutting the chop of the ocean vibrated through the crates and the butterfly wings inside. The ship rolled up and down and heaved to port, and then turned to starboard. The crates didn't move at all, even though the taut wires inside vibrated with the pulse of the steam turbines pushing the screws.

Mabel understood that Mr. Wright would have his revenge. The Smithsonian and Glenn Curtiss, they would all pay. He was taking his treasure, America's treasure, and leaving for the country against which America had fought for independence less than two hundred years earlier. That would show the secretary of the Smithsonian and his lackeys. Langley's machine would never have flown. This Orville knew. If the Smithsonian wanted to try to credit someone else with making the first powered flight, then London would have the prize. Mabel had taken grim pleasure in shipping the *Flyer*. Their outright lies. It was an outrage. This would teach them all.

Ms. Beck had heard there were storms out on the Atlantic. They were not unlike the nor'easters that hit Kitty Hawk. Orville had told her that he and Wilbur had survived more than a few storms, with their tent almost blown away several times. That the plane managed to fly in that wind in 1903 was simply amazing. The wind was blowing at 25 miles an hour that day, and it had been a cheek-biting 35 degrees. Orville said Wilbur would have approved of him taking their flyer away from the men who would do them harm. It was still hard to believe that his brother had been dead for sixteen years.

What Mabel didn't know about was the strange sound coming out of the cargo hold.

Some of the men heard it at night and went down to investigate. They stared at the crates marked *WRIGHT FLYER*. It was a hum, really. What they didn't know was that the strut wires inside the crates were vibrating from the engine of the ship. Wilbur would have known in a second what that hum was. . . . It was the sound of flight.

A TEST OF WILLS—1930

There was an uproar. Orville had the 1903 *Flyer* crated and sent across the ocean to the Science Museum of London. But the new secretary of the Smithsonian, Charles Greeley Abbott, was sticking to the assertion that the secretly altered 1903 Langley aerodrome had been airworthy, even though there was documented proof that it had been modified and Orville's own brother had been witness to the trials. America had lost an important piece of history to the English. Lester Gardner of *Aviation* magazine put the controversy into the public view with an article in which he wrote, "For many years it has been no secret that the original Wright airplane would not be entrusted to the Smithsonian so long as the influences that had conducted the Langley propaganda in this country were in charge. . . . But now [that] Orville Wright has decided to send it to the English Museum the public may awake to some of the damage done by the zeal of Langley's friends."[1]

Secretary Walcott, before he died, had dug in his heels and commissioned a report by Joseph Ames and David Taylor, who were members of the National Advisory Committee for Aeronautics. Although Ames and Taylor were never given a list of the changes that Curtiss made, they backed up Walcott and the Smithsonian by saying that, "structurally the original Langley machine was capable of level and controlled flight."[2] They conceded that the Wrights were the first to fly but stated that Langley, "after years of effort, following a different road, was in sight of the same goal."[3]

Orville Wright saw the report for the whitewash that it was and, in January 1928, the crated 1903 *Wright Flyer* was lifted into the hold of an ocean liner, lashed down, and stenciled. The steamship cleared New York harbor and passed the Statue of Liberty, carrying away the genius of Wilbur and the treasure of the nation.

Letters poured into the Smithsonian. Secretary Abbott developed a form letter to try to establish that the Smithsonian could not admit it was wrong when it wasn't. A lot of the letters were from children. *Why couldn't you just admit you were wrong and get Mr. Wright to bring his airplane back to America?* A lot of the letters were from teachers who complained that they could not explain to their children why the first airplane of manned flight was in London on display but not in America where the Wright brothers had flown.

Secretary Abbott explained that, in fact, the first plane of flight was right here in the Smithsonian. He had changed the plate under Professor Langley's plane to read, "Langley Aerodrome—The Original Langley Flying Machine of 1903 Restored."[4] Abbott then went on to explain that Langley's plane had edged out the Wright brothers' plane by only a few weeks. The teachers did not take the bait. There was a collective sniff on seeing the Langley plane. The question was put forth again: *Why did the Smithsonian not admit that it was wrong and that the Wright brothers were first, so that teachers could then bring their students to see the 1903 Flyer that had flown at Kitty Hawk and solved the problem of flight?*

Abbott had taken over after Secretary Walcott had died in 1927. Secretary Abbott believed the trouble had really begun when Walcott refused the *Wright Flyer* in 1910.[5] Walcott had been intent on rebuilding Langley's reputation and the Smithsonian's, and he had turned down the brothers' offer. He said the Wrights themselves owed Langley a great debt, and he backed up the Smithsonian's assertion with a quote from Wilbur Wright's speech to the Western Society of Engineers in Chicago: "Some years ago Prof. Langley called attention to the great economy of thrust which might be obtained by using very high speeds and from this many were led to suppose that high speed was essential to success in a motor-driven machine."[6] This, along with a letter to Chanute upon Langley's death, in which Wilbur recognized the secretary's contribution to aeronautics: "The knowledge that the head of the most prominent scientific institution of America believed in the possibility of human flight was one of the influences that led us to undertake the preliminary investigation that preceded our active work. He recommended to us the books which enabled us to form sane ideas at the onset. It was a helping hand at a critical time and we shall always be grateful."[7] This also "helped create a false impression over the world that the Wrights had acknowledged indebtedness to Langley's scientific work."[8] Abbott used the presentation of the Samuel P. Langley Medal for Aerodromics by former Secretary Walcott to the Wrights to indicate to the world that they had relied on Langley's data.

That Secretary Walcott had refused the offer of the 1903 *Flyer* in 1910 and asked for other Wright flyers was not important to Abbott, but one sees a plan of positioning in the works. It would not do to have the 1903 *Flyer* when Langley's plane was *the real* inheritor of the title of "first plane capable of flight." Orville Wright wanted a complete retraction; he was basically forcing the Smithsonian to confess that it had lied about Langley's plane and to admit that there was only one plane capable of flight in 1903, and that was Wrights'. That Abbott could not do. It would undo all the hard work Walcott had put in to restoring the public's faith and trust in the Smithsonian. He had pulled Langley's reputation out of the ash heap of history and put it up on the mantle again of the Smithsonian, keeper of all that was great and noble in scientific discovery.

Walcott died in 1927, and a year later Orville shipped his 1903 *Flyer* to London. Abbott had inherited a hell of a mess. No, the teachers would just have to come see Langley's plane and explain that not everything was as it seemed. The fact is Abbott still believed Langley's plane could have flown. As Tom Crouch cites in *The Bishop's Boys*, "The Wrights may have been the first to fly, but Langley had been capable of doing it before them."[9]

This is what Secretary Walcott believed, too, rationalizing that the basics of Langley's plane were there and Glenn had merely adjusted the existing technology. The *Literary Digest* had backed him up and "proclaimed Dr. Langley the Discoverer of the Air," as Crouch points out in his biography of the Wrights.[10] The French publication *L'Aerophile* had also swung in with support and praised the Smithsonian for doing "posthumous justice to a great pioneer."[11] Abbott knew, and Orville knew, that soon history would be rewritten forever, with Langley at the top of the aeronautical pyramid. But there were those from the other side who had called out the Smithsonian. Griffith Brewer had given a lecture in 1914 titled "Aviation's Greatest Controversy."[12] That didn't help. Then articles started appearing: "On a Matter of Fraud" and "The Scandal of the First Man-Carrying Airplane."[13] That all would have died away if Orville had not announced that he was sending the 1903 *Flyer* to the Science Museum of London in 1928.

Abbott had been on the job for only a few years, and he felt like a man keeping his fingers in the dyke. Every time he countered an argument against the Smithsonian, there was another coming in. As stated before, Lester Gardner, founder of *Aviation*, had turned against him as well, pointing out that "the original Wright plane could not be entrusted to the Smithsonian as long as the influences that had conducted the Langley propaganda were in charge. . . . But now that Orville Wright has decided to send it to the English Museum the public may awake to the damage done by the zeal of Langley's friends."[14]

And again, before he died, Walcott had gone on the offensive and commissioned a report by Joseph Ames and David Taylor, two highly respected aviation authorities, who concluded that "structurally the original Langley machine was capable of level and controlled flight."[15]

It did not stop Orville from sending the *Flyer* to London. The 1903 *Flyer* headed overseas, and the letters from teachers and kids continued. Secretary Abbott had not been feeling so great lately. Why couldn't Orville spread around the credit? It wasn't like they had found what nobody else did. Someone would have solved the problem sooner or later. Abbott had to keep telling himself that. Besides, Langley's plane might have flown . . . with a few adjustments.

THE LONE EAGLE—1934

His wings were icing up and he was tired. It was 1927; he was twenty-five; and his plane was whining in the fog. He went lower and lower until he was skimming the tops of the waves. The ice began to melt off the wings, but he could barely keep his eyes open. Twenty-four hours he had been flying. He had taken the dare, and now he was somewhere out over the Atlantic. Somewhere. Dead reckoning. He was flying with a compass, heading due East, hoping to stumble onto Europe, if he didn't end up in the icy Atlantic. The money was on the latter when he took off and barely cleared the telephone wires with his heavy, fuel-laden plane.

And then the voices started. When he would write about it later, people would say it was due to fatigue. Others would make mystical connections. But the voices were there. He was sure. In the darkness, with his consciousness fading in and out, the voices told him to keep going. Was it the dead? Were there lost souls out over the darkest recesses of the ocean? Did they ride on his plane like spirits looking for salvation? They were in the cockpit with him. They were there, and they kept him going.

Lindbergh turned from the window in Orville Wright's home. His flight across the Atlantic had been years ago, but suddenly he felt as if he were back over that dark ocean. Orville stood beside him, a short man with small hands, a mustache, and an oddly fastidious air about him. Charles Lindbergh was the most famous man in the world, and he had come to see another famous man, Orville Wright. But Lindbergh's fame had broken all known barriers. He was a world-famous superstar. People regarded him as if he weren't just someone who flew over the ocean; it was as if he had walked across it. Mass celebrity had broken into universal consciousness.

The man who had invented flight was a shrunken, gray figure; but, to a twenty-five-year-old Lindbergh, most older men seemed that way. But where was the other brother? He had died, of course, and Orville was the surviving one of the pair. Now it was up to Lindbergh to get the most important plane in the world back to America.

Secretary Abbott was desperate and had turned to the most famous man in America to assist him in getting back the most famous plane in the world. As Tom Crouch wrote in *The Bishop's Boys*, "Abbott suggested the creation of a committee to mediate the differences between them [himself and Orville] and proposed that Charles Lindbergh should head the group. Orville accepted."[1] The committee would determine whether or not "the Smithsonian claim that the 1914 Hammondsport tests had demonstrated the capability of the 1903 aerodrome for flight."

If the Smithsonian was right, Orville would bring the plane home from England. If Orville was proved right, then the Smithsonian would "rectify the offenses committed by it in the past in its own publications by printing full corrections in these same publications."[2]

So Lindbergh met with Abbott and then Orville. He had visited Orville before in Dayton and had enjoyed his company. Orville immediately rejected the committee of the secretaries of War, Navy, and Commerce set up by Lindbergh.[3] He recognized that all of the secretaries "had some official connection with the Smithsonian."[4] As the 1903 *Wright Flyer* was displayed in the Science Museum of London and Hitler's rearmament of Germany went on unabated, Orville ignored the committee and gave final terms for return of the *Flyer*. Orville wanted the Smithsonian to say it was misled by the Zahm report, which had claimed that the plane was "nearly as possible in its original condition."[5] And he wanted the Smithsonian to tell its readers to "disregard all of its former statements and expressions of opinion regarding the flights at Hammondsport in 1914."[6]

Walcott had gone to his grave in 1927 sticking to his assertion that the Langley aerodrome was the first airplane capable of flight. That same year, 1927, Charles Abbott changed the label on the aerodrome in the museum from "The First Man-Carrying Aeroplane in the History of the World Capable of Sustained Free Flight"[7] to "Langley Aerodrome—The Original Langley Flying Machine of 1903, Restored."[8] He had the Smithsonian Board of Regents pass a resolution in 1928 stating "to the Wrights belongs the credit of making the first successful flight with a propeller-propelled, heavier-than-air machine carrying a man."[9]

Orville was not moved. He told Lindbergh that he wanted just two things, and then the 1903 *Flyer* could return: "a published list of the differences between the 1903 Aerodrome and the 1914 Hammondsport machine and an admission by the Smithsonian that the craft was heavily modified."[10]

Abbott countered with a full report that could be released, but not an admission by the Smithsonian that the 1903 aerodrome had been modified.[11] Orville saw the list being buried in a report and giving him no satisfaction as to wrongdoing by the Smithsonian. He gave his last response on the subject in 1935. The patent suit had been long settled with Glenn Curtiss by the government's establishment of a patent pool, so this would be his last chance to right the wrongs done to him and his brother by Curtiss and the Smithsonian.

> Instead of a paper such as you have proposed may I offer the following suggestion: That the Smithsonian publish a paper presenting a list of specifications in parallel columns of those features of the Langley machine of 1903 and the Hammondsport machine of 1914 in which there were differences with an introduction stating that the Smithsonian finds that it was misled by the Zahm report of 1914; that through the Zahm paper the Institution was led to believe that the aeroplane tested at Hammondsport was "as nearly as possible in its original condition"; that as a result of this misinformation the Smithsonian had published erroneous statements from time to time alleging that the original Langley machine without modification, or with only such modifications as were necessary for the addition of floats, had been successfully flown at Hammondsport in 1914; that it ask its readers to disregard all of its former statements and expressions of opinion regarding the flights at Hammondsport in 1914 because these were based on misinformation as the list to follow will show.[12]

Orville wanted the Smithsonian to admit it had lied in 1914. Abbott never responded. It was up to Lindbergh now.

Lindbergh knew the Smithsonian would never go for what Orville wanted. To bring the plane back, they had to admit that they were wrong and that Langley's plane could never have flown. They wouldn't do that, and Orville wouldn't bring back the *Flyer*. The Smithsonian, and America, really, had to get the plane back somehow. It was America's. It was not England's.

England had not solved flight, America had. Abbott believed Lindbergh could mediate between the Smithsonian and Orville Wright. The man had flown alone across the ocean. Alone. He could surely deal with this cranky old man and get the damn plane back. Lindbergh was a god in America. He was the first superstar. He was the first mass-media celebrity. He was world-famous. Surely, he could get the *Wright Flyer* back.

So, Orville wrote Lindbergh his demands, which, again, were nothing short of the Smithsonian saying it was totally wrong. Lindbergh tried to reason with Orville and get him to understand that they couldn't really say that. Orville probably didn't think much of Lindbergh. After all, Lindbergh had used his technology and technically speaking he had not paid him a royalty. He could not have flown across the ocean if it were not for Orville and Wilbur's invention. The 1903 *Flyer* paved the way for Lindbergh to become a world celebrity, and it irked Orville that people went so crazy over this man. No one had given him and Wilbur a ticker-tape parade in New York. Now they were trying to say the Wright invention didn't matter. They were trying to say that Samuel Langley had beaten him and his brother and had first invented a plane that would fly. If this was true, then why did they care so much about getting the 1903 *Flyer* back from England? No. The Smithsonian would have to admit its duplicity; confess that it had changed Langley's aerodrome during the trials and then lied about it; and then state for the world that there was only one plane that was capable of flying in 1903—and that was the plane sitting in London.

Apparently the star power of Lindbergh did nothing to change Orville's mind. He basically ignored what Lindbergh and Abbott had proposed: "Orville then proceeded as if the committee proposal had never been made. He sent Lindbergh a list based on Griffith Brewer's 1921 paper with the specific dimensions of the 1903 Langley aerodrome on one side of the page and those of the 1914 machine on the other, so that any reader could see the differences."[13]

Lindbergh passed on the list and proposed that a long article be published by the Smithsonian with the list included, but Orville would have none of it. He responded with the above-mentioned request that the Smithsonian publish an itemized list of specifications showing how the 1914 Hammondsport machine differed from the original Langley machine of 1903.

Essentially, the Smithsonian would have to say that it was wrong and had lied.

Lindbergh eventually gave up. He later wrote in his diary that he believed the fault lay "primarily with the Smithsonian people. But Orville Wright is not an easy man to deal with in the matter. I don't blame him much, though, when I think of the way he was treated for a period of years. He has encountered the narrowmindedness of science and the dishonesty of commerce."[14]

A few years later, Lindbergh then left for Nazi Germany, at the invitation of Adolf Hitler, to see how far the Germans had come in aviation. America had kidnapped and murdered his son, and people would not leave him alone. People needed to be controlled. Democracy was too chaotic. Lindbergh believed in precision, control, and eugenics.[15] He believed in racial superiority. Men like Hitler would change the world. Fascism was the answer.[16] Look at the autobahn, the Volkswagen, and the *Luftwaffe*. Germany was a sterling example of how the world should be. Even Orville Wright, the pioneer of flight, had lost his way in America. Maybe the flyer *should* stay in London. Lindbergh left and did not return to America until 1938.[17]

The tide of public opinion was turning against Abbott and the Smithsonian. "During the next eight years Abbott was bombarded with scores of petitions, most of them a result of a drive by the aviation magazine *Contact* asking that the Smithsonian take the requisite steps to get back the 1903 Flyer. Bills were introduced in Congress calling for an investigation and the creation of a committee to resolve the dispute. . . . A new organization Men with Wings was established to support the return of the airplane from England."[18]

The 1903 *Wright Flyer* would remain in London as the first bombs fell during World War II. Lindbergh became involved with an isolationist movement called the America First Committee to keep America out of the war. He thought the Germans knew what they were doing. He thought fascism was the answer.[19] When the Final Solution was revealed, Lindbergh would denounce the Nazis, but it was too late. When the Japanese bombed Pearl Harbor, he was disgraced forever.[20]

The Germans declared war on America soon after.

35

THE BATTLE OF BRITAIN—1940

Mabel Beck was worried about the 1903 *Flyer*. When World War II broke out and London was bombed, Mabel was alarmed that the *Flyer* might be destroyed. Orville sat down and explained the strategy of the German *Luftwaffe*. He said it was simple. The French had surrendered and the British would surely follow suit. But first the British must be taught a lesson. For the first time in modern warfare, a populace was being bombed from the skies. Incendiary bombs fell from the open cargo holds of German bombers. This was novel. The airplane made civilian populations an easy target. Before, the best an army could do was to lob shells into a city. Now hell could rain down from the skies, and there was only one place to escape: underground.

The London subway system, the Tube, was filled with people cowering from aeronautical terror. The British were stoic and Winston Churchill had said they would never surrender, but this was nothing anyone had experienced before. The bombs killed people in their sleep and didn't discriminate between old people, middle-aged people, children, dogs, or cats. These were dumb bombs, iron tanks of high explosives that rained down with no precision. You couldn't miss. The German pilots looked down, and all they saw were the buildings of London. What an advantage—and only the British Royal Air Force (RAF) was there to stop them.

The army moved the 1903 *Flyer* one hundred miles out of London, into underground storage near the town of Corsham. The *Luftwaffe* was bombing every night. The pilots, high above in the night sky, used radar to hone in on London and let their bombs go. They used their rudders and their ailerons and throttled up their engines and their elevator flaps. The Germans didn't have any idea that below them and deep underground was the reason they were able to fly through the night and drop five-hundred-pound bombs on the city. They used the very controls that were encased in the crates marked *1903 WRIGHT FLYER.*

It had been thirty-seven years since Orville had lifted off for the first twelve seconds and then came back to Earth. Thirty-seven years since Wilbur flew for 59 seconds and then landed back on the sand. If this *Flyer* had not existed, would the planes be trying to destroy it from above?

Mabel had inquired as to what precautions were taken to protect the *Flyer*. People had gone down below to check on the wooden crates. They were soldiers, government officials, and museum officials. They wanted to make sure the 1903 *Flyer* was fine. It had been moved, and would stay where it was until the Germans gave up their bombing attack on Britain. It was hard to say when that would be. They didn't dare think it would end. That would be too optimistic. But, at the same time, they could not risk a piece of world history by moving it. Even if that piece of history was now trying to blow everything to kingdom come. No. They would wait until the war ended. They would wait until that piece of history could go back to America.

Ms. Beck did not feel good about the British assurances, but there was nothing she could do. All her life, men had tried to tell her what to do, and Ms. Beck would rap them across the knuckles every chance she got. Orville had quietly altered his will and stipulated that "the 1903 airplane should remain in London after his death unless the will was amended by a subsequent letter from him indicating a change of heart."[1] All the betting money was on Mabel Beck as the woman most likely to possess such a letter if it had ever been written.

36

THE AUTHORIZED BIOGRAPHY —1943

In the end, history is a writer's story. The cigarettes, the coffee, and the sleepless nights had all produced a manuscript. The story had been told, and it was a writer who would end the standoff between Orville Wright and the Smithsonian. Fred Kelly lit another cigarette and leaned back in his chair. He had been working day and night. His office looked like a tornado had passed through. Eggs were shellacked to plates. Coffee cups were lined up like soldiers. Ashtrays were full. Packs of cigarettes lay crumpled beneath his chair. But he was finished. Books lay all over the floor. He literally walked on them to get to his chair. This was it. He was finished. Kelly leaned back and blew the smoke out tiredly. He looked at the stacked manuscript to the right of his typewriter. The story of the Wright brothers had been told and, more than all that, he now had Orville Wright in his debt—and that meant his book would be published.

Kelly had just gotten off the phone. Abbott did not want the story out there and had agreed to Orville's demands to publish a retraction on the Smithsonian's claims that the Langley plane had been capable of flight first. Abbott had no stomach for seeing a book come out that made the Smithsonian look even worse. Kelly knew this would kill two birds with one stone. Orville would be forever in his debt, and the 1903 *Flyer* could return. Orville would get his version of history published and he, Fred Kelly, would be the sole authorized biographer of the Wright brothers. History was served in the end.

It would take years for later historians to connect the dots on Fred Kelly's maneuvers to get his manuscript published. As Tom Crouch wrote in *The Bishop's Boys*, "Kelly sought to guarantee Orville's continued cooperation and eventual permission to publish the book as an authorized biography. The answer was to put Orville in his debt. There was an obvious way to accomplish that. Kelly wrote to Charles Abbott, suggesting that he would be willing to assist in resolving the long-standing dispute with the Smithsonian by negotiating a statement that would satisfy Orville Wright."[1]

That got Orville back on board with the biography, and it woke up the Smithsonian as well. Kelly had resumed the interviews with Orville, and now it looked like the whole twenty-year controversy would be coming to an end. Nobody could break the standoff; even Lindbergh had given up, citing in his dairy the fault of the Smithsonian people, but also recognizing Orville's stubbornness. The *Wright Flyer* remained in London, and it took a writer to break the impasse. Fred Kelly had a tough client in Orville Wright. Not only did Orville want to go over every page he wrote, but he also held up the threat that he might kill the whole authorized biography and be done with it. But Kelly persevered past the crisis point when Orville wanted to scrap the book.

"Fred Kelly had triumphed. Perhaps because of his assistance in settling the Smithsonian dispute, perhaps simply out of friendship."[2] The *Wright Flyer* had been in London for fifteen years. It was now in deep storage in the small town of Corsham. There was a fear that the 1903 *Flyer* might not survive the war, and Abbott had grown weary. Kelly said he would get the *Flyer* back. Just give him a statement that contained both a list of differences between the 1903 aerodrome and the 1914 machine flown at Hammondsport and a disavowal of the 1914 Zahm report. The statement appeared October 24, 1942, in *Smithsonian Miscellaneous Collections*. An explanatory message preceded the statement:

> This paper has been submitted to Orville Wright and under the date of October 8, 1942, he states that the paper as now prepared will be acceptable to him if given adequate publication.[3]

The fight was over. The Smithsonian had recognized that only one plane was capable of flying in 1903, and that was the *Flyer* that had left the sands of Kill Devil Hills. Orville quietly took steps to ensure that the plane would come back to the United States. In his new will, he wrote a letter in which he stated: "I give and bequeath to the U.S. National Museum of Washington DC; for exhibition in the national capitol only, the Wright airplane (now in the Science Museum, London, England) which flew at Kitty Hawk, North Carolina on the 17th of December 1903."[4] Then he gave the letter to Mabel Beck.

Kelly looked at his typewriter. He and Orville had known each other for almost thirty years now, and it was time to get this book out there. He just had a few more questions for him. He wanted to make sure Orville came across as important as Wilbur did, and that was tricky. Wilbur was the power player and Orville was the little brother. He would never say that to Orville, of course. The man had done very well and was wealthy and respected worldwide. He *was* the Wright brothers. Wilbur had been dead for thirty years, so it had to be that Orville invented the plane as much as did Wilbur. It was fortuitous for the surviving brother. They were fifty-fifty on the invention of flight. Kelly knew there was no one around to say otherwise, and his book would set the record straight for all time. Orville was very smart, and he had a lot of inventions to his name, but this plane business was something else altogether.

Somebody had to have a vision, a drive that came from something other than sheer brilliance. No, this was not just some inventor who cracked flight. This was a man charged with destiny who saw things other men had not. Kelly had not seen the letters between Wilbur and Chanute. But he knew Wilbur was way beyond most people. But he was gone and, somehow, Kelly had to get Orville right in the middle of the whole thing.

Kelly wondered if there was something down at Kitty Hawk that had happened. Maybe some sort of epiphany, something only Orville could claim. Something to do with Kitty Hawk where the plane was invented. Something like: he woke up and, *bam*, he saw the light. That would make a good scene and would put him on equal footing with his brother. Orville did say something about the tail or rudder or whatever it was . . . he would ask him about that later.

Orville Wright finally approved Fred Kelly's manuscript. As Tom Crouch says in *The Bishop's Boys*, "It was not what Wilbur hoped for but it did tell the story in a relatively straightforward fashion."[5] On May 13, 1943, *The Wright Brothers: A Biography Authorized by Orville Wright* was released.[6]

37

WASHINGTON, DC—1943

Orville hated to speak publicly. He would let Wilbur do that, but his brother had been gone thirty-one years. The feud with the Smithsonian was now supposedly over, and the 1903 *Flyer* was coming back to the States. President Franklin D. Roosevelt was to announce the *Flyer's* return. It was an American triumph in a year when the war was not going badly. Orville had been assured that the *Flyer* was perfectly safe down in underground storage. Orville had thought more than once about the irony of the Germans trying to destroy his plane with his planes. He viewed all planes as his. They all used his technology. It didn't matter what the courts or the government said, those bombers were flying with his rudders, his ailerons, his elevators.

And now they wanted him to speak after the president announced that the *Flyer* was to be returned; but the president couldn't come, and they had sent Secretary of Commerce Jesse H. Jones to make the announcement. Orville waited patiently and looked at his watch. He listened to Jones drone on and talk about the return of his plane. Orville sat perfectly still and waited. He was to give the Collier Trophy to General Arnold. Jones finished up his message from the president: "In closing I can think of only one additional tribute to General Arnold. Will you please ask Orville Wright the great teacher, to act for me in handing the Collier Trophy to General Arnold the great pupil."[1] Orville stood up as Jones stepped aside and motioned him to the microphone. It was a national broadcast. People coast to coast leaned close to their radios to hear the voice of Orville Wright. He was a man of legend by now. Orville pressed his lips together and took the trophy from Secretary Jones. The room was silent. Everyone was waiting. Orville Wright was about to speak. The room waited. Secretary Jones waited. General Arnold waited.

Orville stood with the trophy in front of the microphone. Control rooms all over the country checked their sound levels. Had the feed gone dead? This was dead air. A horror in radio. But, no, the feed was good. It was just that Orville Wright was standing in front of the microphone, not speaking.[2]

Orville then moved toward General Arnold. Better to be done with all of this. He hated dinners. He hated ceremonies. He did not like to be around people he did not know. The radio announcer who had been orchestrating the night swung into action. He told the radio audience that the great Orville Wright was now handing the trophy to General Arnold. Arnold took the trophy and then said to the radio audience that there was no one else he would rather receive a trophy from than Orville Wright. Orville nodded stiffly and took his seat. "Orville vowed he would never attend another official dinner in Washington."[3] He crossed his legs. He still hated the Smithsonian. He still hated Glenn Curtiss. Curtiss had killed his brother. The *Flyer* could stay in London, for all he cared. He knew they couldn't move it until the war was over anyway. He could be dead by then for all he knew.

He would be.

38

MABEL BECK—1948

Mabel Beck read in her bed and looked over at her bed stand. The clock ticked. She was now fifty-eight years old, and she heard the freight train down by the station. It was almost nine at night. Mabel looked at the silver-framed picture. Orville Wright was there. He would be there when she went to sleep and when she first awoke. She had kept all his letters and would carefully hide them away in the nook over the stairwell. She had the memories of her life with the man she loved, and she had the letters he had written to her for safekeeping. The nephews who were the executors of the estate of Orville Wright kept calling, but she just hung up on them.

They wanted the letter. Well, she hoped they could find it. Mabel would never help those men. They had all turned against Orville when he was alive, and now they wanted to get their grubby, mendacious hands on his last bequest. She lived alone with her sister, and nobody moved anything.

Judge Love of the probate court would have none of this. He had ordered Harold Miller, executor of the Wright estate, to get the letter. The entire history of aviation now resided with this tight-lipped, brusque woman who since Orville's death had stayed in her home and saw no one. Mabel was used to turning people down. She had met Lindbergh when he had come to see Orville a month after he had flown across the Atlantic. She had been there in the laboratory when he told Orville about how his wings were icing up over the Atlantic when he was twenty-five and it was 1927 and his plane was whining in the fog. He went lower and lower until he was skimming the tops of the waves. The ice began to melt off the wings, but he could barely keep his eyes open. He said he was flying with a compass, heading due east and hoping to stumble onto Europe, if he didn't end up in the icy Atlantic. He said when he took off, he had barely cleared the telephone wires with his heavy, fuel-laden plane.

Mabel had wondered how Orville appeared to the Lone Eagle. Lindbergh had driven with Orville to his home. Lindbergh was just one year old when these two brothers went to Kitty Hawk and solved the riddle of flight that allowed him to stretch man's grasp of the air across the ocean. People were already gathering on the lawn of Orville's mansion when they heard that Lindbergh had come to visit him. It was fitting that he should visit the surviving inventor of the plane. Mabel imagined that Orville seemed more like a lord to the young flier than merely a man who had stretched the boundaries of human existence by cracking the code of flight.

More people were on the lawn, and some had come up on the porch. Years later, Orville Wright's sister-in-law Ivonette recalled the pandemonium of Lindbergh's visit to her brother: "Soon the front lawn was crowded, then the side lawns and hillside at the back. It was not a crowd but a mob, pushing and shoving, trampling the flower beds and bushes, climbing trees, all clamoring for a look at Lindbergh. When the people came up on the porch, the occupants of the house took refuge on the second floor. But the mob persisted, demanding at least of a glimpse of their hero."[1]

Orville approached Lindbergh and asked him if he would mind stepping out and waving to the crowd. Lindbergh had made a promise to financial backers for no more appearances, but he gave in when Orville expressed concern that the mob might enter the house. The two men stepped out on a portico and waved. People marveled at how tall and slim Lindbergh was, and how short Orville Wright was in comparison. The two men then stepped back inside, and Lindbergh left in a chauffeur-driven car.

The phone was ringing. Mabel put down her book. God. Who invented it, anyway? Alexander Graham Bell. Another man who would never get the time of day from her if he had been alive. One of the many who had turned against her lover, her totem, her raison d'être. And now the phone. The phone. So many had called after the death of Mr. Wright. It was ghastly. The family had come to pick his bones now that he was dead. She had made it her life's work to keep those selfish relations away from Orville. The family probably was working for the Smithsonian people who wanted the plane back, and they were the ones who had caused Mr. Wright's death with their duplicity, their lies, and their treachery. Mr. Wright had been correct in sending the *Flyer* to London. He had told her to ship it off, and she had made the arrangements. It was safe in a place where they respected what he and his brother had done. Not like these American men of greed and lies.

Ms. Beck hung up. She took pleasure in the squawk, and then the phone rang again. Boys and men were all the same to her. She picked up the receiver and dropped it again. Ms. Beck rubbed her hands together, sat down, and picked up her knitting. They wanted the letter. It was valuable. Just like the letter she had received from Teddy Roosevelt congratulating Orville on his plane after he had flown in a Wright plane in 1910 with pilot Arch Hoxsey. "Bully!" is what he said when he landed. "Bully!"[2]

Mabel smoothed the covers. The bedside clock ticked. Where did time go? She glanced at the picture of Orville Wright, then turned out the light. Mabel Beck pulled the covers up to her shoulders and looked at the picture. The silver frame glowed in the moonlight; the man with the bushy mustache smiled through the darkness.

"Goodnight, dear," she murmured.

WRIGHT BROTHERS, WRONG STORY

The story of the Wright brothers put forth by Fred Kelly in his authorized biography is in some ways much better than the real one. In Kelly's story, the brothers are one and the same. Both are creative, inventive men who took on the challenge of flight and in perfect synchronicity produced a synthesis of mechanical engineering, physics, aeronautical restructuring, testing, innovating, and inventing—all with equal input and equal epiphanies—and at the other end a plane emerged that was able to ascend to the sky. Manned flight was solved down in the sand dunes of Kitty Hawk.

As a writer, I appreciate a good story, and the mythology generated by this story is massive. The kids' books alone are a cottage industry. The two brothers in their collars and ties and their Ohio values, executing the best of Yankee inventiveness, perseverance, stick-to-itiveness, grit, and tenacity, with a touch of genius sprinkled liberally. It is an American story, a team story. A team of brothers who put their heads together. And what emerged was American values we can all recognize. The bishop father and supportive sister fill out the perfect ensemble cast.

A psychopath knocking out Wilbur's teeth and sending him into a three-year-long spiraling depression does not go along with this story. Orville as a myopic man who was mechanically inclined and who was inventive in his own right but did not have the vision for tackling the problem of flight does not help the story either. A man who did not fit into the world of business, in a bike shop, in a print shop, in college, even in high school is more problematic for the plot line. Two men who never had a sexual encounter with the opposite sex for most of their lives and lived with their sister and father their whole adult lives—that doesn't fit either. None of this would have made it past the Orville Board of Censorship that Fred Kelly had to deal with on every page. Certainly, the real story of Mabel Beck and Orville would have been a deal killer.

The malcontent, the misanthrope, the silent, brooding genius who found a kindred spirit in a brilliant engineer named Octave Chanute and began to crack the science of aeronautics in long polemics going over the known data and then questioning everything also would not give us the same warm fuzzies as the image of the jolly brothers building planes in the bike shop with knowledge pulled out of thin air. The Octave Chanute letters that are in the papers of Wilbur and Orville Wright offered the homeschooling that Wilbur never had. It is the online crash course of 1900 that began with the literature received from the Smithsonian (which would provide great irony later on).

The lone wolf trying to decipher what no one else could is a modern story we are familiar with—whether it be Edison, Bell, Ford, or Mozart. These are all men of genius who blazed new trails and were later recognized. Yes, there are epiphanic moments in teamwork, but someone must lead, someone must have an eye on the bit of stardust that falls down through the heavens on the cold, dark night but inspires and enlightens. Vision is singular, and Orville did not have that vision until his brother pulled him in; and, as late as 1902, he had not flown any of the planes, and he was never pulled into the Wilbur/ Chanute seminars.

It was no accident that Wilbur was the one who published his findings at Kitty Hawk and spoke to the engineers in Chicago. He did this twice. One would think the second go-round would belong to Orville, if we are to go with the Fred Kelly version of events. That would be only fair. But it was Wilbur who presented, Wilbur who was questioned, and Wilbur who was invited by Octave Chanute to give the presentation in the first place.

Orville was perfectly satisfied operating in the bicycle business. He would have been fine with never going to Kitty Hawk to fly a contraption like a kite and then watch his brother fly above him. In fact, he did not go the very first time—Wilbur did. Wilbur went down there alone; and he went alone to find out whether it would be suitable to fly. Wilbur flew the glider in Dayton, alone, before he left. It was never Orville's quest; it was Wilbur's quest to fly, and this makes all the difference. The difference between them was as much as between the pilot and the mechanic. Orville would not fly a glider until 1902; and, even then, it was infrequently, with several flights resulting in crashes and then eventually one fatality in 1906. Wilbur never had a serious crash.

The Wright family culture, as dictated by Bishop Wright, makes this all a blasphemy. He saw the world as evil and full of temptation. He pointed to his older sons as evidence of the difficulty and the duplicity of the world. He made sure Orville, Wilbur, and Katherine would be there when he returned from his travels. There must be a united front against the world, and this demanded plurality, lest one of the corrupted sneaks in. He would slip up and let his true feelings be known, such as when he pointed out the cruelty that Orville and Katherine were expendable but that Wilbur had the gift and he must take no risks.

The gift was simply vision. Somewhere in the three years of reading and nursing his mother as she slowly died, he had a vison that something else lay out there for him. Not business. Not college. Not art. But a unique destiny suited for him—and that dictated his drive and his unfailing focus. He would solve flight. No one else would do so. He would give his brother credit with his clumsy "we" that quickly began to appear in his writings after 1901, but he also would reveal what he really thought when Orville could not hit the mark and justify his part of that plurality.

Orville had two serious crashes: in one, he escaped injury; but in the other, he did not, and it resulted in a fatality. The first was at Kitty Hawk, and the second was in Washington. On both occasions, Wilbur conceded that it was not a mechanical problem but a fault of the operator. On the second serious crash, Wilbur even went so far to say that if he had flown with the army captain instead, the crash would not have occurred. We see his frustration, at times, with having to share his determined quest with his brother. On something like shipping the *Flyer*, he was so hard on his brother that their sister had to ask him to back off.

None of this would play well in the Kelly version of events that set the tone for all historians to follow. It is amazing how this narrative has survived intact, right up to the latest biographies. The truth is that Wilbur was the primary inventor and pilot. His brother assisted him in many steps, but it was Wilbur who set up the wind-tunnel tables, and it was Wilbur who gave this groundbreaking data to Chanute to catalog. It was Wilbur who developed the concept of wing warping and then showed it to his brother, which led to modern ailerons on planes. It was Wilbur who would finally break with his mentor, Octave Chanute.

The discrepancy between the two brothers was so clear that Kelly needed something to put Orville front and center in the "invention process." The winged rudder was the perfect story to make him part of the holy creative process of the plane. The suspicion that Orville might have been just a glorified mechanic assisting his older, smarter, genius brother has haunted the history of the Wright brothers and nibbled at the edges of the kids' books, biographies, movies, CDs, stories, and even *Wikipedia*. There is something there that seeps out between the Kelly story of the midnight, coffee-induced epiphany and the fact that Orville was on the plane when John Daniels snapped the picture.

The picture would cement into history the notion of the brothers being equal and inviolate. Clearly, there is Orville on the plane. There is Wilbur running beside and behind it. Need we say more? Orville and Wilbur together solved the problem of flight at Kitty Hawk, and here is proof of that plurality. But the visionary is really the man on the right, not the man on the plane. We know that Orville will hit the sand after maybe twelve seconds in the air. The real flight that day occurred after the picture was taken—when Wilbur managed to fly for almost a minute. *That* was the first controlled flight of a man in an airplane, and it was done by the man who invented the airplane.

You cannot have coauthors. Not really. Someone is always leading the way, and someone is always following. Someone has the whole thing in his or her head, and someone else has a part. If the author who is following drops off, then another author will be hired. The visionary alone is the indispensable one who must have the entire world in his or her head. If that person quits, then the story, the novel, the film, the inventing of an airplane would truly end right there. This is because the coauthor or mechanic cannot see the next step in the same way that the luminary can. That other person simply doesn't have the vision.

If Orville had gone back to the bicycle business, could he have been replaced? Yes. If Wilbur had been killed or had died of natural causes or had been drafted, could he have been replaced? Would the work go forward on solving human flight without Wilbur? No. There were no other Wilbur Wrights in the world. There were men like Lilienthal, Langley, Chanute, even Curtiss, who had the parts of the problem solved but never the whole. Wilbur Wright not only saw the problem of flight in a unique way, but also solved it intuitively, much like the writer who must finish a very long book and knows where it will end up even as he sets his pen on the first page.

This is genius. This is the flash of insight, which is never taught and never known, but is recognized years later. We can call it destiny, brilliance, genius, or whatever term we can ascribe to what we don't understand. It is the musician who writes the incredible hit, the writer who formulates the bestseller, or the poet who wows the world with three lines. How do they do it? The best we can surmise is that it is something from the heavens.

And then of course the great tragedy occurs. The genius is struck down. Wilbur died in 1912, and that left Orville and the vacuum of history. There was no one else to interpret what really happened at Kitty Hawk before, during, and after. There was only Orville Wright and his friend Fred C. Kelly, and there are the intervening years between the first flight and the first biography describing what happened. There was the long-standing fight with the Smithsonian and the counterclaims that try to take away the very status and credit for the invention of the airplane. But the inventor had died, and that left the brother in the driver's seat.

For thirty-six years, he alone was the voice of the Wright brothers; and the story that he told needed to be airtight because the sharks were circling. As far as Orville knew, Milton was right. The world out there was dangerous and duplicitous, and the Wrights must circle the wagons. Men like Curtiss, Zahm, Walcott, and Langley were the enemy. And so the story was written during this thirty-six-year siege. The war against the Wright brothers brings about the desperate step of taking the very evidence of that flight and holding it hostage unless the story is corrected. That story was being dictated by Orville Wright to Fred Kelly, and it would be an *undisputed* story of two brothers equally talented, equally driven, and equally qualified to solve the problem of flight. It is telling that in the heat of the battle with the Smithsonian, the history of the Wright brothers, the bible of the Wright brothers, was being formulated as if to button up all loose ends. It would be the undisputed truth of the Wright mythology. And it is fitting that that bible would end the decades-long feud.

When all was said and done, the 1903 *Flyer* ended up in the Smithsonian and the story of the Wright brothers was published by Kelly. And there it has remained, unquestioned, like a bible that historians consult, then maybe write a few variations on, but basically retell the same story. It was a story told by one man to another, and it was written during a time of immense stress—a time in which truth was under assault by an array of people and institutions.

Orville would risk nothing to chance and, like the situation where the bombs rained down on the *Flyer* during the blitz of London, the truth would be buried deep underground.

The Wright brothers were two fascinating, talented men. They did have an idiosyncratic family whose lifestyle raised more questions than it provided answers. They did have a hostile view of the outside world. They were both mechanically inclined to a very high degree. They both were remarkably inventive, determined, and resourceful. But Orville Wright operated on a linear plane, whereas Wilbur saw beyond it to the existential moment he discovered while in a dark journey that was brought on by a freak accident and the death of his mother. Somewhere along the way, he had a vision that wedded him to solving the problem of manned flight. His brother would come along for the ride, quite literally, on December 17, 1903, and eventually that brother would write their history.

The Wright brothers were similar in many respects, but it is the difference between the pilot and the mechanic, the visionary and the assistant, the poet and the scribe, that sets them apart. And that is all the difference in the world.

EPILOGUE

Fred C. Kelly had his book, and the Smithsonian would get the *Flyer*. On May 13, 1943, *The Wright Brothers: A Biography Authorized by Orville Wright* was published. History followed. On October 10, 1947, Orville Wright suffered a heart attack while running up the front steps of a building to keep an appointment. On January 27, 1948, he had a second heart attack, and he died three days later. He was seventy-seven years old, and he never again saw the 1903 plane that had flown in Kitty Hawk. John Daniels, the man who had snapped the famous picture of the first flight in 1903, died the day after. Eighteen years earlier, in 1930, Glenn Curtiss had died while going to court in upstate New York. He was on his way to court, responding to a lawsuit brought by his business partner.

In 1948, the *Wright Flyer* of 1903 was loaded on to the ocean liner *Mauretania* in London and shipped to Halifax, Nova Scotia. A representative of the Smithsonian arranged for the rest of the *Flyer*'s journey to Washington on a flatbed truck. On December 17, 1948, a ceremony was held in the Smithsonian's Arts and Industries Building. Charles Lindbergh's *Spirit of St Louis* was moved from its suspended position to the back of the hall to make room for the new centerpiece. The 1903 *Wright Flyer* now hung front and center with a plaque that read:

THE ORIGINAL WRIGHT BROTHERS AEROPLANE

THE WORLD'S FIRST POWER-DRIVEN HEAVIER-THAN-AIR MACHINE
IN WHICH MAN MADE FREE, CONTROLLED, AND SUSTAINED FLIGHT
INVENTED AND BUILT BY WILBUR AND ORVILLE WRIGHT
FLOWN BY THEM AT KITTY HAWK, NORTH CAROLINA, DECEMBER 17, 1903
BY ORIGINAL SCIENTIFIC RESEARCH THE WRIGHT BROTHERS
DISCOVERED THE PRINCIPLES OF HUMAN FLIGHT
AS INVENTORS, BUILDERS, AND FLYERS THEY FURTHER DEVELOPED THE
AEROPLANE, TAUGHT MAN TO FLY, AND OPENED THE ERA OF AVIATION[1]

When Charles Lindbergh was told that his plane was moved back, he said he didn't mind. The first true plane was back in America, but heirs of the Wright brothers put a condition on the returning *Flyer*. If the Smithsonian ever recognized any other aircraft "as having been capable of powered, sustained and controlled flight with a man on board before December 17, 1903, the executors of the estate would have the right to take possession of the machine once again."[2] In other words, the *Flyer* could be shipped away again. Orville's final threat would ensure that no one questioned the Wright brothers again. No one in the Smithsonian, at least.

Katherine Wright finally married in her fifties and left the mansion Orville had built in his later years. He never forgave his sister for marrying and never spoke to her again. On her deathbed in 1929, he relented and visited her. Milton Wright had died in 1917. Orville's final letter directing the return of the *Flyer* to the Smithsonian was in Mabel Beck's possession, and she finally gave it up two weeks after the funeral. The will provided a few surprises. As cited by Roz Young in the *Dayton Daily News*:

> Among his bequests was $300,000 to Oberlin College, Katherine's alma mater, and with the requirement [that] the trustees should pay out of the interest annual stipends to some of his relatives, to one friend Ed Sines, to his mechanic Charles Taylor, to his housekeeper Carrie Grumbach, to his laundress Charlotte Jones and to "my trusted secretary" Mabel Beck. He left her $4,000 annually. The others who worked for Orville received less.[3]

The *Dayton Daily News* reported that "Mabel outlived Orville by 11 years, dying in August 1959, at the age of 68. She had suffered from hypertension and cerebral arteriosclerosis for three years and died three days after a cerebral hemorrhage. She left her estate to her sister Edna."[4] After Orville's death, Mabel Beck and her sister continued to live in her house in Dayton until 1959, and then the house was turned over to the bank.

A woman from the bank and Mabel's friend Mary Francis found a box of letters in a cupboard over the fireplace. The box was tied with a ribbon. Inside were letters from Orville Wright to Mabel Beck. They were the closest thing to love letters that Orville Wright would ever write. The two women read them and then decided to burn them in the fireplace to protect the reputations of Ms. Beck and Mr. Wright.[5] The box returned to its hiding place. History was altered one last time.

In 1985, Professors Fred E. C. Culick and Henry R. Jex analyzed the aerodynamics of the 1903 *Flyer* and declared it to be unflyable by anyone but the Wrights, who had trained themselves on the 1902 glider. On December 17, 2003, Kevin Kochersberger flew an exact replica of the 1903 *Flyer*, but he failed to keep it in the air as Wilbur had done one hundred years before.[6]

Some men are just born to fly.

ACKNOWLEDGMENTS

Following the footsteps of the Wright brothers involves several well-trod trails. First I would like to thank the good folks at the Wright Memorial in Kitty Hawk, North Carolina. Then, of course, the staff of the manuscript division of the Library of Congress, for access to the papers of Wilbur and Orville Wright. The Dayton Public Library and the archivist at the National Air and Space Museum. The Smithsonian, for allowing me to examine the Wright *Flyer* from 1903, and the Henry Ford Museum in Dearborn, Michigan, for an amazing visit to the Wright family home and Wright bicycle shop. Of course to Steven L. Mitchell and the good folks at Prometheus Books, for having the vision that a book on the Wright brothers requires. To my family, for support and everything else that keeps a writer above his garage. Finally, I would like to thank my parents, for taking their recalcitrant son to Kitty Hawk, North Carolina, for many family vacations, which included numerous trips to see where the Wright brothers flew. My fascination began there.

NOTES

Preface: The Wright Myth

1. David McCullough, *The Wright Brothers* (New York: Simon and Schuster, 2016), p. 6.

2. Lawrence Goldstone, *Birdmen: The Wright Brothers, Glenn Curtiss, and the Battle to Control the Skies* (New York: Ballantine, 2015), p. 36.

3. Tom D. Crouch, *The Bishop's Boys: A Life of Wilbur and Orville Wright* (New York: W. W. Norton, 1989), p. 163.

4. Fred Kelly, *The Wright Brothers: A Biography Authorized by Orville Wright* (New York: Harcourt, Brace, 1943).

5. Ibid., p. 26.

6. Ibid., p. 38.

7. Ibid., p. 39.

8. Marvin Wilks McFarland, *The Papers of Wilbur and Orville Wright: Including the Chanute-Wright Letters and Other Papers of Octave Chanute*, vol. 1, *1899–1903* (New York: McGraw-Hill, 2001), p. 3.

9. Crouch, *Bishop's Boys*, p. 118.

10. Kelly, *Wright Brothers*, p. 43.

11. Ibid., p. 45.

12. Ibid., p. 69.

13. McCullough, *Wright Brothers*, p. 6.

14. Crouch, *Bishop's Boys*, p. 117.

15. Ibid., p. 118.

16. Ibid., p. 115.

17. Ibid., p. 118.

18. Rosamond McPherson Young, *Twelve Seconds to the Moon* (Dayton, OH: United States Air Force Museum, 1983), p. 152.

19. Crouch, *Bishop's Boys*, p. 117.

20. Ibid.

21. Ibid., p. 89.

22. Ibid., p. 88.

23. McCullough, *Wright Brothers*, p. 8.

24. Ibid., p. 9.

25. Goldstone, *Birdmen*, p. xii.

26. James Tobin, *To Conquer the Air: The Wright Brothers and the Great Race for Flight* (New York: Simon and Schuster, 2004), p. 92.

27. Goldstone, *Birdmen*, p. xiii.

28. Tom D. Crouch, *A Dream of Wings: Americans and the Airplane, 1875–1905* (New York: W. W. Norton, 2002), p. 224.

29. Crouch, *Bishop's Boys*, p. 14.

30. Ibid., p. 13.

31. Ibid., p. 14.

32. Ibid.

33. Kelly, *Wright Brothers*, p. 285.

34. Douglas, E. Campbell, *Patent Log: Innovative Patents That Advanced the United States Navy* (LuLu.com, 2013), p. 372.

PART 1: PREFLIGHT

1. Tom D. Crouch, *The Bishop's Boys: A Life of Wilbur and Orville Wright* (New York: W. W. Norton, 1989), p. 450.

Chapter 1: The Biographer—1942

1. Fred C. Kelly, "Flying Machines and the War: An Interview with Orville Wright," *Colliers* 55 (July 31, 1915). This article was reprinted in Frank Simonds, *History of the World War*, vol. 1 (Garden City, NY: Doubleday, 1917).

2. Fred Kelly, "How the Wright Brothers Began," *Harper's Magazine*, October 1939.

3. Tom D. Crouch, *The Bishop's Boys: A Life of Wilbur and Orville Wright* (New York: W. W. Norton, 1989), p. 519.

4. Fred Kelly, Fred C. Kelly Papers (Syracuse, NY: Syracuse University, Overview, 1882–1959).

5. Roz Young, "Mabel Beck's Story Part of the Wright Brothers' History," *Dayton Daily News*, November 20, 1993.

6. Katharine Wright, on behalf of Orville Wright, January 1915, Archive of Papers Concerning the Writing and Eventual Publications of a Lengthy Biography of Orville and Wilbur Wright, Christies Fine Printed Books and Manuscripts,

https://www.christies.com/features/The-Wright-Brothers-revealed-in-their-letters
-and-photographs-7961-1.aspx (accessed July 24, 2018).

7. Crouch, *Bishop's Boys*, p. 476.

8. Young, "Mabel Beck's Story."

9. Crouch, *Bishop's Boys*, p. 516.

10. Ibid., p. 519.

Chapter 2: The Letter—1948

1. Roz Young, "Orville Did More Than Invent in His Shop—Years Can't Erase Memories," *Dayton Daily News*, December 4, 1993.

2. Tom D. Crouch, *The Bishop's Boys: A Life of Wilbur and Orville Wright* (New York: W. W. Norton, 1989), p. 476.

3. Roz Young, "Wilbur's Death Left Mabel to Insinuate Herself into Orville's Life," *Dayton Daily News*, November 27, 1993; Roz Young, "Mabel Beck's Story, Part of the Wright Brothers' History," *Dayton Daily News*, November 20, 1993.

4. Crouch, *Bishop's Boys*, p. 476.

5. Young, "Mabel Beck's Story"; Young, "Orville Did More than Invent."

6. Ibid.

7. Ibid.

8. Young, "Mabel Beck's Story."

9. Ibid.

10. Ibid.; Roz Young, "Mabel Alone after Orville's Death," *Dayton Daily News*, December 11, 1993.

11. Ibid.

12. Crouch, *Bishop's Boys*, p. 525.

13. Ibid., p. 526.

14. Ibid.

Chapter 3: The Murderer—1884

1. Paul Pfeifer, "Wilbur Wright and the Hockey Stick," *Highland County Press*, August 2016.

2. "Cocaine in Coca-Cola," Snopes, published May 19, 1999, updated April 8, 2017, https://www.snopes.com/fact-check/cocaine-coca-cola/.

3. Tom D. Crouch, *The Bishop's Boys: A Life of Wilbur and Orville Wright* (New York: W. W. Norton, 1989), p. 65.

4. Ibid., p. 74.

5. Pfeifer, "Wilbur Wright and the Hockey Stick."

6. Crouch, *Bishop's Boys*, p. 75.

7. Ibid.

8. David McCullough, *The Wright Brothers* (New York: Simon and Schuster, 2016), p. 14.

9. Lawrence Goldstone, *Birdmen: The Wright Brothers Glenn Curtiss and the Battle to Control the Skies* (New York: Ballantine, 2015), p. 35.

10. Crouch, *Bishop's Boys*, p. 22.

11. Ibid., p. 25.

12. McCullough, *Wright Brothers*, p. 11.

13. Ibid., p. 14.

14. Crouch, *Bishop's Boys*, p. 90.

15. Ibid., p. 91.

16. Fred Howard, *Wilbur and Orville: A Biography of the Wright Brothers* (New York: Dover, 2013), p. 205.

17. Crouch, *Bishop's Boys*, p. 77.

18. McCullough, *Wright Brothers*, p. 17.

19. Thos R. Coles, "The 'Wright Boys' as a Schoolmate Knew Them," in *Out West Magazine* 32–33 (January 1910).

20. Crouch, *Bishop's Boys*, p. 77.

21. Ibid., p. 76.

22. Ibid., p. 110.

23. Ibid., p. 93.

24. Orville Wright and Wilbur Wright, *Published Writings of Wilbur and Orville Wright*, ed. Peter L. Jakab and Rick Young (Washington, DC: Smithsonian, 2016), p. 60.

25. Crouch, *Bishop's Boys*, p. 94.

26. Ibid., p. 95.

27. Ibid., p. 96.

28. Ibid.

29. McCullough, *Wright Brothers*, p. 21.

30. James Tobin, *To Conquer the Air: The Wright Brothers and the Great Race for Flight* (New York: Simon and Schuster, 2004), p. 46.

Chapter 4: Steam Bugs—1896

1. Tom D. Crouch, *The Bishop's Boys: A Life of Wilbur and Orville Wright* (New York: W. W. Norton, 1989), p. 132.

2. Ibid., p. 134.

3. Ibid., p. 139.

4. Lawrence Goldstone, *Birdmen: the Wright Brothers, Glenn Curtiss, and the Battle to Control the Skies* (New York: Ballantine, 2015), p. 20.

5. Ibid.

6. Frank Harris, *Fortnightly Review* 52 (New York: Leonard Scott, 1892): 445.

7. Goldstone, *Birdmen*, p. 20.

8. Ibid., p. 22.

9. Crouch, *Bishop's Boys*, p. 138.

10. Ibid., p. 139.

11. Stephen Goddard, *Race to the Sky: The Wright Brothers versus the United States Government* (Jefferson, NC: McFarland, 2003), p. 40.

12. Crouch, *Bishop's Boys*, p. 140.

13. Tom D. Crouch, *A Dream of Wings: Americans and the Airplane, 1875–1905* (New York: Norton, 2002), p. 159.

14. Ibid., p. 160.

15. Goddard, *Race to the Sky*, p. 24.

16. Crouch, *Dream of Wings*, p. 160.

17. Ibid., p. 162.

18. American Engineer and Railroad Journal, *Proceedings on the International Conference on Aerial Navigation Held in Chicago*, August 1, 2, 3, and 4, 1893 (Cambridge, MA: Harvard University Graduate School of Business Administration, Baker Library, 1894).

19. Crouch, *Bishop's Boys*, p. 149.

Chapter 5: Typhoid—1896

1. Bronwyn Rae, "Water, Typhoid Rates, and the Columbian Exposition in Chicago," *Public Health Review* 2 (2015).

2. Emil C. Gotschlich, "Bullets and Bacilli: The Spanish American War and Military Medicine," *Journal of Clinical Investigation* 115, no. 1 (January 3, 2005).

3. Kurt Ray, *Typhoid Fever* (New York: Rosen, 2002), p. 13.

4. Richard Maurer, *The Wright Sister: Katherine Wright and Her Famous Brothers* (New York: Macmillan, 2016), p. 88.

5. Tom D. Crouch, *First Flight: The Wright Brothers and the Invention of the Airplane* (Washington, DC: Government Printing Office, 2002), p. 24.

6. Ibid., p. 25.

7. Tom D. Crouch, *The Bishop's Boys: A Life of Wilbur and Orville Wright* (New York: W. W. Norton, 1989), p. 113.

8. Thomas Means, *Aeronautical Annual* (New York: W. E. Clarke, 1894), p. 25.

9. David McCullough, *The Wright Brothers* (New York: Simon and Schuster, 2016), p. 22.

10. Ibid., p. 24.

11. Crouch, *First Flight*, p. 29.

12. McCullough, *Wright Brothers*, p. 29.

13. Etienne Jules Mary, *Popular Science Monthly* 6 (1874): 248.

14. Marvin Wilks McFarland, *The Papers of Wilbur and Orville Wright: Including the Chanute-Wright Letters and Other Papers of Octave Chanute*, vol. 1, *1899–1903* (New York: McGraw-Hill, 2001), p. 4.

15. Ibid., p. 5.

16. Crouch, *Bishop's Boys*, p. 160.

17. *Washington Post*, December 24, 1897.

18. Crouch, *Bishop's Boys*, p. 160.

19. McFarland, *Papers of Wilbur and Orville Wright*, vol. 1, *1899–1903*, p. 5.

20. Wilbur Wright, "The Story of Flight," *Aeronautics* 15 (1914).

21. Terrance MacDonald, *Firsts in Flight: Alexander Graham Bell and His Innovative Airplanes* (Halifax, NS: Formac, 2017), p. 37.

Chapter 6: Inventors—1900

1. Cecil Roseberry, *Glenn Curtiss: Pioneer of Flight* (Syracuse, NY: Syracuse University Press, 1972), p. 3.

2. Ibid.

3. Ibid.

4. Ibid., p. 27.

5. Ibid.

6. Ibid.

7. Samuel Langley, *Langley Memoir on Mechanical Flight*, vols. 1–2 (Washington, DC: Smithsonian Institution, 1911), p. 280.

Chapter 7: School of One—1900

1. Fred Kelly, *The Wright Brothers: A Biography Authorized by Orville Wright* (New York: Harcourt, Brace, 1943), p. 300.

2. Tom D. Crouch, *The Bishop's Boys A Life of Wilbur and Orville Wright* (New York: W. W. Norton, 1989), p. 110.

3. Ibid.

4. Tom D. Crouch, *First Flight: The Wright Brothers and the Invention of the Airplane* (Washington, DC: Government Printing Office, 2002), p. 34.

5. Kelly, *Wright Brothers*, p. 34.

6. Marvin Wilks McFarland, *The Papers of Wilbur and Orville Wright: Including the Chanute-Wright Letters and Other Papers of Octave Chanute*, vol. 1, *1899–1903* (New York: McGraw-Hill, 2001), p. 11.

7. Fred Howard, *Wilbur and Orville: A Biography of the Wright Brothers* (New York: Courier, 2013), p. 35.

8. McFarland, *Papers of Wilbur and Orville Wright*, vol. 1, *1899–1903*, p. 11.

9. Ibid., p. 15.

10. Ibid., p. 17.

11. Ibid., p. 16.

12. Ibid., p. 18.

13. Ibid., p. 238.

14. Ibid., p. 15. Italics added.

15. Howard, *Wilbur and Orville*, p. 39.

16. McFarland, *Papers of Wilbur and Orville Wright*, vol. 1, *1899–1903*, p. 18.

17. Ibid., p. 20.

18. Howard, *Wilbur and Orville*, p. 37.

19. David McCullough, *The Wright Brothers* (New York: Simon and Schuster, 2016), p. 41.

20. McFarland, *Papers of Wilbur and Orville Wright*, vol. 1, *1899–1903*, p. 21.

21. Ibid., p. 22.

22. Ibid.

23. Ibid.

24. Ibid., p. 23.

25. Ibid.

PART 2: FLIGHT

Chapter 8: The Pilgrim—1900

1. Marvin Wilks McFarland, *The Papers of Wilbur and Orville Wright: Including the Chanute-Wright Letters and Other Papers of Octave Chanute*, vol. 1, *1899–1903* (New York: McGraw-Hill, 2001), p. 24.

2. Ibid.

3. Ibid.

4. Ibid.

5. Ibid.

6. David McCullough, *The Wright Brothers* (New York: Simon and Schuster, 2016), p. 44.

7. McFarland, *Papers of Wilbur and Orville Wright*, vol. 1, *1899–1903*, p. 24.

8. Ibid.

9. Ibid., p. 25.

10. Ibid.

11. Renee Wright, *Explorer's Guide North Carolina's Outer Banks and Crystal Coast* (New York: Countryman, 2013), p. 81.

12. McFarland, *Papers of Wilbur and Orville Wright*, vol. 1, *1899–1903*, p. 12.

13. David Stick, *An Outer Banks Reader* (Chapel Hill, NC: University of North Carolina Press, 1998), p. 233.

14. McFarland, *Papers of Wilbur and Orville Wright: Including the Chanute-Wright Letters and Other Papers of Octave Chanute*, vol. 2, *1906–1948*, p. 1161.

15. Patty Wilson, *Haunted North Carolina, Ghosts, and Strange Phenomena of the Tar Heel State* (Mechanicsburg, PA: Stackpole, 2009), p. 47.

16. Orville Wright and Wilbur Wright, *Published Writings of Wilbur and Orville Wright*, ed. Peter L. Jakab and Rick Young (Washington, DC: Smithsonian, 2016), p. 284.

17. Fred Howard, *Wilbur and Orville: A Biography of The Wright Brothers* (New York: Courier, 2013), p. 45.

18. McFarland, *Papers of Wilbur and Orville Wright*, vol. 1, *1899–1903*, p. 25.

19. Ibid., p. 26.

20. McCullough, *The Wright Brothers*, p. 46.

21. Wright and Wright, *Published Writings of Wilbur and Orville Wright*, p. 281.

22. McFarland, *Papers of Wilbur and Orville Wright*, vol. 1, *1899–1903*, p. 34.

23. Ibid.

24. Ibid.

25. Ibid., p. 26.

26. Ibid.

27. Ibid.

28. Ibid.

29. Tom D. Crouch, *The Bishop's Boys: A Life of Wilbur and Orville Wright* (New York: W. W. Norton, 1989), p. 188.

30. Ibid., p. 163.

31. Ibid., p. 124.

32. Ibid., p. 163.

33. Ibid., p. 188.

34. John E. Walsh, *One Day at Kitty Hawk: The Untold Story of the Wright Brothers and the Airplane* (New York: Crowell, 1975), p. 104.

35. McFarland, *Papers of Wilbur and Orville Wright*, vol. 1, *1899–1903*, p. 38.

36. Ibid., p. 32.

37. Ibid., p. 39.

38. Ibid.

39. Ibid., p. 33.

40. Ibid., p. 32.

41. Ibid., p. 31.

42. Ibid., p. 39.

43. McCullough, *Wright Brothers*, p. 49.

44. McFarland, *Papers of Wilbur and Orville Wright*, vol. 1, *1899–1903*, p. 29.

45. Ibid., p. 30.

46. Ibid.

47. Ibid., p. 39.

Chapter 9: The Wright Sister—1900

1. Richard Maurer, *The Wright Sister: Katherine Wright and Her Famous Brothers* (New York: Macmillan, 2016), p. 128.

2. Charles Yrigoyen and Susan Warre, *Historical Dictionary of Methodism* (Lantham, MD: Scarecrow, 2013), p. 362.

3. Tom D. Crouch, *The Bishop's Boys: A Life of Wilbur and Orville Wright* (New York: W. W. Norton, 1989), p. 87.

4. Maurer, *Wright Sister*, p. 30.

5. Ibid.

6. Ibid., p. 31.

7. Ibid.

8. Ibid.

9. Ibid., p. 35.

10. Ibid.

11. Ibid., p. 53.

12. Ibid.

13. Marvin Wilks McFarland, *The Papers of Wilbur and Orville Wright: Including the Chanute-Wright Letters and Other Papers of Octave Chanute*, vol. 1, *1899–1903* (New York: McGraw-Hill, 2001), p. 27.

14. Ibid., p. 28.

15. Ibid.
16. Ibid., p. 27.

Chapter 10: Kill Devil Hills—October 18, 1900

1. Marvin Wilks McFarland, *The Papers of Wilbur and Orville Wright: Including the Chanute-Wright Letters and Other Papers of Octave Chanute*, vol. 1, *1899–1903* (New York: McGraw-Hill, 2001), p. 31.
2. Ibid., p. 38.
3. Ibid.
4. Ibid.
5. Ibid.
6. Ibid., p. 46.
7. Ibid., p. 30.
8. Tom D. Crouch, *The Bishop's Boys: A Life of Wilbur and Orville Wright* (New York: W. W. Norton, 1989), p. 191.
9. Lester Garber, *The Wright Brothers and the Birth of Aviation* (Ramsbury, Marlborough, Wiltshire: Crowood, 2005), p. 95.
10. Crouch, *Bishop's Boys*, p. 276.
11. David McCullough, *The Wright Brothers* (New York: Simon and Shuster, 2016), p. 55.
12. Crouch, *Bishop's Boys*, p. 190.
13. Ibid.
14. Ibid.
15. Fred Howard, *Wilbur and Orville: A Biography of the Wright Brothers* (New York: Courier, 2013), p. 52.
16. Crouch, *Bishop's Boys*, p. 198.
17. Howard, *Wilbur and Orville*, p. 53.
18. McFarland, *Papers of Wilbur and Orville Wright*, vol. 1, *1899–1903*, p. 106.
19. Larry Tise, *Conquering the Sky: The Secret Flights of the Wright Brothers at Kitty Hawk* (New York: St. Martin's, 2009), p. 24.
20. McFarland, *Papers of Wilbur and Orville Wright*, vol. 1, *1899–1903*, p. 43.

Chapter 11: The Mentor—1901

1. Marvin Wilks McFarland, *The Papers of Wilbur and Orville Wright: Including the Chanute-Wright Letters and Other Papers of Octave Chanute*, vol. 1, *1899–1903* (New York: McGraw-Hill, 2001), p. 40.

2. Tom D. Crouch, *The Bishop's Boys: A Life of Wilbur and Orville Wright* (New York: W. W. Norton, 1989), p. 201.

3. McFarland, *Papers of Wilbur and Orville Wright*, vol. 1, *1899–1903*, p. 41.

4. Ibid., p. 43.

5. Ibid.

6. Ibid., p. 44.

7. Ibid., p. 45.

8. Ibid.

9. Ibid., p. 54.

10. Ibid.

11. Ibid., p. 58.

12. Ibid.

13. Ibid., p. 61.

14. Ibid.

15. Ibid., p. 41.

16. Ibid., p. 44.

Chapter 12: Dangerous Times—1901

1. Scott Miller, *The President and the Assassin: McKinley, Terror, and Empire at the Dawn of the American Century* (New York: Random House, 2013), p. 302.

2. Western Society of Engineers, *Journal of the Western Society of Engineers* 2 (1897): 595.

3. Cecil Roseberry, *Glenn Curtiss: Pioneer of Flight* (Syracuse, NY: Syracuse University Press, 1972), p. 35.

4. Ibid., p. 36.

5. Ibid., p. 40.

6. Ibid.

7. Ibid., p. 42.

8. Ibid., p. 43.

9. Ibid., p. 45.

10. Lawrence Goldstone, *Birdmen: The Wright Brothers, Glenn Curtiss, and the Battle to Control the Skies* (New York: Ballantine, 2015), p. 47.

11. Marvin Wilks McFarland, *The Papers of Wilbur and Orville Wright*, vol. 1, *1899–1903* (New York: McGraw-Hill, 2001), p. 56.

12. Ibid., p. 56.

13. Ibid.

14. Ibid., p. 57.

15. Orville Wright and Wilbur Wright, *Published Writings of Wilbur and Orville Wright*, ed. Peter L. Jakab and Rick Young (Washington, DC: Smithsonian, 2016), p. 227.

16. Tom D. Crouch, *The Bishop's Boys: A Life of Wilbur and Orville Wright* (New York: W. W. Norton, 1989), p. 205.

17. McFarland, *Papers of Wilbur and Orville Wright*, vol. 1, *1899–1903*, p. 63.

18. Ibid., p. 66.

Chapter 13: Return to Kitty Hawk—1901

1. Marvin McFarland, *The Papers of Wilbur and Orville Wright: Including the Chanute-Wright Letters and Other Papers of Octave Chanute*, vol. 1, *1899–1903* (New York: McGraw-Hill, 2001), p. 55.

2. Ibid., p. 70.

3. Ibid., p. 68.

4. Ibid.

5. Ibid., p. 72.

6. Ibid., p. 73.

7. Steven Hensley and Julia Hensley, *The Unwelcome Assistant: Edward C. Huffaker and the Birth of Aviation* (Johnson City, TN: Overmountain, 2003), p. 101.

8. Fred Howard, *Wilbur and Orville: A Biography of the Wright Brothers* (New York: Courier, 2013), p. 61.

9. McFarland, *Papers of Wilbur and Orville Wright*, vol. 1, *1899–1903*, p. 69.

10. Ibid.

11. Ibid., p. 70.

12. Ibid., p. 73.

13. Ibid., p. 74.

14. Ibid.

15. Ibid.

16. Ibid.

17. David McCullough, *The Wright Brothers* (New York: Simon and Shuster, 2016), p. 60.

18. McFarland, *Papers of Wilbur and Orville Wright*, vol. 1, *1899–1903*, p. 108.

19. Ibid.

20. Ibid., p. 108.

21. Ibid., p. 81.

22. Tom D. Crouch, *The Bishop's Boys: A Life of Wilbur and Orville Wright* (New York: W. W. Norton, 1989), p. 209.

23. Wilbur Wright, "Some Aeronautical Experiments," *Journal of the Western Society of Engineers* 6 (1901): 501.

24. McFarland, *Papers of Wilbur and Orville Wright*, vol. 1, *1899–1903*, p. 75.

25. Smithsonian National Air and Space Museum, "Correcting Smeaton," https://airandspace.si.edu/exhibitions/wright-brothers/online/fly/1901/smeaton.cfm.

26. Crouch, *Bishop's Boys*, p. 210.

27. Wright, "Some Aeronautical Experiments," p. 503.

28. McCullough, *Wright Brothers*, p. 62.

29. McFarland, *Papers of Wilbur and Orville Wright*, vol. 1, *1899–1903*, p. 77.

30. Patrick Nolan and John Zamonski, *The Wright Brothers Collection* (Columbus, OH: Wright State University, 1977), p. 165.

31. Crouch, *Bishop's Boys*, p. 212.

32. Ibid.

33. Orville Wright and Wilbur Wright, *Published Writings of Wilbur and Orville Wright*, ed. Peter L. Jakab and Rick Young (Washington, DC: Smithsonian, 2016), p. 32.

34. Crouch, *Bishop's Boys*, p. 213.

35. McFarland, *Papers of Wilbur and Orville Wright*, vol. 1, *1899–1903* (New York: McGraw-Hill, 2001), p. 81.

36. Crouch, *Bishop's Boys*, p. 213.

37. Stephen Goddard, *Race to the Sky: The Wright Brothers versus the United States Government* (Jefferson, NC: McFarland, 2003), p. 101.

38. McFarland, *Papers of Wilbur and Orville Wright*, vol. 1, *1899–1903*, p. 83.

39. Howard, *Wilbur and Orville*, p. 67.

40. Ibid.

41. Crouch, *Bishop's Boys*, p. 210.

42. Ibid.

43. Ibid., p. 213.

44. McFarland, *Papers of Wilbur and Orville Wright*, vol. 1, *1899–1903*, p. 84.

45. Ibid., p. 150.

46. Crouch, *Bishop's Boys*, p. 213.

Chapter 14: Wilbur Unleashed—1901

1. Marvin Wilks McFarland, *The Papers of Wilbur and Orville Wright: Including the Chanute-Wright Letters and Other Papers of Octave Chanute*, vol. 1, *1899–1903* (New York: McGraw-Hill, 2001), p. 91.

2. Ibid., p. 92.

3. Ibid.

4. Ibid., p. 99.

5. Ibid., p. 93.

6. McFarland, *Papers of Wilbur and Orville Wright*, vol. 1, *1899–1903*, p. 99.

7. Ibid.

8. Ibid.

9. Ibid., p. 95.

10. Ibid., p. 116.

11. Ibid.

12. Ibid., p. 100.

13. Ibid.

14. Ibid., p. 99.

15. Ibid., p. 100.

16. Ibid., p. 103.

17. Orville Wright and Wilbur Wright, *Published Writings of Wilbur and Orville Wright*, ed. Peter L. Jakab and Rick Young (Washington, DC: Smithsonian, 2016), p. 32.

18. Wilbur Wright, "Some Aeronautical Experiments," *Journal of the Western Society of Engineers* 6 (1901): 506.

19. McFarland, *Papers of Wilbur and Orville Wright*, vol. 1, *1899–1903*, p. 115.

20. Ibid., p. 116.

Chapter 15: Tunnel Vision—1901

1. Orville Wright and Wilbur Wright, *Published Writings of Wilbur and Orville Wright*, ed. Peter L. Jakab and Rick Young (Washington, DC: Smithsonian, 2016), p. 32.

2. David McCullough, *The Wright Brothers* (New York: Simon and Schuster, 2016), p. 69.

3. Marvin Wilks McFarland, *The Papers of Wilbur and Orville Wright: Including the Chanute-Wright Letters and Other Papers of Octave Chanute*, vol. 1, *1899–1903* (New York: McGraw-Hill, 2001), p. 156.

4. Lawrence Goldstone, *Birdmen: The Wright Brothers, Glenn Curtiss, and the Battle to Control the Skies* (New York: Ballantine, 2015), p. 53.

5. McFarland, *Papers of Wilbur and Orville Wright*, vol. 1, *1899–1903*, p. 185.

6. Ibid., p. 115.

7. Ibid.

8. Ibid., p. 183.

9. Ibid.

10. Ibid., p. 187.

11. Ibid., p. 183.

Chapter 16: The Smithsonian—1902

1. Marvin Wilks McFarland, *The Papers of Wilbur and Orville Wright: Including the Chanute-Wright Letters and Other Papers of Octave Chanute*, vol. 1 (New York: McGraw-Hill, 2001), p. 261.

2. Ibid., p. 257.

3. Orville Wright and Wilbur Wright, *Published Writings of Wilbur and Orville Wright*, ed. Peter L. Jakab and Rick Young (Washington, DC: Smithsonian, 2016), p. 25.

4. Fred Howard, *Wilbur and Orville: A Biography of the Wright Brothers* (New York: Courier, 2013), p. 96.

Chapter 17: The Movable Rudder—1902

1. Marvin Wilks McFarland, *The Papers of Wilbur and Orville Wright: Including the Chanute-Wright Letters and Other Papers of Octave Chanute*, vol. 1, *1899–1903* (New York: McGraw-Hill, 2001), p. 260.

2. Fred Kelly, *The Wright Brothers: A Biography Authorized by Orville Wright* (New York: Harcourt, Brace, 1943), p. 78.

3. McFarland, *Papers of Wilbur and Orville Wright*, vol. 1, *1899–1903*, p. 269.

4. David McCullough, *The Wright Brothers* (New York: Simon and Schuster, 2016), p. 77.

5. McFarland, *Papers of Wilbur and Orville Wright*, vol. 1, *1899–1903*, p. 260.

6. Fred Howard, *Wilbur and Orville: A Biography of the Wright Brothers* (New York: Courier, 2013), p. 89.

7. McFarland, *Papers of Wilbur and Orville Wright*, vol. 1, p. 470.

8. Ibid.

9. Howard, *Wilbur and Orville*, p. 82.

10. McFarland, *Papers of Wilbur and Orville Wright*, vol. 1, *1899–1903*, p. 281.

Chapter 18: United States Patent Office—1903

1. Tom D. Crouch, *The Bishop's Boys: A Life of Wilbur and Orville Wright* (New York: W. W. Norton, 1989), p. 246.

2. Ibid., p. 254.

3. Thomas Hill, "Status of the Wrights' Suits," *Aeronautics* 5–7 (1909): 122.

4. Stephen Goddard, *Race to the Sky: The Wright Brothers versus the United States Government* (Jefferson, NC: McFarland, 2003), p. 117.

Chapter 19: The Western Society of Engineers—1903

1. Orville Wright and Wilbur Wright, *Published Writings of Wilbur and Orville Wright*, ed. Peter L. Jakab and Rick Young (Washington, DC: Smithsonian, 2016), p. 13.

2. Ibid., p. 11.

3. Ibid., p. 231.

4. Ibid., p. 9.

5. Ibid., p. 10.

6. Marvin Wilks McFarland, *The Papers of Wilbur and Orville Wright: Including the Chanute-Wright Letters and Other Papers of Octave Chanute*, vol. 1, *1899–1903* (New York: McGraw-Hill, 2001), p. 323.

7. Ibid., p. 597.

8. John Klooster, *Icons of Invention*, vol. 1 (Santa Barbara, CA: ABC-CLIO, 2009), p. 382.

9. Wilbur Wright, "Observations in Soaring Flight," *Journal of the Western Society of Engineers* 8 (August 1903): 410.

10. Ibid., p. 415.

11. Ibid., p. 416.

Chapter 20: The Great Embarrassment—1903

1. Lawrence Goldstone, *Birdmen: The Wright Brothers, Glenn Curtiss, and the Battle to Control The Skies* (New York: Ballantine, 2015), p. 77.

2. Ibid., p. 78.

3. Ibid., p. 79.

Chapter 21: Great Things—September 23, 1903

1. David McCullough, *The Wright Brothers* (New York: Simon and Schuster, 2016), p. 85.

2. Ibid., p. 86.

3. Marvin McFarland, *The Papers of Wilbur and Orville Wright: Including*

the Chanute-Wright Letters and Other Papers of Octave Chanute, vol. 1, *1899–1903* (New York: McGraw-Hill, 2001), p. 357.

    4. Ibid., p. 356.

    5. Ibid., p. 359.

    6. Ibid., p. 365.

    7. Ibid., p. 367.

    8. Fred Howard, *Wilbur and Orville: A Biography of the Wright Brothers* (New York: Courier, 2013), p. 115.

    9. McFarland, *Papers of Wilbur and Orville Wright*, vol. 1, *1899–1903*, p. 364.

    10. Ibid., p. 373.

    11. Orville Wright and Wilbur Wright, *Published Writings of Wilbur and Orville Wright*, ed. Peter L. Jakab and Rick Young (Washington, DC: Smithsonian, 2016), p. 230.

    12. McFarland, *Papers of Wilbur and Orville Wright*, vol. 1, *1899–1903*, p. 374.

    13. Howard, *Wilbur and Orville*, p. 117.

    14. McFarland, *Papers of Wilbur and Orville Wright*, vol. 1, *1899–1903*, p. 378.

    15. Ibid., p. 381.

    16. Ibid., p. 379.

    17. Ibid.

    18. Ibid., p. 380.

    19. Ibid., p. 381.

    20. Ibid., p. 383.

    21. McCullough, *Wright Brothers*, p. 99.

    22. McFarland, *Papers of Wilbur and Orville Wright*, vol. 1, *1899–1903*, p. 388.

    23. Ibid., p. 389.

    24. Ibid., p. 390.

    25. Lawrence Goldstone, *Birdmen: The Wright Brothers, Glenn Curtiss, and the Battle to Control the Skies* (New York: Ballantine, 2015), p. 79.

    26. McFarland, *Papers of Wilbur and Orville Wright*, vol. 1, *1899–1903*, p. 390.

    27. Ibid., p. 385.

    28. First Flight Foundation, "Coin Toss," https://firstflightfoundation.org/coin-toss/.

    29. Ibid., p. 392.

    30. Ibid.

    31. Ibid.

    32. Ibid.

    33. Ibid.

Chapter 22: The Photograph—December 17, 1903

1. Marvin McFarland, *The Papers of Wilbur and Orville Wright: Including the Chanute-Wright Letters and Other Papers of Octave Chanute*, vol. 1, *1899–1903* (New York: McGraw-Hill, 2001), p. 394.

2. Fred Howard, *Wilbur and Orville: A Biography of the Wright Brothers* (New York: Courier, 2013), p. 135.

3. McFarland, *Papers of Wilbur and Orville Wright*, vol. 1, *1899–1903*, p. 394.

4. Ibid., p. 395.

5. Ibid.

6. David McCullough, *The Wright Brothers* (New York: Simon and Schuster, 2016), p. 105.

7. Ibid.

8. Ibid.

9. McFarland, *Papers of Wilbur and Orville Wright*, vol. 1, *1899–1903*, p. 358.

10. Ibid.

11. Ibid.

12. Ibid., p. 397. Please note, this initial telegram was incorrect; the fourth flight lasted 59 seconds.

13. Smithsonian National Air and Space Museum, "1903 Wright Flyer Fabric Taken to Moon: Apollo 11," https://airandspace.si.edu/multimedia -gallery/430-l1-s1hjpg.

14. Ibid. The initial telegram was erroneous; the fourth flight had a duration of 59 seconds.

15. Ibid., p. 403.

16. Orville Wright and Wilbur Wright, *Published Writings of Wilbur and Orville Wright*, ed. Peter L. Jakab and Rick Young (Washington, DC: Smithsonian, 2016), p. 212.

17. McFarland, *Papers of Wilbur and Orville Wright*, vol. 1, *1899–1903*, p. 403.

18. Ibid., p. 396.

19. Ibid., p. 395.

20. Ibid.

21. Torenbeek Wittenberg, *Flight Physics: Essentials of Aeronautical Disciplines and Technology, with Historical Notes* (Dordrecht: Springer Science and Business Media, 2009), p. 1.

22. McFarland, *Papers of Wilbur and Orville Wright*, vol. 1, *1899–1903*, p. 396.

23. Ibid.

PART 3: LANDINGS

Chapter 23: Fliers or Liars—1906

1. Cecil Roseberry, *Glenn Curtiss: Pioneer of Flight* (Syracuse, NY: Syracuse University Press, 1972), p. 52.

2. James Tobin, *To Conquer the Air: The Wright Brothers and the Great Race for Flight* (New York: Simon and Schuster, 2004), p. 250.

3. Roseberry, *Glenn Curtiss*, p. 63.

4. Ibid., p. 48.

5. Ibid., p. 71.

6. Ibid., p. 51.

7. Ibid.

8. Ibid., p. 52.

9. Ibid.

10. Ibid.

11. Tom D. Crouch, *The Bishop's Boys: A Life of Wilbur and Orville Wright* (New York: W. W. Norton, 1989), p. 284.

12. David McCullough, *The Wright Brothers* (New York: Simon and Schuster, 2016), p. 120.

13. "The Wright Aeroplane and Its Fabled Performances," *Scientific American* 94, no. 2, January 13, 1905.

14. Crouch, *Bishop's Boys*, p. 271.

15. Fred Kelly, *The Wright Brothers: A Biography Authorized by Orville Wright* (New York: Harcourt, Brace, 1943), p. 105.

16. Ibid., p. 106.

17. Marvin Wilks McFarland, *The Papers of Wilbur and Orville Wright: Including the Chanute-Wright Letters and Other Papers of Octave Chanute*, vol. 1, *1899–1903* (New York: McGraw-Hill, 2001), p. 409.

18. *Popular Aviation*, December 1928, p. 14.

19. Kelly, *Wright Brothers*, p. 109.

20. Crouch, *Bishop's Boys*, p. 274.

21. Ibid., p. 277.

22. Ibid.

23. Ibid.

24. *Harper's Magazine*, 1940, p. 288.

25. McFarland, *Papers of Wilbur and Orville Wright*, vol. 1, *1899–1903*, p. 437.

26. McCullough, *Wright Brothers*, p. 126.

27. McFarland, *Papers of Wilbur and Orville Wright*, vol. 1, *1899–1903*, p. 514.

28. Kelly, *Wright Brothers*, p. 138.

29. Herbert Molloy Mason, *The United States Air Force: A Turbulent History* (New York: Charter, 1976), p. 5.

30. McCullough, *Wright Brothers*, p. 128.

31. Crouch, *Bishop's Boys*, p. 277.

32. Ibid., p. 313.

33. Ibid., p. 132.

34. Kelly, *Wright Brothers*, p. 136.

35. Ibid.

36. Roseberry, *Glenn Curtiss*, p. 53.

37. Ibid.

38. Ibid., p. 54.

39. Ibid., p. 81.

40. Ibid., p. 82.

Chapter 24: Death in the Sky—September 17, 1908

1. Tom D. Crouch, *The Bishop's Boys: A Life of Wilbur and Orville Wright* (New York: W. W. Norton, 1989), p. 376.

2. Marvin McFarland, *The Papers of Wilbur and Orville Wright: Including the Chanute-Wright Letters and Other Papers of Octave Chanute*, vol. 2, *1906–1948* (New York: McGraw-Hill, 2001), p. 907.

3. Mark Eppler, *The Wright Way: 7 Problem Solving Principles from the Wright Brothers* (New York: AMACOM, 2003), p. 182.

4. Ibid.

5. Cecil Roseberry, *Glenn Curtiss: Pioneer of Flight* (Syracuse, NY: Syracuse University Press, 1972), p. 124.

6. Crouch, *Bishop's Boys*, p. 376.

7. McFarland, *Papers of Wilbur and Orville Wright*, vol. 2, *1906–1948*, p. 907.

8. Crouch, *Bishop's Boys*, p. 260.

9. Lawrence Goldstone, *Birdmen: The Wright Brothers, Glenn Curtiss, and the Battle to Control the Skies* (New York: Ballantine, 2015), p. 137.

10. McFarland, *Papers of Wilbur and Orville Wright*, vol. 2, *1906–1948*, p. 937.

11. Goldstone, *Birdmen*, p. 140.

12. McFarland, *Papers of Wilbur and Orville Wright*, vol. 2, *1906–1948*, p. 925.

13. Ibid., p. 900.

14. Goldstone, *Birdmen*, p. 130.

15. McFarland, *Papers of Wilbur and Orville Wright*, vol. 2, *1906–1948*, p. 954.

Chapter 25: Return to Eden—1908

1. Fred Howard, *Wilbur and Orville: A Biography of the Wright Brothers* (New York: Courier, 2013), p. 53.

Chapter 26: The Injunction—1910

1. Lawrence Goldstone, *Birdmen: The Wright Brothers, Glenn Curtiss, and the Battle to Control the Skies* (New York: Ballantine, 2015), p. 149.
2. Ibid.
3. Ibid.
4. Ibid., p. 262.
5. Ibid., p. 180.
6. Ibid., p. 181.
7. Ibid., p. 185.
8. Ibid.
9. Ibid., p. 186.
10. Ibid.
11. Ibid.
12. Ibid., p. 189.
13. Ibid., p. 181.
14. Ibid., p. 182.

Chapter 27: Warped by the Desire for Great Wealth—1911

1. David McCullough, *The Wright Brothers* (New York: Simon and Schuster, 2016), p. 203.
2. Ibid.
3. Ibid., p. 204.
4. Ibid., p. 207.
5. Ibid.
6. Ibid., p. 219.
7. Ibid., p. 224.
8. Ibid., p. 221.
9. Marvin Wilks McFarland, *The Papers of Wilbur and Orville Wright: Including the Chanute-Wright Letters and Other Papers of Octave Chanute*, vol. 2, *1906–1948* (New York: McGraw-Hill, 2001), p. 862.
10. Lawrence Goldstone, *Birdmen: The Wright Brothers, Glenn Curtiss, and the Battle to Control the Skies* (New York: Random House, 2014), p. 202.

11. McFarland, *Papers of Wilbur and Orville Wright*, vol. 2, *1906–1948*, p. 962.

12. Ibid., p. 972.

13. Ibid., p. 979.

14. Ibid., p. 981.

15. Ibid.

16. Ibid., p. 983.

Chapter 28: Final Flight—1912

1. Tom D. Crouch, *The Bishop's Boys: A Life of Wilbur and Orville Wright* (New York: W. W. Norton, 1989), p. 447.

2. Fred Howard, *Wilbur and Orville: A Biography of the Wright Brothers* (New York: Courier, 2013), p. 380.

3. Crouch, *Bishop's Boys*, p. 447.

4. Marvin Wilks McFarland, *The Papers of Wilbur and Orville Wright: Including the Chanute-Wright Letters and Other Papers of Octave Chanute*, vol. 2, *1906–1948* (New York: McGraw-Hill, 2001), p. 1043.

5. Ibid., p. 1044.

6. Flying Association, "Flying," *Journal of the Flying Association* 1 (1912), p. 52, cited in Crouch, *Bishop's Boys*, p. 449.

7. Crouch, *Bishop's Boys*, p. 451.

8. Ibid., p. 460.

9. "Wright Curtiss Litigation Ended, Patent Upheld," *Aeronautics* 14, January 31, 2014, p. 21.

10. Ibid.

11. McFarland, *Papers of Wilbur and Orville Wright*, vol. 2, *1906–1948*, p. 1073.

12. Lawrence Goldstone, *Birdmen: The Wright Brothers, Glenn Curtiss, and the Battle to Control the Skies* (New York: Random House, 2014), p. 262.

13. Ibid.

Chapter 29: The Great Flood—1914

1. Lawrence Goldstone, *Birdmen: The Wright Brothers, Glenn Curtiss, and the Battle to Control the Skies* (New York: Random House, 2014), p. 262.

2. Ibid., p. 450.

3. Ibid.

4. Ibid.

5. Ibid., p. 454.

6. Roz Young, "Mabel Beck's Story," *Dayton Daily News*, November 20, 1993.
7. Ibid.
8. Ibid.

Chapter 30: To Fly Again—1914

1. Tom D. Crouch, *The Bishop's Boys, A Life of Wilbur and Orville Wright* (New York: W. W. Norton, 1989), p. 485.
2. Ibid.
3. Ibid.
4. Ibid., p. 486.
5. Ibid.
6. Ibid.
7. Ibid.
8. Ibid.

Chapter 31: Hammondsport, New York—1915

1. Tom D. Crouch, *The Bishop's Boys: A Life of Wilbur and Orville Wright* (New York: W. W. Norton, 1989), p. 486.
2. Ibid., p. 489.
3. Ibid.
4. Marvin Wilks McFarland, *The Papers of Wilbur and Orville Wright: Including the Chanute-Wright Letters and Other Papers of Octave Chanute*, vol. 2, *1906–1948* (New York: McGraw-Hill, 2001), p. 1090.
5. Ibid., p. 1091.
6. Ibid.
7. Ibid.
8. Ibid.
9. Ibid., p. 1092.
10. Ibid.
11. Crouch, *Bishop's Boys*, p. 487.
12. Ibid.
13. Ibid.
14. Ibid.
15. Ibid., p. 492.
16. Ibid.
17. Ibid., p. 481.

Chapter 32: Middle of the Atlantic Ocean—1928

1. Orville Wright and Wilbur Wright, *Published Writings of Wilbur and Orville Wright*, ed. Peter L. Jakab and Rick Young (Washington, DC: Smithsonian, 2016), p. 247.
2. Ibid.
3. Ibid.
4. Tom D. Crouch, *The Bishop's Boys: A Life of Wilbur and Orville Wright* (New York: W. W. Norton, 1989), p. 491.

Chapter 33: A Test of Wills—1930

1. Tom D. Crouch, *The Bishop's Boys: A Life of Wilbur and Orville Wright* (New York: W. W. Norton, 1989), p. 492.
2. Ibid.
3. Ibid.
4. Ibid., p. 493.
5. Ibid., p. 488.
6. Marvin Wilks McFarland, *The Papers of Wilbur and Orville Wright: Including the Chanute-Wright Letters and Other Papers of Octave Chanute*, vol. 1, *1899–1903* (New York: McGraw-Hill, 2001), p. 115.
7. Marvin Wilks McFarland, *The Papers of Wilbur and Orville Wright: Including the Chanute-Wright Letters and Other Papers of Octave Chanute*, vol. 2, *1906–1948* (New York: McGraw-Hill, 2001), p. 737.
8. Crouch, *Bishop's Boys*, p. 488.
9. Ibid., p. 490.
10. Ibid.
11. Ibid.
12. Ibid.
13. Ibid., p. 491.
14. Ibid., p. 492.
15. Ibid.

Chapter 34: The Lone Eagle—1934

1. Tom D. Crouch, *The Bishop's Boys: A Life of Wilbur and Orville Wright* (New York: W. W. Norton, 1989), p. 493.
2. Ibid.

3. Ibid., p. 494.
4. Ibid.
5. Crouch, *Bishop's Boys*, p. 495.
6. Ibid.
7. Ibid., p. 487.
8. Ibid., p. 493.
9. Ibid.
10. Ibid., p. 494.
11. Ibid.
12. Ibid., p. 495.
13. Ibid.
14. Ibid.
15. Susan Hertog, *Anne Morrow Lindbergh: Her Life* (New York: Anchor, 2000), p. 345.
16. Ibid., p. 324.
17. Ibid.
18. Crouch, *Bishop's Boys*, p. 495.
19. Ruth Sarles, *A Story of America First: The Men and Women Who Opposed US Intervention in World War II* (New York: Greenwood, 2003), p. 56.
20. Max Wallace, *The American Axis: Henry Ford, Charles Lindbergh, and the Rise of the Third Reich* (New York: St. Martin's, 2003), p. 374.

Chapter 35: The Battle of Britain—1940

1. Tom D. Crouch, *The Bishop's Boys: A Life of Wilbur and Orville Wright* (New York: W. W. Norton, 1989), p. 496.

Chapter 36: The Authorized Biography—1943

1. Tom D. Crouch, *The Bishop's Boys: A Life of Wilbur and Orville Wright* (New York: W. W. Norton, 1989), p. 520.
2. Ibid.
3. Ibid.
4. Ibid.
5. Ibid., p. 521.
6. Ibid.

Chapter 37: Washington, DC—1943

1. Fred Howard, *Wilbur And Orville: A Biography of the Wright Brothers* (New York: Courier, 2013), p. 440.
2. Ibid.
3. Ibid.

Chapter 38: Mabel Beck—1948

1. Tom D. Crouch, *The Bishop's Boys: A Life of Wilbur and Orville Wright* (New York: W. W. Norton, 1989), p. 503.
2. Ibid., p. 431.

Epilogue

1. Tom D. Crouch, *The Bishop's Boys: A Life of Wilbur and Orville Wright* (New York: W. W. Norton, 1989), p. 529.
2. Ibid., p. 527.
3. Roz Young, "Mabel Beck's Story, Part of the Wright Brothers' Story," *Dayton Daily News*, November 20, 1993; Roz Young, "Mabel Alone after Orville's Death," *Dayton Daily News*, December 11, 1993.
4. Ibid.
5. Ibid.; "Letters of Love: Correspondence Reveals Orville's Feelings for Mabel," *Dayton Daily News*, January 22, 1994.
6. Associated Press, "Wright Flyer Replica Fails to Fly," *Wired*, December 17, 2003.

BIBLIOGRAPHY

Abbott, C. G. "The 1914 Test of the Langley 'Aerodrome.'" *Journal of the Aeronautical Sciences* 10, no. 1 (1943): 31–35.

American Engineer and Railroad Journal. *Proceedings on the International Conference on Aerial Navigation Held in Chicago.* August 1, 2, 3, and 4, 1893. Cambridge, MA: Harvard University Graduate School of Business Administration, Baker Library, 1894.

Associated Press. "Wright Flyer Replica Fails to Fly." *Wired,* December 17, 2003.

Bauer, Charles J. "Ed Sines, Pal of the Wrights." *Popular Aviation,* June 1938, p. 40.

Beck, Mabel. "The First Airplane after 1903." *US Air Services,* December 1954, pp. 9–10.

Campbell, Douglas E. *Patent Log: Innovative Patents That Advanced the United States Navy.* LuLu.com, 2013.

Coles, Thos R. "The 'Wright Boys' as a Schoolmate Knew Them." In *Out West Magazine* 32–33 (January 1910).

Collections. Washington, DC: Smithsonian Institution Press, October 24, 1942.

Combs, Henry, and Martin Caidin. *Kill Devil Hill: Discovering the Secrets of the Wright Brothers.* Boston: Houghton Mifflin, 1979.

Crouch, Tom D. *The Bishop's Boys: A Life of Wilbur and Orville Wright.* New York: W. W. Norton, 1989.

———. *A Dream of Wings: Americans and the Airplane, 1875–1905.* New York: W. W. Norton, 2002.

———. *First Flight: The Wright Brothers and the Invention of the Airplane.* Washington, DC: Government Printing Office, 2002.

Downing, Sarah. *Hidden History of the Outer Banks.* Charleston, SC: History, 2013.

Eppler, Mark. *The Wright Way: 7 Problem Solving Principles from the Wright Brothers.* New York: AMACOM, 2003.

First Flight Foundation. "Coin Toss." https://firstflightfoundation.org/coin-toss/.

Flying Association. "Flying." *Journal of the Flying Association* 1 (1912), p. 52.

Foulois, Benjamin D. *From the Wright Brothers to the Astronauts.* New York: McGraw-Hill, 1968.

Garber, Lester. *The Wright Brothers and the Birth of Aviation.* Ramsbury, Marlborough, Wiltshire: Crowood, 2005.

Goddard, Stephen. *Race to the Sky: The Wright Brothers versus the United States Government*. Jefferson, NC: McFarland, 2003.

Goldstone, Lawrence. *Birdmen: The Wright Brothers, Glenn Curtiss, and the Battle to Control the Skies*. New York: Ballantine, 2015.

Gotschlich, Emil C. "Bullets and Bacilli: The Spanish American War and Military Medicine." *Journal of Clinical Investigation* 115, no. 1 (January 3, 2005).

Harper's Magazine, 1940.

Harris, Frank. *Fortnightly Review* 52 (New York: Leonard Scott: 1892): 445.

Hatch, Alden. *Glenn Curtiss: Pioneer of Naval Aviation*. New York: Messner, 1942.

Hensley, Steven, and Julia Hensley. *The Unwelcome Assistant: Edward C. Huffaker and the Birth of Aviation*. Johnson City, TN: Overmountain, 2003.

Hertog, Susan. *Anne Morrow Lindbergh: Her Life*. New York: Anchor, 2000.

Hildebrandt, Alfred. "The Wright Brothers Flying Machine." *American Magazine of Aeronautics* 2, no. 1 (January 1908): 13–16.

Hill, Thomas. "Status of the Wrights' Suits." *Aeronautics* 5–7 (1909): 122.

Howard, Fred. *Wilbur and Orville: A Biography of the Wright Brothers*. New York: Dover, 2013.

Jakab, Peter L. *Visions of a Flying Machine: The Wright Brothers and the Process of Invention*. Washington, DC: Smithsonian Books, 1990.

Kelly, Fred C. "Flying Machines and the War: An Interview with Orville Wright." *Colliers* 55, July 31, 1915. Reprinted in Simonds, Frank. *History of the World War*. Vol. 1. Garden City, NY: Doubleday, 1917.

———. Fred C. Kelly Papers. Syracuse, NY: Syracuse University, Overview, 1882–1959.

———. "How the Wright Brothers Began." *Harper's Magazine*, October 1939.

———. *Miracle at Kitty Hawk: The Letters of Wilbur and Orville Wright*. New York: Da Capo, 2002.

———. *The Wright Brothers: A Biography Authorized by Orville Wright*. New York: Harcourt, Brace, 1943.

Klooster, John. *Icons of Invention*. Vol. 1. Santa Barbara, CA: ABC-CLIO, 2009.

Langley, Samuel. *Langley Memoir on Mechanical Flight*. Vols. 1–2. Washington, DC: Smithsonian Institution, 1911.

"Letters of Love: Correspondence Reveals Orville's Feelings for Mabel." *Dayton Daily News*, January 22, 1994.

Lilienthal, Otto. *The Problem of Flying*. Washington, DC: US Government Printing Office, 1894.

MacDonald, Terrance. *Firsts in Flight: Alexander Graham Bell and His Innovative Airplanes*. Halifax, NS: Formac, 2017.

Mackersey, Ian. *The Wright Brothers: The Remarkable Story of the Aviation Pioneers Who Changed the World*. London: Time Warner, 2004.

Mary, Etienne Jules. *Popular Science Monthly* 6 (1874): 248.

Mason, Herbert Molloy. *The United States Air Force: A Turbulent History*. New York: Charter, 1976.

Maurer, Richard. *The Wright Sister: Katherine Wright and Her Famous Brothers*. New York: Macmillan, 2016.

McCullough, David. *The Wright Brothers*. New York: Simon and Schuster, 2016.

McFarland, Marvin Wilks. *The Papers of Wilbur and Orville Wright: Including the Chanute-Wright Letters and Other Papers of Octave Chanute*. Vol. 1, *1899–1903*. New York: McGraw-Hill, 2001.

———. *The Papers of Wilbur and Orville Wright: Including the Chanute-Wright Letters and Other Papers of Octave Chanute*. Vol. 2, *1906–1948*. New York: McGraw-Hill, 2001.

McMahon, John R. *The Wright Brothers: Fathers of Flight*. Boston: Little, Brown, 1930.

Means, Thomas. *Aeronautical Annual*. New York: W. E. Clarke, 1894.

Miller, Scott. *The President and the Assassin: McKinley, Terror, and Empire at the Dawn of the American Century*. New York: Random House, 2013.

Newton, Byron. "Watching the Wright Brothers Fly." *Aeronautics* (June 1908): 8.

Nolan, Patrick, and John Zamonski. *The Wright Brothers Collection*. Columbus, OH: Wright State University, 1977.

Parramore, Thomas C. *Triumph at Kitty Hawk: The Wright Brothers and Powered Flight*. Raleigh, NC: Division of Archives and History, 1993.

Pfeifer, Paul. "Wilbur Wright and the Hockey Stick." *Highland County Press*, August 2016.

Popular Aviation, December 1928.

Rae, Bronwyn. "Water, Typhoid Rates, and the Columbian Exposition in Chicago." *Public Health Review* 2 (2015).

Ray, Kurt. *Typhoid Fever*. New York: Rosen, 2002.

Root, A. I. "Our Homes." *Gleanings in Bee Culture*, September 1, 1904, and January 1, 1905.

Roseberry, Cecil. *Glenn Curtiss: Pioneer of Flight*. Syracuse, NY: Syracuse University Press, 1972.

Sarles, Ruth. *A Story of America First: The Men and Women Who Opposed US Intervention in World War II*. New York: Greenwood, 2003.

Short, Simine. *Locomotive to Aeromotive: Octave Chanute and the Transportation Revolution*. Urbana: University of Illinois Press, 2011.

Smithsonian National Air and Space Museum. "Correcting Smeaton." https:// airandspace.si.edu/exhibitions/wright-brothers/online/fly/1901/smeaton.cfm.

———. "1903 Wright Flyer Fabric Taken to Moon: Apollo 11." https:// airandspace.si.edu/multimedia-gallery/430-l1-s1hjpg.

Stick, David. *An Outer Banks Reader*. Chapel Hill: University of North Carolina Press, 1998.

Taylor, Charles. "My Story of the Wright Brothers." As Told to Robert S. Ball. *Collier's Weekly* 122, no. 20 (December 25, 1948): 26–27.

Tise, Larry. *Conquering the Sky: The Secret Flights of the Wright Brothers at Kitty Hawk*. New York: St. Martin's, 2009.

Tobin, James. *To Conquer the Air: The Wright Brothers and the Great Race for Flight*. New York: Simon and Schuster, 2004.

Wallace, Max. *The American Axis: Henry Ford, Charles Lindbergh, and the Rise of the Third Reich*. New York: St. Martin's, 2003.

Walsh, John E. *One Day at Kitty Hawk: The Untold Story of the Wright Brothers and the Airplane*. New York: Crowell, 1975.

Washington Post, December 24, 1897.

Western Society of Engineers. *Journal of the Western Society of Engineers* 2 (1897): 595.

Wittenberg, Torenbeek. *Flight Physics: Essentials of Aeronautical Disciplines and Technology, with Historical Notes*. Dordrecht: Springer Science and Business Media, 2009.

Wohl, Robert. *A Passion for Wings: Aviation and the Western Imagination, 1908–1918*. New Haven, CT: Yale University Press, 1994.

Wolko, Howard, ed. *The Wright Flyer: An Engineering Perspective*. Washington, DC: Smithsonian Institution, 1987.

Wright, Katharine, on behalf of Orville Wright. January 1915. Archive of Papers Concerning the Writing and Eventual Publications of a Lengthy Biography of Orville and Wilbur Wright. Christies Fine Printed Books and Manuscripts. https://www.christies.com/features/The-Wright-Brothers-revealed-in-their-letters-and-photographs-7961-1.aspx.

Wright, Milton. *Diaries: 1857–1917*. Dayton, OH: Wright State University Libraries, 1999.

Wright, Orville. "The Wright Brothers Aeroplane." *Century Magazine*, September 1908, pp. 641–50.

Wright, Orville, and Wilbur Wright. *Published Writings of Wilbur and Orville Wright*. Edited by Peter L. Jakab and Rick Young. Washington, DC: Smithsonian, 2016.

Wright, Renee. *Explorer's Guide North Carolina's Outer Banks and Crystal Coast.* New York: Countryman, 2013.

Wright, Wilbur. "Observations in Soaring Flight." *Journal of the Western Society of Engineers* 8 (August 1903): 410.

———. "Some Aeronautical Experiments." *Journal of the Western Society of Engineers* 6 (1901): 501.

———. "The Story of Flight." *Aeronautics* 15 (1914).

"Wright Aeroplane and Its Fabled Performances, The ." *Scientific American* 94, no. 2, January 13, 1905.

"Wright Curtiss Litigation Ended, Patent Upheld." *Aeronautics* 14 (January 31, 2014): 21.

Young, Rosamond McPherson. "Mabel Alone after Orville's Death." *Dayton Daily News*, December 11, 1993.

———. "Mabel Beck's Story, Part of the Wright Brothers' History." *Dayton Daily News*, November 20, 1993.

———. "Orville Did More Than Invent in His Shop—Years Can't Erase Memories." *Dayton Daily News*, December 4, 1993.

———. *Twelve Seconds to the Moon.* Dayton, OH: United States Air Force Museum, 1983.

———. "Wilbur's Death Left Mabel to Insinuate Herself into Orville's Life." *Dayton Daily News*, November 27, 1993.

Yrigoyen, Charles, and Susan Warre. *Historical Dictionary of Methodism.* Lantham, MD: Scarecrow, 2013.

INDEX

bicycle business, 41, 53, 67
at Columbian Exposition
World's Fair (1893), 49
at Dayton County Fair,
185–86, 193–94
differences and similarities
between, 9, 12, 16–17,
134–35, 259
different roles in Kitty Hawk
(1900), 105–106
disbelief about flights of,
192–93
father treating as equals, 9–10
Glenn Curtiss and, 187–88,
194–95, 197
indebtedness to Langley's
work, 236–37
in Kelly biography, 248,
254–59
at Kill Devil Hills (1900),
100–106
at Kitty Hawk (1902), 143,
144, 147–49
media coverage on 1903
flight at Kitty Hawk and,
188–90
Orville version, in bio-
graphical information on,
10–11, 12
patent wars, 204–205,
206–207
photograph of December 17,
1903 flight and, 180–81

pioneer patent ad, 218–19,
223–24
portrayed as perfect men, 15
printing business, 40–41
renewed test flights of 1903
Langley flyer and, 230
secrecy by, 190–91, 193
sexual relations, 11–12, 13
trip to Kill Devil Hills
(1903), 165–82
trip to Kitty Hawk (1901),
120–30
wing-warping idea (*see* wing-
warping concept)
See also Wright, Orville;
Wright, Wilbur
Wright Brothers, The
(McCullough), 10, 210
*Wright Brothers: A Biography
Authorized by Orville Wright,
The* (Kelly), 10–11, 12, 146–47,
148, 149, 246–48, 254–55
Wright Cycle Exchange, 41, 53
Wright, Dan, 35
Wright Flyer
damaged after December
1903 flights, 182
delivered to Kill Devil Hills
(1903), 167
displayed at MIT as world's
first airplane, 230–31
displayed at the Smithsonian,
229, 230, 231